THROUGH A SOLDIER'S EYES

2/8/15

To: My Sister in Christ

May God Bless you always.

THROUGH A SOLDIER'S EYES

TO IRAQ AND BACK

D. R. TOOLE

TATE PUBLISHING
AND ENTERPRISES, LLC

Published by Tate Publishing & Enterprises, LLC
127 E. Trade Center Terrace | Mustang, Oklahoma 73064 USA
1.888.361.9473 | www.tatepublishing.com

Tate Publishing is committed to excellence in the publishing industry. The company reflects the philosophy established by the founders, based on Psalm 68:11,
"The Lord gave the word and great was the company of those who published it."

Cover design by Jan Sunday Quilaquil
Interior design by Joana Quilantang

Published in the United States of America

ISBN: 978-1-62510-207-2
1. Psychology / Psychopathology / Post-Traumatic Stress Disorder (PTSD)
2. Biography & Autobiography / Military
13.02.20

DEDICATION

I would like to dedicate this book to my friends and family who have stood by my side and provided support and encouragement.

My family stood by my side even when I tried to push them away. At times you gave me the strength to take my next breath. You saw me through my darkest days and held my hand when I needed a comforting touch. I'm not a man that can admit weakness, but with your love and encouragement, I found the courage to open my heart and allow it to flow into the pages of this book.

To all of my friends and comrades at the Veterans Administration in Albuquerque, New Mexico, you are the reason for this book. You have often told me that I put your feelings into my words and helped you to communicate to your friends and families the words that you just couldn't find. It is my sincere hope that this book speaks to you and others and provides a venue for a deeper understanding about war and Post Traumatic Stress Disorder.

To my doctors and counselors, you have seen me through many ups and downs. You have been flexible and tailored your care to my particular needs. You understand that we are individuals and more than just our disabilities. You have always treated me with dignity and respect. I know from experience that good people in your fields are not easy to come by. I have been blessed to have you pulling for me.

ACKNOWLEDGMENTS

I would like to thank the following people for their contributions. At times you have provided me with help in editing and storytelling and gave me the time and encouragement to tell my story.

My beautiful wife, Helen Toole
My stepsons, Diego Ortiz, David Ortiz, and Daniel Ortiz
My daughter, Cherestine Toole
My son, Ryan Toole
My mother and father, Janice and Damon Toole
My sister and brothers, Sharon Vescovo, Craig and Brad Toole
My counselor, Kathy Girod
All of the members of the 720th Transportation Company

PROLOGUE

I'm an ordinary man with a modern "yours, mine, and ours" family. We are a tight-knit group with four boys widely varying in age from adult to adolescent and one preteen girl. My wife, Helen, is a bit older than me, but she is very spry. She is a beautiful woman in appearance and heart. She's a petite woman, only four feet ten inches tall, though she tries to steal an inch every now and again. She has long platinum hair that frames her little round face well. She has a dainty nose, big brown eyes, and a smile that could brighten the darkest night. She spends her time catering to everyone around her and I am no exception.

My name is Damon Toole Jr. I am named after my father, who is now and always will be my mentor and hero. He is the hardest working man I know; he painstakingly put his time in providing for his family until he got hurt on the job and was forced an early retirement. I have two older brothers and one older sister. My mom has been the glue that holds us all together. We all seem to look up to one another, so there is no room for animosity or sibling rivalry. Of course, that wasn't always true, but we learned our lessons as we grew, and we all became very close.

I followed in my father's footsteps by joining the Marine Corps and then going into the propane business, where he worked for most of his life. However, business has changed over the years, and now I spend my time jumping from job to job, trying to claw my way up the corporate ladder. I am a dreamer who always sees myself at the next level of whatever I am doing. I am a hard worker, a real workaholic, a trait that appears to run in the family. I put in the time it takes to make things happen. I'm that guy who does all the groundwork so the boss can take the credit. I don't mind making him look good just so long as he throws me a bone now and again. I have had the privilege of working for some really good managers and a few not so good. I guess that just helps you to know what not to do.

After my five and a half years in the corps, I have been in and out of the New Mexico Army National Guard. It's a difficult transition going from a highly disciplined, well-trained soldier to the unorthodox, relaxed temperament of the Guard. I guess that's why I didn't stick around. I felt awkward and out of place, not that there weren't good people in the Guard, it was just so different.

It all seems so long ago, and it was. It feels almost as if I was a different person entirely as war changes you at your core, I remember so little about what life was like before. It truly is as if I died and came back to live again. You leave as a husband, father, friend, and you return as a stranger. Life goes on without you. All that you left behind is gone for good. It is impossible to pick up where you left off. The best that you can hope for is that your family and friends can accept the new you and you have the strength and courage to accept them as they have grown without you. This is a story about war and its effects on a family. The accounts that you are about to read are true to the best of my recollection. The names of the soldiers in this story have been changed to protect the privacy of each individual.

CHAPTER 1

On the morning of September 11, 2001, my life changed as did the life of every American. We were no longer safe and were a little less free in our country that was born of freedom. With smoke billowing from the Twin Towers, the blood that was shed stained every American. It was a shocking blow that took us all to our knees, but by the time the towers fell, America rose up as one. The sleeping giant was now awake for the first time in decades. Somebody was going to get their butts kicked though it would take a while to figure out who that somebody was.

I was in shock and caught up in the moment as I'm sure everybody was. You couldn't turn on your TV without the horrific pictures staring you in the face. It was on every channel at every time of the day. If it wasn't a replay of the towers falling, then it was the cleanup or simply questions. When are we going to react, how are we going to react, and will there be more attacks? There was always speculation, but there were defiantly more questions than answers.

I struggled with a decision: do I stay, or do I go? I know that my family needs me, but I know that I could make a difference for my countrymen. Then when I convinced myself that it was my job to ensure that my children had a right to the same freedom that I was so fond of, the choice became clear. I was going to war. I was going to make a difference. The decision seemed to take forever, but by September 18, 2001, I was once again a member of the New Mexico Army National Guard.

Helen and I sat our three youngest children down, Daniel, age fourteen; Cherestine, age twelve; and Ryan, age four, to talk about what was happening and about my plans to go back into the Guard. My family stood by me in my decision though I'm not sure that they fully understood what that might mean. I tried to explain that at some point I was going to get called upon to serve and that would take me away for some time. They didn't like the idea, but they were proud of their dad just the same.

We live in the moment; who is to say what will happen next? How will decisions we make today affect what we'll be tomorrow? Foresight has never been my strong point, but I am leaving my children in capable hands. My wife is strong; she will keep the home fires burning. I have a duty and a calling that I must answer. My unit has not yet been called, but I know that it is just a matter of time.

I'm worried about what all of this is doing to my family, but it seems that while many people are up in arms, the kids are still kids. They get bored watching the same old thing on the news and would much rather frolic and play than let any of this get them down. They don't understand the magnitude of what they are seeing, and why should they? They are only children.

Time was moving at a snail's pace. It seemed to take forever before we could take action against the guilty parties, yet the news networks replay the footage of the destruction and announce the growing daily body count. America is due her retaliation. The masses were fired up and ready for action, but weeks would pass before justice could begin. This was no ordinary attack. It did not come from a particular nation. This was the work of independent radicals, radicals that would have to be hunted down in areas of the world that were not particularly America-friendly.

Early on, the majority of the world appeared sympathetic to America with the exception of a few individuals. Some of whom would say that we brought the attacks upon ourselves, but this was not the rule. Most understood that we would not take anything off the table when it came to our certain retaliation. There was even speculation that a nuclear attack was possible. I had my doubts about that, but the thought filled me with nervous energy.

It wasn't long before the world support dwindled, and even NATO wasn't fully behind our apparent plans to strike back. We would go it alone if need be. America was growing weary of the UN as they are always quick to hold out their hands for aid but just as quick to demean our policies. Many Americans would like to see this alliance of fair-weather friends abolished. I was also of this mentality, but it was not anything that had any hope of coming to fruition.

The terrorist organization al-Qaeda headed by Osama bin Laden claimed responsibility for the horrific attacks on America. Al-Qaeda was heavily based in Afghanistan. Now that we had a face to put with the attacks, we could begin working on a plan for our retaliation.

Politics were being played as mean-spirited as ever. The Democrats and Republicans were doing battle long before the actual war would begin. The masses were standing behind the president, at least for now, so with poles on their side, the Republicans were armed and ready for whatever the Dems could throw at them. On October 6, 2001, the battle between the parties was at an all-time high. When is Bush going to react? We should have begun by now, many would say, while others would say that we shouldn't act at all. The wind was all taken out of their sail when the war in Afghanistan began on the morning of October 7, 2001.

I was overjoyed when I woke up to the news that the war was on. Al-Qaeda was going to pay the price for the attacks on America as would anybody that had the bad judgment to attack our citizens. Now the question is, when would it be my turn? With the limited number of troops that we sent into Afghanistan, I began to think that my time may never come.

With the war in Afghanistan well into its second year, things seemed to be heating up in Iraq. There was a lot of speculation as to whether we could fight a war on two separate fronts. This was, of course, just talk. We would never get the approval from the UN to invade Iraq even though they thumbed their noses at every Security Council sanction. President Bush continued to push for action in Iraq, and with each day that passed, it became increasingly more likely that a war with Iraq would come to be.

Helen was growing more concerned by the day. The anticipation of not knowing if or when I would be called was weighing heavy on her mind. She knew that I had to go, and she knew why. I still carried a lot of guilt for not going to the Gulf War as a young marine. I should have gone, but due to family reasons at the time, my command labeled me nondeployable. It was what I had trained for my entire military career, and when they said that my place was at home, it was almost more than I could take. They discharged me for humanitarian reasons. That alone left a hole in my heart. Now this was my opportunity to somehow make up for that. I fully realize that one could not fully make up for the other, but I knew that I could use my experiences to make a difference now.

Though we were still months away, the writing was on the wall. Many troops were already building up and in the area. Not us, at least not yet. We were just guardsmen, weekend warriors. We knew how to drink, not how to kill. We had quite a mix of people from professionals to those on probation. Some of us had prior service; some were just clueless. We were a unit that knew how to work when it came down to it, and nobody was more capable of getting the job done than the 720th Transportation Company. We were a medium-truck company composed of Freightliner trucks and forty-foot flatbed trailers. Our job was to transport much needed supplies to the forward elements.

We had quite a variety of characters within our unit. Johnson was a crusty old fart; he once had a heart attack on a two-mile run during his annual fitness test. He loved to cuss, and his claim to fame was the story he told about how he dropped a turd on his boss's desk one day after he pissed him off. I couldn't imagine anybody even thinking about that, but he was definitely a different individual. He was a good guy in spite of himself. We were talking one day about how our training had been stepped up and about world events. We both agreed that we were being prepped for what was coming, and we were fired up. I couldn't wait for the inevitable. We were going, and I was ready. I would miss my family, but they would understand. They had been anticipating this day since 9/11, and so had I.

Shadows have dimmed as day fades to night. Helen and I retreated to our backyard. It was small and cozy. We had a hot tub on a deck with an overhead arbor, a small pond complete with waterfalls, and a couple of well-developed fruit trees. We loved to go outside at night, listen to the trickling water, and stare up at the fiery night sky. With a house full of kids, it is hard to get time for ourselves, but late in the evenings was our time.

"Lover," I said.

"What?" Helen replied.

"I think we are getting close to deploying."

"What makes you say that? Did they say something?"

"No, but it's different. They have stepped up our training and even the type of training we are doing. It's more in-depth than ever before. I think that we must be getting close."

"Well we knew that this was going to happen sooner or later." She takes my hand in hers and says, "We'll miss you."

"Me too."

Then I move in for a short kiss. We both sit back, cuddling until the night grows cold. We retreat to bed soon thereafter as it will be an early morning for me and another Guard day.

I was up early Sunday morning. I got dressed and headed for the door. I wonder what the day will hold in store. We always have a plan for the day, but the plans change without notice. It's always good to see the clan, Neilson, Palo, and Bella to name a few. We never get together or even talk to one another away from drill, but it's nice to see them once a month. We always make time to shoot the breeze and catch up with one another, but when it's time to work, we all get right to it. Rank doesn't mean much. With this group, we all lend a hand and work together well.

This day is all about inventory. First, it is our personal equipment, but then we will inventory our trucks and trailers. After lunch, we will break up into small groups. Some will help with weapons, supply, and the tool room, and the rest will do the tents. We will need all of our gear for training over the next few months. Next month, we will be going to Santa Fe for field training and evaluation. They want to see what they are getting. If we pull this one off, we will be going for sure.

I head for home after a long day, hell, a long weekend. I pull up into the driveway, and before I can get to the door, the boy, Ryan, and the girl, Cherestine, run to greet me. They miss their weekend when I am away. I try to make up for lost time. This usually includes some roughhousing. They team up to try to get the best of me. I can usually hold my own. It's not as easy as you would think. They just keep coming and keep coming, and I have to subdue the mighty duo without hurting them. This usually continues until someone crashes; when laughter turns to tears, it's time to bring it to an end.

I grab a couple of beers, and Helen and I retreat to the backyard.

"Have I ever taken you night fishing?"

"No," said Helen, "you've never taken me."

"It's truly a remarkable experience. I'll have to take you when life gets a little less complicated, perhaps when I return. I love to go. I go partly for the fishing but even more for the serenity. It can be quite romantic as well. The journey begins by embarking from a well-lit dock, but as you push off, you find that you are somewhat blinded by the light as you steer out into the black of night. It's a bit eerie at first, but as you get away from the light, a whole new world appears right before your eyes. You must take this trip slow and easy. You feel the gentle rocking of the craft as the water passes beneath you. All you hear is the quiet hum of the motor and the peaceful patting of the rippling water as it slaps against the hull. As you regain your vision, the first thing you will notice is the glow of the moon welcoming you to the night. Its soft glow emits just enough light to see the world in a new way. You can look to the horizon and see a glimpse of the rugged, rocky terrain. It feels as if it's a million miles away. The moon shines upon the water, reflecting its never-ending light as if it were a pathway to the abyss. As you look up at the night, you will see infinity, so many stars going on and on, perhaps a soft black pearl of a cloud casts its shadow against the endless field of fiery projectiles streaming through the sky. It's as if this world was created just for you and yours to share with whom you desire. Just another one of God's miracles I am dying to share with you."

"Sounds wonderful. Are you sure that you want to take me?"

"Of course. I can't think of anyone better. I love to run my fingers through your hair. It's so long, soft, beautiful, and it smells good too."

"I love it too. I feel so safe with you."

"How many years has it been now, ten?"

"I think that it is closer to nine."

"Still, I can't see myself with anybody but you. You complete me."

"Do you mean that?"

"I'm still here, aren't I?"

"You're a brat, and I suppose that if you ever change your mind, you will let me know."

"You look so beautiful with the moonlight gleaming off your hair."

She moves in for a kiss. It's amazing how lucky of a man I could be. I'm married to a woman who just happens to be my best friend, and after nine years, you would think that we are still newlyweds. It hasn't all been a bed of roses. We have never had time for ourselves. We have had a house full of kids from day one. Mixing a family is full of challenges, but I am now, and have been since the beginning, proud of every one of them. We have been cross from time to time, but I have loved them from the beginning.

It's Monday morning and back to the grind. I get up early with my bags packed for the week. I have been recently promoted to the position of sales manager for a beverage company operating out of Albuquerque. I am responsible for all of the convenience stores in all of our large-coverage area. I am staying with my sister-in-law during the week then go home for the weekend.

My sister-in-law keeps me busy with honey dos of her own. It's almost like having two wives, and that becomes a little inside joke of its own. I help with chores, a few bills, and whatever task is at hand. It works well, and I think that she was glad to have me there. I stayed in the guest room and always kept it tidy, not tidy enough however because every day when I got home, the throw pillows were always rearranged on my bed. I found it a little funny and probably left them out of order on purpose just to see if I was mistaken, but I wasn't. The rest of the house could fall into disorder, but my bed was always just so. It was nice to have a place to stay and be off the road every night. Liz and I got along well, and our friendship grew during this time. We spent the evenings after dinner and cleanup watching whatever program that she was accustomed to. I'm not much for TV, so I would often turn in early for the night.

The weekend will begin with a new set of honey dos as I have been gone all week, and I still have to make up for last weekend. You never really get caught up. There just isn't enough time for all that needs doing. I go to bed exhausted and fight to get to sleep.

Morning breaks way too early. With my mind racing, I didn't get much sleep. It's Sunday morning. No work today, and since I'm up early, it might be a good chance to get a little fishing in. I keep the boat stocked and ready for such an opportunity. It's an hour-and-a-half drive to Conchas Dam. Conchas Lake is a local-people lake; not too many outsiders come around. It's one of our best-kept secrets. It's a medium-sized lake big enough for great skiing but always has a quiet cove to fish for some nice bass. One guy caught what would have been the state record but threw it back to avoid publicity. I bet that old buck has to be about eleven pounds or better by now. It's a beautiful winter morning, thirty-five degrees and not even a hint of a breeze. The lake will be like glass. I'm almost happy that I couldn't sleep. I drive through the long straights then down mesa with its steep winding path. The huge rock and red earth make this place like no other. The sparse cottonwood trees are haggard and still. They await spring with great anticipation. There is just enough early morning sun to cast dark, ominous, and eerie shadows along the ground. I am getting anxious as I round the last corner before the lake comes into full view. It's as spectacular a scene as I figured it would be. The lake is smooth as glass, not so much as a ripple on it. Fishing may be slow this time of year, but I will enjoy every minute. I pull to the dock to launch my small aluminum craft with a twelve-horse, two-cycle Evinrude motor, while next to me an, older gentleman launches his Triton 21HP bass boat. "Boy! Someday," I told myself, "I will have a boat like that." For now, I am content. I putter away from the dock, cast my line, and troll the shoreline to my favorite fishing hole. Along the way, I see a few old diehards casting from the shoreline. I give a shout-out on occasion to see if they are having more luck than me. It is as I figured; fishing was slow. Just around the bend now is where an old log lay on a sandy bottom in about eight feet of water. My friend and I had gotten my truck stuck on the beach three years ago when they drained the lake to work on the dam. We tied the winch to this old tree, and as we pulled, the rotten wood gave way and then fell. Eventually, we got the truck out, but when the lake filled back up, I knew that it would be the making of a wonderful new fishing hole. I attach my favorite lure. It's a dark green salmon deep-diving plug. I cast out just past the trunk of the tree. My lure slides against the sandy lake bottom and then bumps up the side of the log, catches just slightly at the top, then bumps and drops off the other. It was the perfect cast, a slow retrieval, and then—nothing. I make the same cast over and over again with the same results. I try a few tricks; I change my lure several times, but nothing apparently is going to tempt the fish today. It is about two o'clock, and I think I will call it a day. No fish today, but the day has been good. I feel like I was able to get my head clear, at least a bit. Maybe I can get some sleep tonight.

The next Guard weekend in Santa Fe was one filled with long cold days. This was to be a MUTA-6, which translates to Friday, Saturday, and Sunday. We were at the rifle range all day Friday. With the wind ripping at about thirty miles per hour, the cold cuts straight through our meager cold-weather gear. The next day was a round-robin. This is where you go from station to station, taking in training, from first aid to land navigation to squad tactics and on and on. Sunday was convoy ops; this was our specialty. Everything to this point was fruitless as far as I was concerned. We were truck drivers, not ground pounders. This was the area where we could really shine. Sure enough, by the end of the day, we had passed our evaluation. Now it was just a matter of time.

CHAPTER 2

We get the call. We will be heading out to Fort Bliss within a week. I have to tell everyone. With mixed emotions, I call Helen. She will be devastated, but we should only be gone for about six months. These were the words from my command: plan on being gone for at least six months. Being a Guard unit, I couldn't imagine that it could be much longer than that. I try to conceal the excitement in my voice as I speak to my wife.

"Helen, we got the call." A brief silence followed as if she was afraid to ask what call. She knew anyway.

"When will you be leaving?" she asked.

"By the end of the week," I said. Then another brief silence followed.

"Well, I guess that it's no surprise," she said as she tried to keep her composure. "You will have to break the news to the kids."

"I know. I will do it tonight when everyone is there together."

"Okay then, I'll see you tonight. Love you."

"I love you too. Good-bye."

Once we both get home, the kids are already there. We call them altogether, and Helen says, "Daddy has something to tell you."

I take the floor and I get right to it. "We have been activated." Cherestine's eyes instantly well up with tears. Danny looks saddened and somewhat surprised, and the boy Ryan is waiting for clarification but is scared by the older two's reaction. "I will be heading to Iraq soon. We will be at Fort Bliss by the end of the week."

Now the boy knows what I am talking about and runs to my side, grabs on to my leg, looks up to me with big sad eyes, and says, "Don't go, Daddy!"

"I have to buddy. I should only be gone about six months or so. The time will fly." I tried to believe my own words as saying them felt like someone stuck a knife through my chest. I knew that telling them would be difficult, but with my feelings at this moment, I don't know how I will ever say good-bye.

Being only a part-time soldier, there are a million and one things to consider when you will be leaving your job for some time. First is the family; they never really think of you as a soldier or that you are really capable of being gone for any length of time. Even if they were told in advance, they never believe that it could happen. We were some of the first troops called, so they didn't have any real expectations. All that I could do was to pass the information that was passed to us, that we would be deployed for at least six months, but I knew in my heart that it would be longer than that. This was not going to be as quick as the Gulf War. We would be going into a foreign country, taking over their government, and occupying until a new government was in place. Telling this to other soldiers, many didn't believe me, so how was my family to understand. I told them to plan for the worst and hope for the best. I couldn't take away any hope that they had because that was all that they had.

Then the whole income thing. Would I make enough to pay our bills? Would I have a job when I get back? What about insurance for my family? What if I don't come back, what will become of my family? Some of these questions would be answered in the days and weeks to come. In fact, we received so much information in the next few days that it would make your head spin. It was hard to keep everything straight. The more information that I would come home with, the more questions Helen would have.

We worked long days with a whole lot of "hurry up and wait" time. It gets frustrating sitting around when you want to spend time with your family. Every moment is precious. How do you say good-bye to a family that means the world to you, especially not knowing when or if you will see them again? The kids are growing so fast. The boy at age four looks to me for everything. He will be in school by the time I return. The girl is a beautiful preteen who puts me on a pedestal and thinks of me as her hero. She will have gone from a little girl to a young woman by the time I return. Danny, already a young man, needs guidance to help find a place within this troubled world. By the time I return, will it be too late? As for my lovely wife, I know that she has the strength to carry this burden and the love and devotion to wait for me no matter how long it takes. Still, she will face long cold nights; she will worry for every moment until my return. All I can do is pray for her. I can't provide the strength that she will need to carry on. That will have to come from within.

At this time, I cannot fathom what I will face in Iraq or what my family will face at home. All that I can do is speculate, anticipate, and worry. I know that I will carry their love with me onto the battlefield. It will provide me with courage and a desire to survive and return. I will also carry the love and prayers of many; I will take all that I can.

My mother, father, sister, and brothers as well as in-laws will carry the burden of concern for me as I venture out on this quest. War touches many. For every soldier who goes into combat, there are dozens of people left at home in the shadows. Everyone has their own concerns for safety. They will not truly rest until your safe return.

I am and always will be my mother's baby. My father is proud. My sister respects my decision but silently wonders what it is all for. Maybe they all do. My brothers would just as soon go in my stead or at least by my side. Life holds something different for all, and none of us know what our purpose is, and most will spend their entire lives in search of it. For the moment, I believe I know what my purpose is; it's to keep my brethren safe and to help as many as possible come home. This is what made everything worthwhile for me. My family would survive without me, but without me, some of my comrades may not. I could be the difference between life and death, and that was reason enough to go.

The guilt and pain that I have from leaving my family this way has left a memory block that won't fully allow me to reflect on this time. A soldier has a duty to reach beyond the heartache and pain that he or she feels and carry on. There is no place for tears or to admit your fear; a soldier's life is do-or-die. You must bury things like sorrow, guilt, and fear. How else does one go forth into danger when all of your natural instincts tell you to go in the opposite direction? The military does a fine job of converting ordinary men into machines for death and destruction. We must prepare to face multiple battles day in and day out for as long as it takes to get the job done. This is as close to the definition of *insanity* as I ever care to seek. We will kill as often as need be in the name of righteousness and risk our own lives for the same.

The last night before we headed out to Fort Bliss, Texas, was a bit somber, to say the least. Everyone is showing strength and trying to believe that somehow it will be but a dream. They will wake up and I will still be there. This, of course, is not the case. After tonight, God only knows when or if I will see my family again. The pain of this realization is gut-wrenching. My family is my life. Tonight may be the last time that I kiss my children good night and hold my lover in my arms. I can't bear what tomorrow will bring, and it will likely be one of the hardest days of my life.

My family is up early and by my side. They will go to the armory with me then head to the roadside as we parade out of town. As we head down the road, I see their faces for the last time. They are sad but full of pride as so much of the community has come out to show their support. I feel my heart break as they leave my sight, but now is the time for strength, so I shrug off any emotion and focus on the mission.

Truck 112 with the first squad leader, Jason Baca, and his co-driver, Neil Otero, lead the convoy. The next truck contained the assistant squad leader, Walter Sanchez, and his co-driver, Jose Pena. The rest of the platoon followed with sequential order. I was in the last truck within our squad; Young Feller was my co-driver. Young Feller was of the youngest troops within our squad. His name was Carlos Trujillo, but his nickname caught on quickly and was known by all. We had a radio to communicate with the different elements of the convoy.

"143 to 112, over."

"This is 112. Go."

"We're ready to roll, over."

"Roger," said 112.

"Let's get this mother rolling!" I told Young Feller.

We were off on a journey that was way too long in the making. In a few short weeks, we will be kicking butts and taking names in Iraq, but for now, we will take one day at a time.

We spend the next few days standing in line after line. We were drawing gear from supply, filling out paperwork, going through medical, updating shots. It is all necessary, but all the hurrying and waiting will drive you crazy. We are on lockdown at night, and alcohol was strictly forbidden. Yeah right. Telling the 720th that they are not allowed to drink is like telling anyone else not to breathe. Our command knows better. What they mean by "we are not allowed to drink" is that we had better keep it low key and not disrupt anyone. Even that was near impossible for some members of our company. One night, two guys from maintenance got rowdy drunk then started chasing each other from room to room; they then found themselves out on the balcony, trying to throw each other over the side. That cost them a couple of nights' extra duty but then was washed away like yesterday's laundry. Everyone's stress level was way up; it wasn't unlikely that some would blow off a little steam.

Everybody always assumes that we are sending our children off to war, but the median age for our company was about thirty-three, with a range of nineteen to sixty. Everybody has a life beyond the military, and we bring these specialties along with us. We had policemen, nurses, correction officers, mechanics, professional drivers, and probably our share of crooks as well. We definitely didn't have the military discipline of the regular forces, but we did have the people with real-life experience beyond the battlefield to train our troops.

Days turned into weeks then weeks into months. It seemed as if we would never leave. We trained daily for every different scenario that we could imagine. We had several veterans from the previous war in our company, but this promised to be a much different fight. We were going to be fighting in their homeland. It was thought that we may find ourselves in an urban-warfare environment. Door-to-door, house-to-house, we checked and cleared blocks of homes at a time. Nobody was looking forward to this type of environment, but we had to be as ready as possible for anything. Being a transportation company, some took the training lightly. "We would never get in this kind of a situation," they would say. You can bet that others took every possibility as a serious venture. Over and over again, this was the norm. Some people would not take any of the training seriously, and I figured these were the people who would be coming home one piece at a time.

After several weeks, we were granted days off, and our families were allowed to come to Fort Bliss to see us. That was a real morale booster. Helen, the girl, and the boy came up the first weekend that they could. We took them to the PX, where the boy was bought a set of mini fatigues so he could look like Daddy. Many soldiers saluted as he walked by in his uniform, and the boy swelled with pride. This was the first of many weekends. Our ship date was pushed back due to the fact that Turkey changed their minds about us using their country for the invasion. Kuwait became so backed up that we did not leave Fort Bliss until mid-April.

CHAPTER 3

The day finally comes. We're standing on the tarmac in full battle rattle, waiting for the commercial 747 that will carry us halfway around the world. The sun is beating down, and the heat radiates off the blacktop. As uncomfortable as it is, we all know that this is nothing compared to the forthcoming environment. Every face carries its own character and emotion, from the stone-chiseled, cold-eyed sergeant to the baby-faced private and everything in between. Young or old, we all had our demons, and we would face them when called on to do so. As we board the airplane, the nervous energy begins to build and then releases with a motivating battle cry—whoaaaaaaaaaah—when we feel the big bird's wheels leave the ground. All of the 167 soldiers are caught up in this moment, and for the first time, we are one.

We arrive in Kuwait, and none of us know what to expect. We are hurried to our feet and shuffled to the door. When the door opens, the intense sunlight is instantly blinding, and the radiant heat wave covered us all like a giant blanket. We quickly moved our gear from the plane to the busses that were pre-staged and awaiting our arrival. Our busses are buttoned up tight. The windows are covered, and I can't help thinking that they are there to shield our identity from the locals. Later, I realized that they kept the windows covered to keep the strong sun shut out, allowing the air conditioners a chance to work. When the busses stopped, we were again hurried to get off of the bus and to ground our gear. The army is full of hurrying and waiting, and wait we did. We are set out to bake in the hot sun while this overcrowded transfer base figures out what they're going to do with so many new troops. I thought it would be nice if the entire tour could be as efficient as the busses appeared to be. Fat chance. This theory was squashed from the get-go.

They staged us next to the biggest Porta John city that I had ever seen. There must be at least a hundred or so. They are set up back-to-back and row after row. The air is heavy and still. With nothing to move the smell from this city, I was afraid that the stench would stick to our hot, sweaty bodies. I guess it's crazy to think that they may have running water. Damn, it's bright. As I peer through my almost closed eyes, I see that everything, including the sand, is almost white, intensifying the blinding sun. The camp was anything but army. All of the tents were Middle Eastern-style like you would see in an old Saturday-morning cartoon. They looked quite large, but we were soon to find out how wrong we were. Each tent was designed to house about 50 or 60 troops, so we were a bit surprised to find that this one tent would be the temporary home for all 167 of us, men and women alike. We are arranged in squad order, and each of us had the space of one bedroll. Side by side, each bedroll was touching the next, and a six-inch walkway was allowed between the first and second row, the third and fourth row, and the fifth and sixth row. Our gear was staged from floor to roof in the remaining space. We are practically living on top of one another. Day two and the tent already smells like stale sweaty socks. Army field showers are available, and we are all happy to have that. Still, living in this hot climate, in close proximity, and without so much as a fan to move the air around, it was bound to get ripe.

After a few days, we are becoming a bit more comfortable with our new surroundings. The billeting sergeant barges into our tent and begins bellowing that we need to make room for another hundred troops. *You've gotta be kidding me*, I thought to myself. *Our tent is busting at the seams already!* He states that these tents are designed to hold three hundred troops with gear. The entire tent is in protest and refuses to move, and after overwhelming resistance, the sergeant walks out. "Neilson, can you believe this crap?" Neilson is Neil Otero, a man of medium build, black hair, and a complete horndog. There is nothing frightening about Neil except his appetite for porn and sex in general. He always has a story to tell, and for now, he's my best friend. Neil replies, "If that SOB wants me to move anywhere, he had better bring a lot more guys!"

"Or only one chick and you would follow him anywhere," I said.

"She'd have to be a good looking chick!"

That was his only denial. He talked a good game and he had a history to back it up, but for now, he was devoted to his one and only. A few minutes later, the sergeant returns with his captain. After only a moment, Lieutenant Clark, our executive officer (XO) and second in command, starts to buckle and informs us that we are going to have to tighten up. Again, huge protests come from the inhabitants, and the lieutenant begins to regain some of his nerve. He holds the captain off until our commander could be summoned. Our commander was a spitfire redhead, who was about six foot one. And while he was only a captain himself, he carried the persona of a much greater man. We never heard from the billeting command for the rest of our stay. Although we never knew exactly what was said, there were rumors of heroism, and our commander was gaining our respect. As our commander was elevated, our XO lost a notch on the respect belt, and we began to fear what we were in for if he ever assumed command.

Days later, we were sent from the transfer point to Camp Arifjan. This was an area that had several aluminum warehouses and more of the Middle Eastern style tents. The newly formed base was still under construction for the most part. They house all of us in one of the huge warehouses along with several other transients. We were still a little cramped for space, but it was nothing like the troop transfer base. Here we had actual military bunks, and there were a couple of huge portable swamp coolers. The coolers were over spaced and didn't offer much relief from the near unbearable heat. They were nice to sit in front of if you needed to cool down for the moment. It was only April, and we knew that we were in for much worse conditions in the coming months.

Camp Arifjan was definitely a step up. They had a PX (post exchange) like a Wal-Mart, only this would be more like an empty Wal-Mart. The line at the front door was always long. Neilson and I would stay in line for nearly an hour to get a glimpse at any potential new inventory. More often than not, the supplies were limited and we would leave with a Coke labeled in standard Arabic script and some form of pogie bate (junk food) to help fight away the boredom.

Tomorrow we will break up into groups. Some of us will be going to the shipping port to gather our anxiously awaited equipment, and others will stay behind to construct our new quarters in the rapidly growing tent city. All of this was too long in the making.

We found our way to the docks, and we were attempting to find our equipment among the thousands of other units' equipment that had already been off-loaded and staged. We asked a number of people that were in charge of the many staging areas only to find that this was one major Charlie Foxtrot (cluster f—). The officers in charge of the staging areas didn't really know what they had, and that information would prove valuable later on. Our equipment was found to be still aboard the ship. It was behind an abundance of tanks and other tracked vehicles, road construction equipment, and numerous other wheeled vehicles. We offered our assistance to move other equipments from the ship to the staging area in order to expedite the process. They told us that they would love to have our help, and the fun begins. We run like kids to a carnival ride, trying to pick out their favorite character. Some were nervous and wanted to only drive what they knew, while others would jump on anything. If we could figure out how to start them, then we were halfway there. We had to take extreme caution as we slowly moved the huge trucks and tracks from the boat. This also provided a bit of time to learn how to control, turn, start, and stop the equipment. It was like driving a tractor trailer through an overcrowded parking garage. In fact, at times that's exactly what we did. Once off the ship, we still had a slow ride to the end of the pier, but from there, it was as if the green flag dropped and the race was on. It was truck against truck and track against track all the way to the staging area. The excitement was enhanced because most of the stuff we had only just taught ourselves how to operate in a few hundred yards and at a snail's pace. After becoming a little bored with the standard equipment, I jumped on the saddle of a huge steamroller. It takes a moment to figure out how to start the humungous beast, but soon, I found the right combination of levers, switches, and pedals, and the monster comes to life with a powerful roar. I put the machine into gear and release the parking brake, and as I release the clutch, the horn sounds as the mass inches forward. I push the clutch back in, and the horn and machine stop. I check the gauges and fluid levels. All are okay, so I take off again with the horn continuing to sound. As the green flag drops at the end of the pier, I shift from gear to gear, going faster and faster, all the while the horn continues to sound. Irritated by the loud horn, I didn't realize the attention that I was attracting. When I looked around, I could see all of my comrades laughing, and I couldn't help but to join them. That took my attention away from my path, and at full speed, I was barreling down on a Kuwaiti guard shack. I regain my attention and see the wide-eyed guard. He is frozen in place as the steamroller rapidly approached with its horn blaring. I steer away with little more than a spare moment, and all of the laughter erupts into near hysterics. I never could figure out what the horn thing was all about, but it did provide highlights for an already action-packed day.

There is a conflict brewing between officers as the XO and the first platoon commander are in competition to see who the first hero will be. Lieutenant Clark and Lieutenant Summers both want to command the first mission into Iraq. When the first mission is assigned from our Battalion Headquarters only days after we get our equipment, we find that we have bigger problems than who will lead. Apparently, we were supposed to draw our initial combat load of ammo from Fort Bliss before we left the States. We are making a name for ourselves, and that name was the Walking Charlie Foxtrot. We are making history, the first company in history to go to war without ammo. It is going to be an uphill climb to pull our name out of the mud pit that we are starting out in. The mission goes down, and we borrow ammo from another company within our new battalion. Our witty commander has chosen both officers and all of the NCOs who are in leadership conflicts to go on this first mission. I guess he figured that they would have to learn to work together or risk getting their butts shot off. My truck had an overheating problem that started on the way to Fort Bliss, and our maintenance team didn't feel the need to fix it when we had all of our lag time. I will be on the sidelines until they get the parts to repair it. That could be a problem since the supply chain is still missing a few links.

They rigged a few of our trucks with MTS systems. This is the government's overly complicated piece-of-crap answer for GPS. The system has some good points though, like the fact that each one is plotted on to a central computer system and you can track your convoy's progress from the company headquarters. As our first mission heads out, we plot their route on the mainframe. They start okay, but soon things go wrong. Our XO doesn't seem able to orient a map either. We are beginning to wonder if there is anything that he can do. As the darkness falls upon them, they are lost in the desert. They should be safe and spending the night at a secure checkpoint, but somehow they managed to leave the MSR (main service road) and took the road less traveled. We watch their progress as they go from halt to travel again and again. They are going in circles. We would have been in fear for them except for the fact that they never made it out of Kuwait. They almost made it out once, but they were wrongfully headed to the Jordanian border instead of Iraq. Eventually, they found a way to get their heads in the game and complete the mission.

With my truck being down, I was volunteered to drive our company bus. It was a piece-of-crap brand-new four-cylinder, fifteen-passenger Mitsubishi bus. It had pretty good pickup and power for such a small engine. We were tasked with running a regular route taking troops from the main base back to the numerous tent cities that were popping up. We also used the bus to take our people and equipment from the truck staging area to our tent city. It was the least I could do. I felt bad that I was not able to go on missions, but at least for now, most missions never left Kuwait. Neilson and Daniel Palomino were my bus groupies. Daniel is also known as Palo or Ox. He was built like an ox, so that fit him quite well. He stood only about five foot five and was almost as wide as he was tall. He was not fat though he often joked that he was a fat man. He loved life and deep conversation. He had a great sense of humor and was always respectful to anyone he thought deserving. They were always with me when they were not on missions themselves. They came for two reasons. Number one, we were good friends, the kind that you knew would be there when you needed them, which was really important to have in a combat environment. The second was because the bus had air-conditioning, a commodity seldom found on base and not at all in the tent city. With the temperature now hitting in the high 120s, it made for a nice escape. When the bus was full of passengers, I was reserved and tried to drive responsibly. But when empty or when it was just Neilson, Palo, and me, I would let it all hang out. We would cruise through the desert paths, not really roads yet, and ramp the bus over sand dunes that would build up from the blowing sand. There was always some excitement to be created and seldom a dull moment when we were together.

My truck wasn't the only broken truck that we had, and with parts not readily available, we took matters into our own hands. Remember when I said that the lot commanders at the dock didn't know what they had? This is where that information comes into play. We work our way back to the dock and pick up a few extra pieces of equipment. We take them back to our camp, and after a quick number change, we have our parts. We make quick work to strip down the trucks then tow the shells to a live-fire artillery-impact area and blend them in with the other targets. We make one last check to ensure that they can't be traced back to our unit, and we run away clean. Things are finally looking up.

With things finally falling into place, I was reminded of how much I miss my dear wife back at home. I think that I will go to the PX to see if I can find a greeting card worthy of how I feel about her. After an hour of waiting in line and enduring the heat, it's my turn to enter. I make my way to the greeting card section, and while there is not much of a selection, one caught my eye. It's soft, yellow in color, and has a bright red ribbon flowing around the script. When I picked it up, the edges were dirty and tattered as if it had been read a hundred times. I almost put it back right then and there, but I was compelled to at least see what it said. As I read it, the words rolled off my tongue and straight into my heart. The card spoke my words, at least what I would want them to be if I could get them out. It's perfect. I reach to the shelf to get an envelope, and it is gone. I search the entire rack, and to my dismay, there is not a single envelope that the card would fit in. I begin to get disheartened, and I begin to doubt my choice. I start to put it back on the rack but then decided to give it another read to see if it is truly worth the trouble. Again, the words ring out like a majestic choir. I take my search beyond the card rack to see if I can find anything that I could possibly mail this wonderful card in, and to my dismay, it just wasn't meant to be. I laid the card on the rack and left the PX with my head hung low. During my walk back to my tent, I began to perk up just a bit when I decided that I would still send her a letter.

> Hello, Lover,
>
> I miss our time together. How are the kids? It's hotter than hell already. I can't bear to think what it will be like when it really gets hot. My truck is still broken, so I'm not running any missions as of yet. Neilson and Palo say hi. We are always together. It's nice to have such great friends. They help make this place bearable.
>
> The bus that I am driving is really small. It looks like an oversized Volkswagen, bus but it is made by Mitsubishi. I had it on the highway the other day. Its top speed was about fifty-seven and shakes profusely from about fifty on. What a piece of crap. It's still fun to go hopping sand dunes with, and it does have AC, so it's not all bad. I even sleep in it on occasion to stay out of the dust and heat.
>
> I found a card that was absolutely perfect and said everything I would love to be able to say myself. Unfortunately, the card was dirty, tattered, and unworthy of purchase, but the message was pure poetry. It stated that true love could endure the distance that we face and the trials that we have already bared. Of course, it was stated in a way that

> I could only dream of. What the card really said is that I love you and miss you with all of my heart.
>
> I Love and miss you!
>
> Damon

This would be the first of many letters home. For now, it is our only way to communicate. I wrote a couple of times a week. It made me feel closer to home as I let my heart open and spoke to my beloved family. Helen was good about answering every letter that I sent and kept me up-to-date with everything on the home front. I received more mail than almost anybody on post and was envied for it. I was always ready to share information as Helen kept in touch with many of the other wives, so she would often have a few words for the others. I lived for the letters to and from home. They made the world just a little smaller as I felt closer to home.

Many of my friends didn't bother to write and only received a few letters here and there. I could see them growing distant and building great disdain for everything that the deployment was. I could tell that they were primarily just homesick, but for them, staying close by writing just reminded them of all that they were missing back home. They would just as soon, keep their family at bay, deny their feelings, and hope that we wouldn't be gone for long.

CHAPTER 4

Through the children's eyes, I see how we are received on my first trip into Iraq. They stand just beyond the border, greeting us with friendly waves and the occasional thumbs-up. These people have nothing except the hope that we bring for a brighter future. The broken down shacks they live in rest on a barren dust bowl. Many of these shacks had less than four crumbling adobe walls, and roofs were a rare commodity. These places would not be fit for livestock back home, I thought to myself. For as far as the eye can see, there is not so much as a tumbleweed, and I wonder how they feed the few goats and sheep that are present.

The children stand by the roadside, waiting for a soldier to toss them food, water, or some small trinket. As the troops pass, the kids run barefoot on the scorching hot blacktop highway. They dodge in and out of traffic, risking life or limb to gain some new treasure. Our troops think that they are doing these children a favor by tossing their gifts of charity, but one life lost to this foolishness is too much. Most of these people have never had anything other than the basic necessities of life. They didn't feel cheated or in need of anything else, but when we see them we feel pity and wonder how anybody can live so meagerly and still be happy. So we introduce them to our trinkets and turn their tranquility into chaos as they fight and build internal animosity. It occurs to me that our way isn't always better. What did they do before we came? I wonder how many others asked themselves this question. Surely they had better things to do with their time than stand at the side of the road. It has always been easier to give and give from the heart than to rationally think about not only what they did before but what they will do when the gravy train runs dry. Not unlike the "give a man a fish or teach a man to fish" saying, we need to help these people, but handouts will become expected and result in animosity.

Our convoy consisting of twenty-five M915 tractors (single-cab Freightliners) towing forty-foot triple-axle flatbed trailers, one recovery vehicle, and the lieutenant leading in his HMMWV pushes north toward our destination at Camp Anaconda. We are traveling on MSR Tampa, a supply road that has only bits of blacktop. We are running with windows down and weapons at the ready. With almost no wind, the air becomes heavy with a thick cloud of dust, and at speeds of up to fifty miles per hour, we are driving blind. If you slow down, you risk getting hit from behind, and if they slow down in front, you're just plain screwed. The convoy commander feels that speed is our best defense from hostiles, but I fear that traveling like this, we could become our own worst enemy.

After a few hours into the trip, we pull off to the side of what you would call a road, I guess, for a short break. As we come to a halt, the empty desert comes to life. Hodgie men and children seemed to appear from nowhere. I can't see any visible signs of existence other than the people themselves. They have come to peddle their goods: Old Iraqi money, bayonets, whiskey, and numerous other items. It was a regular Hodgie mart. They don't quite have the hang of this free enterprise as each peddler carries the same merchandise as the last, and nobody seems to understand why only the first couple of salesmen are having any luck. We grab what we can during the short stop, all the while maintaining a high level of distrust and vigilance. Then it's back to the dusty trail, and the people seem to disappear back into the desolate desert.

The small patches of blacktop increase the farther north that we venture. It is a huge relief to actually see the road and beyond. The tension drops just a bit, but it wouldn't last very long. Soon, we found ourselves in the city of Samawah, engulfed by the population. It was Young Feller's turn at the wheel. His eyes grew wide, and I'm sure his butt was puckered tight. He didn't have much experience driving a tractor trailer in the first place, and this environment was new for the both of us. Lieutenant comes on the radio: "Scorpion 1 to all elements, keep it tight and don't let any civilians into the convoy." I acknowledge his request, "143 copy, out." Then I start barking commands to Young Feller to get in tight. "Get close! Closer! Damn it, I don't want to see as much as air get between us and the truck in front of us!" Young Feller gets a very determined look on his face and honors my command, actually bumping up against the truck in front of us several times. "Good job! Damn good job!" I told him, and his face now shows pride in addition to determination. My focus now turns to the crowd as well as other parts of the convoy who were not doing the job near as well as my young rookie driver.

We remain tight as we come up to the circle of death. This is one of these traffic circles where the intersection merges several streets together without stopping. Everybody is expected to merge into the circle then dart off onto whatever street they desire. This circle is tough to maneuver our twenty-wheel tractor trailer around. Then you add not letting any civilians into the convoy and it is tougher yet, but our security depends on it. So I didn't feel too bad when a broken-down, not-fit-for-travel

Hodgie car bumps off of our trailer tires. We communicated our intent, but these people drive as if they never had traffic laws. They drive pedal to the metal and only stop when they hit something or reach their destination. We had our mission, and we were not about to miss our turn.

None of these cars look like they would be fit for travel. The only cars on the road are twenty-plus-year-old Japanese imports mixed with a few new BMWs and Mercedes. It was like time stopped for the poor and middle class. This was likely due to the trade blockade imposed by the previous administration. People think that war is inhumane, but these trade embargos affect the general population in a much more direct manner. The people who are connected with the local government live lavishly on the rations while the poor and general population must live off the few remaining scraps. This is truly inhumane. It's easy to see why the masses are happy with our invasion. I wonder if they would be as happy if they realized that we were also somewhat responsible for their poverty.

We clear the city, and the population and activity fades to a much more manageable level. Only an occasional dwelling exists along the two-lane highway beyond the city limits. The traffic is easily kept at bay though they are quite persistent. The job of the rear truck in the convoy is to keep anybody from passing and getting within the main body. As somebody attempts to pass from the rear, the rear truck pulls into the opposite lane and blocks their approach. It seems that no matter how many times these people are blocked, they continue to try. They just don't seem to get it.

The farther we travel north, it becomes more apparent that a war actually took place. The road is lined with the remnants of Iraqi tanks and a few of our own vehicles. Structures once thriving with activity are now crumbling masses of charred destruction. The people who escaped the wrath of the powerful weaponry now seek refuge along the streets, creating shelter out of what others have thrown away. Black smoke billows into the sky as if there was some urgency to consume it.

Baghdad is the ultimate paradigm of rags or riches. Some of the houses are lavishly large, well kept, and in good repair, while others were small, and trash appears to be piling up just beyond their doorways. The war didn't seem to affect the general population. Most of the buildings that were destroyed were on former Iraqi military bases, bases that we now occupy. One thing that peaks my curiosity—no dwellings, no matter how grand or meek, appear to have glass for their windows. I just found this odd and wondered why.

We plan to spend the night at Saddam International Airport. As we make our way through the narrow two-lane road, I can't help thinking that perhaps I have been here before. I know that it's not possible, but the area looks much like the farming community in the San Joaquin Valley near Bakersfield, California. About the only difference is the lack of machinery and farm equipment. Here, things are still done by hand, and the labor is done primarily by the women. In fact, almost all of the work is done by the women. I remember earlier today I saw women carrying heavy bundles while the donkeys walking beside them carry only a few supplies. I guess I know how most women are regarded here.

We cross through the back gate and make our way to the staging area where we will bed down for the night. There are a few small planes parked around, but for the most part, other than gate guards, this place is completely abandoned. We park our trucks in what at one time would have been the plane taxi area. Then we set up our cots and bedrolls and slowly break up into our peer groups for companionship and light conversation. Everyone has their own stories, and each has their own perceptions of what we have seen today. Someone has managed to score some beer from one of the many Hodgie marts along the way. This should make the night a bit more interesting.

Neilson, Palo, and I congregated by my truck, and someone handed me a tall, sixteen-ounce brew from Holland. All the beer that we bought from the Hodgies was European, the good stuff, and it should have been for twenty bucks a case. Hell, you could buy whiskey for five dollars a fifth, the not so good stuff. Palo also had a beer, but Neilson only drank on a rare occasion. He didn't need it. Neilson would talk your ear off either way. If he wasn't telling you a story about one of his sexual encounters, then he was complaining about the heat. Palo was different. He would talk about the ranch or one of his relatives. It was always interesting and never disrespectful. We all liked to make fun of one another, and for me, the beer aided in the *carilla* (Spanish for ribbing). Jokes in general flow easier once I have tipped a few. They just seem to come to me. My favorite was a Johnny joke; it goes kind of like this. Little Johnny was out in his backyard, playing bus driver (stop me if you've heard it). Anyway, Johnny was out in his backyard, playing bus driver. His mother was proudly watching out of the kitchen window as Johnny pulls up to his first stop and says, "All you mothers getting on, get on! And all of you mothers getting off, get off!" Johnny's mother couldn't believe what she thought she just heard until little Johnny pulls up to the next stop and again he says, "All you mothers getting on, get on! And all of you mothers getting off, get off!" There is no mistaking this time, and Johnny's mother runs out to the yard, yanks Johnny up by the arm, spanks his butt, and sends him to his room. Three hours later, Johnny's mother comes in and asks him if he thinks he can play nice now, and after a brief assurance, Johnny runs back outside and jumps into his make-believe bus, then it is off to the next stop. As Johnny makes his stop, he says, "All you nice people getting on, get on. And all of you nice people getting off, get off. And all of you mothers complaining about the three-hour delay, talk to the b— in the kitchen!" Cracks me up every time.

The next morning, we are off again. The lieutenant was looking at a map and decides on a shorter alternate route. What he didn't know is that this route would take us straight through downtown Baghdad. The locals were as surprised to see us as we were to see them. It's not often you would see a twenty-five-truck convoy on a road so close-quartered that our mirrors stretched from one side of the road to the other. We were again at a snail's pace as we tried not to run over any of the marketers that filled up what was left of the crowded road. "What the hell was the lieutenant thinking?" I told Young Feller. "He wasn't, apparently," said Young Feller. He wasn't indeed. We probably would have been taken apart if anybody would have had foresight to think that somebody would have been stupid enough to take this route. We were lucky, and I would rather be lucky than good. As we finally pull to the gate of Camp Anaconda, our final destination, we receive intel that a convoy that was where we were supposed to be was taken apart by an ambush. Like I said, I would rather be lucky than good.

On the trip back, we took the road most traveled. We had all of our gear as we were en route to what would become our new home for the unforeseen future. Southbound we traveled past Scania then past Samawah then onto a patch of dirt that had just been cleared of all signs of life only a mile or so from Nasiriyah. This would be our new home.

CHAPTER 5

Welcome to Camp New Cedar. Later, they dropped the *new* as people forgot that there was ever an Old Cedar. This was a camp midway between Baghdad and Kuwait. Our mission was to resupply the North with all combat-essential items: food, water, clothing, ammo, and just about anything else you could think of. Our base was the relay point between northern and southern Iraq. As we pull up to an empty patch of dirt, we all felt that somewhere along the way we must have pulled the short straw.

"So this is it," I told Young Feller, "home sweet home." Just then, some first sergeant shows up and says, "Nope, you guys are supposed to be on that patch of dirt over there." There was absolutely no difference from one patch to the other. So we moved five hundred yards to a new empty patch of dirt. "Let's see what the hell they tell us now," I said. We have been moved time and time again, so now we were reluctant to unload any gear. They first told us that our home would be Camp Anaconda, so we were surprised to find ourselves here.

I jump from my truck, and the soft, deep sand seems to explode into a dust cloud. This was nothing like anything I had ever seen before. The dirt was the consistency of baby powder, and you couldn't walk without a cloud following you.

I walk up to Nielson's truck and said, "I feel like Pig-Pen from Charlie Brown with this dust cloud following me everywhere."

"Not only do you look like Pig-Pen but you smell like him too!" Neilson replied.

"Thanks," I said.

"No problem," he replies.

We continue to converse through the open window of his truck. Neilson wasn't about to get out of his air-conditioned truck until he had to.

After an hour or so, our platoon sergeant returns with the plan; he then gives the signal to rally around him. George Gregory was our platoon sergeant. He was a good-looking former marine, about medium build, and had short silver hair. Some called him the Silver Fox, but I just called him George. George says, "This will be our motor pool. We will set up our camp way in the hell on the other side of the base." Many groans come from the crowd. George responded by barking, "That's the way it is. We don't have a choice. Get used to it." George was a nice guy but tried to pull off the hard-nosed marine act when he was in front of the whole platoon. It just didn't fit. He was a friend to most of us, and you either respected him or you didn't. There wasn't much in between.

That night, we slept under the stars just as we had every night since we first ventured into Iraq. The nights were cool, at least compared to the days. I always found peace at night as I would stare into the amazing star-filled sky. It was so dark that you could see every constellation, and I would fall asleep every night to their fiery glow. It was so peaceful that it was hard to imagine that a war was still going on.

The next morning, about half of us prepare to return to Camp Anaconda while the others will stay behind to construct our new home. Each of the three platoons that made up our company would have two tents for the soldiers and then a common mess area. We had prebuilt our showers and shitters back in Kuwait. They were rough and makeshift, but they did the job. This tent city is what I returned to after our uneventful trip to Anaconda and back.

Our days were set out for us from this point on. One day we would have a down day; this consisted of work details such as filling shower water, burning shitters, or policing the camp. Then we would report to the motor pool for preventative maintenance, refueling, and anything else required to get ready for the next day's mission. Then, in the afternoon, we would do laundry, write letters home, or other personal things. The next day, you would get up at two in the morning, pick up your load, and head for Camp Anaconda. Once there, we would wait to get unloaded, and by about 10:00 p.m., we would finally return to our staging area and bed down for a few hours. The next morning, we were up early to get loaded with trash, old tires, and anything needing to go back down south. It was a grueling schedule, and then add the 130-plus-degree heat, not to mention the enemy activity, it made for very long stressful days.

We would clean our laundry in washtubs like back in the good old days. We didn't have washboards, just one wash pail, one rinse bucket, and a scrub brush. When we got our clothes all nice and clean, we would hang them from the tent ropes to dry. If you were lucky, they dried before the wind came up blowing the powdery sand into your not-so-clean clothes. There was always a dust cloud over Camp Cedar even if the rest of the county was calm. So our laundry was never really clean. I guess it had something to do with the engineers clearing the land before we arrived. In any case, you could see the base from miles away.

We are up early for this day's mission. We go to the TTP (trailer transfer point). This is where we pick up our loads, and like many days, the tie-downs were pathetic. The goods would never make the trip like this. Everybody helps out, and we get the loads secure. We have some of the best teamwork that I have ever seen. I would match this group against any team in the armed forces for cohesion. It looks like we may make our spot time. This is the time that our convoy was due to depart. It becomes a big deal when you're trying to balance the traffic for the entire theater. We have a quick safety brief, then we are on our way.

As we run down MSR Tampa, the Hodgies follow close behind the convoys to pick up anything that rattles loose on the rough, washboard road. We have seen them pull knifes and even guns on one another to fight over a simple tire that fell from one of our loads. It was nothing worth stopping an entire convoy over. They never challenged us, but it seems on this day they have come up with new tactics. They have started digging small trenches in the road to jar our loads loose. This was unacceptable. Our lieutenant and the rear trailer less Freightliner truck or (bobtail) stop to chase the Hodgies away from our convoy. It becomes apparent that we will need to start using MSR Jackson from now on.

We have to examine our loads after the Hodgies' efforts. This will require an off-scheduled stop. We hate to stop; it always gives the bad guys added time to set up ambushes. They shouldn't need more time as they could almost set their watches to our schedule. I guess they get agitated if we are late. I do know that the attacks become more numerous when we are a little off schedule.

We make up a little time and arrive in Scania only about ten minutes late. The lieutenant leaves to check in and get the latest intel report. He returns in short order and calls us all together to spread the word. IEDs (improvised explosive devices) are expected between BIAP (Baghdad International Airport, formerly Saddam International Airport) and Samawah. Then he went on to say that the enemy has begun firing at convoys from their vehicles as they pass. We proceed with diligence, taking heed from the latest intel.

We pass through Samawah without incident, and then we move on to the three-lane highway. We run in the center lane in an attempt to keep the IEDs as far away from the convoy as possible. The last two vehicles will be the only trucks to alternate lanes as needed to block oncoming traffic from entering our convoy. Then we would run at speeds of up to seventy miles per hour. A moving target is hard to hit; a fast moving target is harder to hit. We used everything at our disposal to better our chances.

We are about halfway to BIAP when a huge blast comes from the center median. The blast shook my tractor like an earthquake. The sound was heard by the lead vehicle a mile and a half away, but our speed paid dividends this day as only small rocks and bits of shrapnel peppered our trailer. Our adrenaline spiked, and from that point on, it was apparent that we were part of this war. My emotions were all over the place. One moment I was angry, the next I was thankful with a little fear thrown in from time to time. At that moment, I was transformed from truck driver to warrior.

The lieutenant radios back through the convoy, "Did everyone make it through?" I reply, "We're all good." Then I proceed to give a situation report. We really didn't see anything other than the blast through the side mirror. We were lucky, and again, I would rather be lucky than good. Our awareness went up a notch, and we were always careful to ensure that we wore our protective gear even if it was outdated. At least it was something.

We passed by BIAP and on to MSR Sword without further confrontation. MSR Sword was the highway that took us through Baghdad and on to Camp Anaconda. To say the least, this was a dangerous area. It was highly populated and attacks could come from anywhere and often did. There were a great number of buildings to hide a sniper, trash piles all along the highway to conceal IEDs, overpasses to take potshots, and the terrain was as such to easily set up all-out ambushes. This was definitely a target-rich environment. Unfortunately, we were the targets more often than not. Today, we had already had all the action that I cared to handle. Thankfully, it was all the action we had to endure as we reach our destination.

We unload and head back to our staging area before chow. We made good time in spite of all that had happened. I have taken to sleeping on the hood of my truck. It was easier than setting up a cot, and the day's heat would radiate out as the night chill took over.

As darkness washes the day away, we hear a familiar sound. *Thunk, thunk, thunk.* Then there was an eerie whistle as mortars were sent flying into the base. We can see them fly overhead like skyrockets on the Fourth of July. Then the ensuing blasts!! They occur over and over again until the choppers go airborne to chase them away. I wonder if anybody is hurt, and I pray for one and all before fading to sleep.

We are up at the first morning light. I shit and shower but did not shave today. We can get away without shaving on mission days. They say that it was so the helmet strap didn't irritate your freshly shaven face, but I think the command was just throwing us a bone to keep up morale. Whatever the reason, I was more than happy to partake. Then we grab a quick bite as the chow hall first opens. We must make it quick so that we get our loads and can be the second out the gate. This was a balancing act. You never wanted to be first out because you were more likely to get hit, but you wanted to get out so that you could be off the road before dark. Today, we were a little too good and the first out. Our luck may be running down as we are forced to make a quick stop just inside Baghdad in the heart of MSR Sword. I have the back door and remember the intel from the previous day. Small arms fire as vehicles pass the convoys. I was still a bit jumpy from the IED and very determined to keep our convoy safe.

I pushed the traffic to the far left lane as we were parked on the right shoulder. I take a quick glance into every car and truck as they pass and then peer down the line to see if any looked more suspicious than the others. One catches my eye. It is an old 1970s-style Volkswagen bus; it was solid white, not decked out in some psychedelic paisley print like those back home. The windows were up, and the side door was wide open. It was early but already over ninety degrees outside. I can't imagine why they would have the windows rolled up but have the side door open. I still evaluate each vehicle as they slowly pass. If a vehicle comes too fast or erratic, my weapon comes to the ready, and I take aim on the driver. Then they must make the choice to yield or die. So far, I'm happy with their choices as everyone has chosen to live. The bus is now only one car away. I bring my weapon to the ready and switch the selector lever from safe to burst. I will only have a split second to make the call. My heart pumps adrenaline through my pulsing arteries. The tension builds, and my finger starts to squeeze the trigger. *I have to keep my people safe* keeps running through my mind, and the few seconds feel like an eternity. At the last moment, bearing down on the target, a little girls face appears in my sights. I pull away as I see a woman and little girl proudly waving as they pass. No lives were lost this day, but my virtue will be forever scarred for what almost just happened.

Two days and two life-changing events; I just wanted this mission to be over. There was no chance as our day was just beginning. It was about two hundred long miles from Camp Cedar to Camp Anaconda, and every mile held its own challenges. I am grateful to find out that we will be taking MSR Jackson home today. MSR Jackson was a nicer route. It was totally paved, but we would have to travel through more towns with possible hostiles. Everyone agrees that it is worth the risk. I don't think I could bear the dusty trail today. The route cuts our travel time by nearly an hour, and I'm happy to get back to our meager existence. I'm happy for the dusty cot, cold shower, and lousy food. I will never look at life the same. We were home, if only for a day, and for that, I was thankful.

That evening I met with Neilson to discuss the recent events. He knew of the IED but had no idea about the incident with the woman and child. Neilson said, "Man, I would have blown them away!" I damn near did, I thought. He wouldn't have wanted to have been in my shoes, and for that matter, neither did I. But I would have to put this one behind me and the only way I could, would have been to die that day. So I did, at least in my mind. I gave up on the idea that I would ever make it home; that let me give my all every time I entered on to the battlefield.

The next mission, Young Feller was given the day off, and I was volunteered to babysit the sergeant major. He was from Puerto Rico, and with the way he spoke, he was the butt of many jokes. He loved to talk about "saucer." You and I know it as soccer, but he had his way. I actually gained some respect for him on this mission. High-ranking people seldom put themselves in the trenches, but he wanted to know exactly what his troops were going through on a daily basis.

We took MSR Tampa on this trip to give him the full taste. I was tasked with putting him through the wringer, and I gave it all that I had. While driving blind on the dusty road, I was never more than a few feet off the bumper of the truck in front of me. We were the last truck in the convoy, so I could play it as if this was the only way to know where the road actually was. That wasn't far from the truth, but I had run this route enough to know where I was. It was almost second nature by now.

We stop in Scania, and the sergeant major was on major Hodgie watch. If any would come close to the convoy, he would pull his sidearm and run them off. I wanted to tell him to chill a bit, but that's not something that you could say to a sergeant major on his first mission. As the intel report comes down, he gets even more keyed up. IEDs, small-arms fire, and RPGs (rocket propelled grenades) were reported between BIAP and Anaconda. Then we were under way.

In the town of Samawah, traffic begins to back up, and then we are forced to halt. The sergeant major again draws his sidearm but this time for good reason. Anytime you are forced to halt is a good reason for concern. Today, it appears to be an accident between two Hodgies, and they are blocking the road. We race to the front of the convoy on the shoulder of the road. No one appears to be hurt, so we push the blockage out of the way with my tractor and the convoy passes, but the Hodgies don't take kindly to our level of concern for their property. "F— dem," said the sergeant major, and I had to laugh out loud.

The sergeant major would draw his weapon in every little town from Samawah to Baghdad. Once in Baghdad, he stayed at the ready. He almost looked like a soldier, and somehow I found that strange. The trip home was almost a carbon copy of the trip up except for the blockade in Samawah. Once home, the sergeant major was very appreciative for the experience and shared his enthusiasm with my immediate command.

You can bet that I took a razzing for being the sergeant major's driver. It didn't matter that I didn't have a choice. It made me an easy target. From that day on, I had a newfound respect, but I couldn't convince any of the others or at least not that anybody was ready to admit.

I received a package upon my return. It was from Helen. She always found interesting and useful items to send. Bug spray, flea collars, pogie bate, and in this box were ten pounds of pinto beans. We would have our company cooks make up a batch for a hometown treat at some point, but it was hard to find time when we were all together.

Helen would send a package just about every other week. Mail, however, was unpredictable, so I would often receive several packages at once. I would share much of what I was sent. Everyone appreciated it, and besides, there wasn't very much room to store a lot of stuff, so you had to make quick use of anything that you received. One day, she sent me a set of sheets. This was one of the nicest ideas that Helen had. They were cool to sleep in and provided coverage from the sand fleas. We were still sleeping on cots, so no one thought of asking for sheets, but once again, I became the envy of my tent.

Little things make a big difference when you are living in hell. Helen always took the time to send me a little piece of home. I know that she would do her best to be creative, and she was. The kids would on occasion send some pictures or homemade artwork. These were always treasures. We still didn't have any luxuries; the nearest PX was miles away, and we seldom had an opportunity to go. Camp Anaconda had a small PX, but by the time we got there and down loaded, we were too exhausted to go for the meager inventory that they carried.

With all of the love pouring in from home through correspondence, it made it hard to think of myself as already gone, but I had to. If I was going to function on the daily missions, I had to accept death and face it head-on. It was the only way. So from this point on, I would go on every mission as if I would never see home again, leave everything on the battlefield every time out.

It didn't take long to follow my guts and instinct; I even welcomed confrontation. It was exciting, and I was now fearless. Every day on the road became just another day at the office. I wasn't trying to die; I didn't have a death wish. I just made my peace with it.

CHAPTER 6

It's July third and a down day for us. That means that we will be heading out on the fourth for Anaconda. We anticipate stepped-up enemy activity to help us celebrate our holiday. After a quick preventive maintenance check on my tractor, I go to look for Neilson. I find him where I knew I would, sitting in his air-conditioned truck. I jump up on the step, and we begin to speculate as to what we can expect for tomorrow.

"What's up, my brother?" I said.

Neil replied, "It's freakin' hot!"

"It's not that bad, at least not yet," I told him.

It was still early. The temperature was probably nearing one hundred, but the mercury would travel much higher before the day was over.

Again, I ask, "So other than the temperature, what's up?"

He replies, "It's freakin' hot! When I get home, I'm going to fill the bathtub with ice and just lay there for a week!"

Neil was a little dramatic when it came to the heat. He was starting to talk about going home in a couple of weeks. I told him that I thought we would be here for some time to come. He said, "Fine, you stay here, but I'm going home in a few weeks." He was beginning to act a little crazy, but as far as I know, it was just an act. He really didn't want to talk about the mission tomorrow, so I didn't force the issue.

That evening, we heard that there had been major attacks both on Camp Anaconda and on convoys. Twenty-two soldiers were killed including the first KIA (killed in action) from our battalion. He was one of us, a truck driver; it could have been any of us, but somebody had to be the first. For many soldiers, this was a place of honor, the ultimate sacrifice. We all have to go, and if you can go doing something that you believe in, then somehow you've won.

With all of the risk factors adding up, we thought that perhaps they would cancel our mission. There wasn't much of a chance for that; the war must go on. Our battalion commander once provided us with his great words of wisdom, and for many of us, it gave us something to cling to. He said, as many were bitching about our extended stay, "Suck it up. This is war, pussies!" In war, it is accepted and expected that some people will die. The hope is that more of their people die than ours. So anything other than business as usual would be unacceptable.

Morning comes hours before the sunrise. I grab a cool shower before anybody else begins to stir. I hate waiting in line for a shower, and just about every other time of day, that is exactly what you do. It's like going with your girlfriend to a shoe store during a clearance sale. The lines are long, and the service is slow. At night, if you wait too long, then the water supply cools off to a less than comfortable level. If you get there by one or two in the morning, the water carries enough residual heat from the previous day's sun that it is still tolerable.

We have something to look forward to this evening: steak and lobster for dinner. I can't remember the last time I had a good steak. I guess it has only been about four months, but it seems like a lot longer. We ate MREs (meals ready to excrete) every meal for two months before they finally built the chow hall. Even then, the meals were less than desirable. The chow hall was the only semi-rigid building on the entire base. It was air-conditioned and had real ice for your drinks, so it was a nice place to go to get out of the dust for a few minutes a day. For Neilson, it was a little piece of heaven right smack down in the middle of hell. If they would have had women working it instead of Hodgies, you wouldn't have been able to pry him out with a crowbar.

At the safety brief prior to the mission, we are told that we will be taking MSR Tampa this morning due to the increase in enemy activity. This was not good news, but it was understandable. We had always been our own worst enemy on this route. We had a number of minor accidents resulting in lost equipment but never any enemy activity.

With great apprehension, we depart from the gate of Camp Cedar. Then, as we make the cross over to MSR Tampa, our convoy comes to a halt. "Not already!" I said to Young Feller. This was too soon for enemy activity; we weren't five minutes beyond Camp Cedar. Then the lieutenant comes on the radio, "Scorpion 1 to all elements, there is a blockage in the road. I'm going forward to check it out." We all exit our vehicles and set up a five-twenty-five security. This is when you first patrol the first five meters from your truck then turn your focus to the next twenty-five meters. That was about the best that you could hope for in the dark of night.

The lieutenant returns with a slight alteration in our route. By now, the sun was beginning to peak over the horizon, and the desert was beginning to take shape in ominous shades of shadowy grey. As we move around the blockage, I look over to see the remnants of a 915 tractor still smoldering after an RPG attack.

The loaded trailer was still attached, so the convoy must have been in a hurry to get the hell out of the area. This is going to be a long Fourth of July, and the Hodgies are providing the fireworks.

We make good time on the dirt road today as we had a favorable breeze that kept the dust at bay. The Hodgies will also be kept at bay today. As far as we were concerned, this was our holiday and the Hodgie mart was closed. That didn't stop them from trying, but we shut them down. As we pass other convoys, I can tell that they were not alone in this thinking. While we were in solidarity, I doubt the Hodgies understand. As far as they knew, it was just a slow day at the market.

As we pull into Scania, the lieutenant says that if we need the restroom, we had better use it quickly. He said that he was going to get the intel brief but would send it out over the radio to speed things up a bit. We had been taken off our mark early this morning, and we needed to get back on track. The lieutenant returns in about five minutes, and by the sixth, we were rolling. Then he comes back on the radio. "Scorpion 1 to all elements. Stand by for intel report, break. We all know what took place yesterday. Today we are expecting more of the same. Heavy IED attacks. They are setting them up in daisy chains." Daisy chains are where they set out a number of IEDs in a row, covering up to several hundred meters, all wired to go off simultaneously. As you can imagine, this makes escaping the blast area nearly impossible. The lieutenant continues, "They will try to use these IEDs to separate our forces then will likely have ambushes set up to inflict heavy casualties. Allow extra following distance and engage any and all targets while maintaining movement." This was our SOP (standard operating procedure). If any truck goes down for any reason, the last three trucks in the convoy would stop to provide security and/or recovery while the rest of the convoy suppressed fire and headed for the next predetermined rest point.

It's all quiet from Scania to BIAP, but as we pass BIAP, we hear a voice over the radio say, "Contact right front! Contact left front!" We were in a cross-fire ambush. As I heard these words, my senses peaked. I can hear the faint but distinct sounds from their AK-47s over the palpitating sound of our diesel engine. They are still a ways off but should come into view in a few short moments. I begin to peer out, looking for the forthcoming gunman but also not losing focus on the sides of the road. This would be a great place for them to set up secondary IED attacks. I then see the right-side gunman ducking behind a sandbar at about my two o'clock and about fifty meters off the MSR. The left-side gunman must have already been taken out as we are not taking fire. Young feller lays down suppressive fire from the driver's seat. I radio out their location then switch my selector lever to burst. I take a bead, pull the trigger, and watch as my rounds fall just short. I adjust fire, but it's difficult to get a clear shot from our fast-moving vehicle. My next shots were affixed to their position, and as one magazine empties, I slap the next one in. The encounter only lasted a few seconds, but everything seemed to go in slow motion, and I can recall every burst from my M16. I can no longer tell if my rounds are hitting their targets, and as they fade from my sight, the only thing I know for sure is that they are no longer firing at us. I will never know if I killed anyone today or not, but it did not matter to me either way. I fulfilled my objective and that was to aid our convoy in completing our mission. As we clear the area, the lieutenant radios to the MPs to police what may be left of the unsuccessful combative antagonists.

With my body still trembling from the excitement and my ears ringing from the echoing truck cab, I shout to Young Feller, "That was awesome!" Young Feller appeared to be a bit shaken by the experience but tried to match my enthusiasm. I don't know what I found more exciting, the shooting or being shot at, but it was truly the experience of a lifetime. The rest of the journey was uneventful, but that didn't matter because as we cross into the gate at Camp Anaconda, I am still beaming with excitement. I can hardly wait to get unloaded. First, we will go for the holiday feast, and then we will get together and talk about the day's events.

We enter the chow hall, and the cool air is filled with the smell of seafood and a hint of smoke coming from the barbecues. For a moment, it was like being transported back home to a nice surf-and-turf restaurant. The meal looks great too. They continuously bring in fresh steaks from the grill and fill the chow line. To complement the feast, they had baked potatoes and corn on the cob. Butter and fresh lemon were provided, and it seems the only thing missing is sour cream. I guess we all must make sacrifices. I sit down at the first open table and make the first cut into my steak only to find that it was very well done and tougher than nails. *Oh well*, I thought, *I still have lobster to enjoy*. As I plunge my fork into the meaty lobster tail, the fork appears to go right through. I have never seen lobster that you can cut with your fork. I dip a piece into the greasy melted butter then pop it into my mouth. The next thing I knew, I was spitting the morsel into my napkin. This lobster was so over boiled that it had the consistency of canned cat food and probably tasted just about as good. Everything was overcooked to the point of cremation. The only thing that wasn't overcooked was the potato, and that was still a little crisp. They ruined the entire meal. I was so disgusted that I dumped the meal in the trash and lost my appetite. Some people looked as if they were actually enjoying the meal; maybe I would have too if I didn't set the bar so high to start with.

I returned to my truck and waited for Neilson to return from chow. At the end of the day, it feels good to remove your top, unlace your boots, and relax in pools of your own sweat. Most of us had brought fold-up camping chairs from home, and they came in handy to relax in during the evenings and into the night. I still had the better part of a case of beer that I had been saving for this mission. When Neilson came back from chow, he passed right by me without saying a word. He headed straight to his truck cab then took his cooler from his truck and dumped its contents over his head, then he let out a scream like a little schoolgirl. Neil had been acting strange, and this event concerned me. You see, this wasn't just ice water, it was Hodgie ice water. This ice was brown when purchased, and God only knows what kind of parasites and other organisms it carried. I used the ice to cool my beer and sodas, but I always made an attempt to sterilize them with the whiskey before use. Neilson, then dripping wet, comes over and says again, "I'm going home in two weeks." I told him that if he believed that, then he truly was crazy. "Watch me," he says. I made an attempt to turn the conversation to today's mission, but Neil didn't want any part of it. I guess this place is really getting to him. He retires to his truck as the sun begins to set.

"Young Feller, grab us a beer."

"You bet," he says as he quickly appears with a cold one.

I could talk to Young Feller about anything—religion, politics, or just about any other topic. He seemed genuinely interested in my opinion, and I am happy to have an inquisitive audience. I am a right-wing Christian conservative who loves politics but hates politicians. For as long as I can remember, I have kept abreast with the issues. I don't mind people having opposing views just so long as they know why they have the views that they do. I find more people who call themselves liberal and vote as such but have no idea what a candidate stands for or even who their candidate was in extreme cases. I suppose that we have some on our side as well, but as far as I know, I've never met one. Young feller was admittedly on the fence; he was curious about the issues on both sides. He did, in fact, live up to his nickname and was still trying to define the person that he was to become.

After a little more conversation and a few more beers, I crawl up to the hood and my bedroll. As I look into the sky, *thunk, thunk, thunk*. I was waiting for that, but they won't last long tonight as the choppers were already airborne waiting for the ensuing strike. Several bursts from the mighty guns in the sky and the mortars are silenced. I lay on top of my bedroll dressed in my sleeping shorts, and the gentle breeze softly kissed my exposed skin and feathered through my fine hair. It was just like a whisper on my skin. With the sudden chill, I pull over the cover, look back into the sky, and ponder over the day's events. I have been pulled in many directions during the past couple of weeks. I wonder what Helen and the kids are going to do today. They should be waking up soon. The time difference from Iraq to home is ten hours, so morning comes at home shortly after night falls here. I'm thankful for my family, and I miss them like crazy. It seems funny; even though I miss them, they make it easier for me to be here. It's easier to risk your life when you're fighting for those that you love.

In the morning, I catch up to the lieutenant on the way to the chow hall. He tells me about an idea he has for gun trucks—mobile gun trucks that are hardened with steel plates that could not only draw fire away from the convoy but could actually chase down and engage the enemy. That sounds good to me. I wouldn't mind getting into something like that though I really didn't want to give up my truck. The lieutenant had other ideas for me. He wanted to put me in the rotation for convoy commander. That was a job I could sink my teeth into. I was honored by his confidence. This was unheard of for a young E-5. The convoys were always led by E-6 and above, and there were going to be many people who outranked me in my convoys. This could prove to be difficult, but I would have to show my strength as a leader if I am to gain their trust.

The lieutenant felt like there was no time like the present and had me take over as the CC (convoy commander) for the trip home. It was my convoy, and I was making the calls. I would say when we go, where we stop, how fast, what route, and who would go where within the convoy. I had my own ideas, and so far, everyone else seemed satisfied with the status quo. I was going to shake things up a bit and possibly ruffle a few feathers along the way, not for this trip though for now I will learn the ropes. Next time, it will be all on me, but that will take a week or two before I come up again in the rotation. They say that every good leader is also a good follower, and I am content to follow, but I would rather take the reins.

Neilson continued to act a bit crazy, and his insistence that he was going home never faded. After a week had passed, he started counting down the days. Then, the morning at the end of his countdown, as he wakes, he looks at me and smiles. "I'm going home today," he said. The next thing I knew, Neil turned as pale as a ghost. He said that he didn't feel well, and he didn't look very well either. George had me usher Neil to sick call, and by the time we reached the doc, his temperature was spiking at 105 degrees. He was starting to go into convulsions, and the doctors had to put him in an ice bath to bring his temperature down to a safe level. Neil was getting everything that he predicted, including the ice bath. The doctors couldn't figure out what was wrong with Neil, and by that afternoon, he was on a medevac to Germany. The SOB did it. I don't know how, but he did. I have some speculation but nothing that I could pin down. His symptoms and fever were real. If he did anything to trigger a life-threatening fever, then he truly was crazy.

CHAPTER 7

A few of us took a ride to Tallil Air Base. It's still early in the morning, so I will have a chance to make a few phone calls before my family goes to bed. It is always good to hear a familiar voice. Helen tells me all of the things that she sees every day on the news. I have to this point made light of the danger here. I kept telling her that the headline-grabbing media was blowing things out of proportion. I knew that Helen was worried sick to have me over here; I couldn't bear to justify her fears.

We spoke for about half an hour. While it was great to talk to her and hear about all of the things that I am missing back home, it really put a lump in my throat to think about how lonely I am. Then she had me say hi to the kids. It was hard enough talking to Helen but talking with the kids would almost completely rip my heart out of my chest. It was always worth the pain; my lonely heart may have been ripped from my chest but it was then refilled with joy the more we spoke. By the time I hung up, I would deny any feeling of guilt or heartache and hold on to the love that I have for them all.

When I hang up with Helen and the kids, I look around to see several empty phone lines; this makes it okay to make another call. I take turns calling my mom and my sister. They both love to hear from me as I do from them. We are all very close. Today it was my mom's turn as I spoke to my sister a couple of weeks ago. I dial the many numbers that it takes to make a calling card call from overseas. Within a few rings, my mom answers.

"Hello."

"Hi, Mom."

"How are you?"

I can always tell that she is especially happy to hear from me. She clings to every word that I speak. She always has questions about different things on the news. I do my best to set her at ease. She tells me that she had spoken to Helen and, by her words, made me realize that I wasn't doing anybody any favors by holding back all that we have been going through. I tell my mom that I am going to set everything straight, but the waiting line for the phones are growing quickly, so I have to cut my call short. "Love you, Mom. Send my love to Dad and let everyone else know that I say hi. I have to go. Bye." I hear her good-bye as I hang up the phone.

I pick up a few needed items at the PX and then wait for the others to head back to the base. Once I get there, I waste no time. I get out my pen and paper and write a very detailed fifty-seven-page letter to Helen. I told her every detail about what we had been doing, about the near misses, about the highs and lows and everything in between. I was from this moment on going to tell her everything; she was seeing it on the news, and now hearing from me, she could decide what was blown out of proportion by the media. I wrote before during and after every mission. Every spare moment I spent writing. It was good for me. It helped me keep things in perspective, and it made me feel closer to my family as well. I wrote so much that people would kid me about writing a book. Before long, I realized that I could use the letters as notes to tell my story.

I had a few missions under my belt as the CC and the changes that I made while in command became the norm. All I did was take favoritism out of the mix and arranged the trucks to better stage our firepower. I did ruffle a feather or two, but I was completely correct for doing so. My convoys had run well even when some of the higher ranking individuals tried to challenge my authority. I was quick to set them in line, and they never stepped over again.

This next mission would be a true test of my abilities. They are making the little redhead girl assume the role of CC, and I am to assist her. The little redhead girl was Veronica Chavez. Veronica was not quite five feet tall, a little on the heavy side with red hair and a round petite face. She was a nurse but then took a job as the training NCO for our company shortly before our activation.

The night before a mission is when the work of the CC begins. You had to collect all of your paperwork (i.e., movement orders, the latest intel, and a list of equipment, weapons, and personnel). Then you would have to construct the order of march, ensuring the people and weaponry were dispersed properly throughout the convoy. Then finally, you would write down the pre-convoy and safety brief that you will talk through in the morning. This would include the rate of march, rest points, route, and every scenario that you could think of for preplanning. Much of this information was not ready until late afternoon or evening, so the CC always had a late night.

After I walked her through all of the paperwork, I headed for bed. This would be a short night. As I drift off to sleep, I instantly begin to dream. It's a bloodbath of which I cannot escape though it's not my blood. It's an ocean of deep red with pounding waves crashing down, leaving behind a soft pink residue along the shoreline. I run around searching, looking for answers. Who did this? Whose blood is this? And why do I get trapped at every turn? I take a path far from the last only to end up at the same place I started. I change my approach, I change the game and the task, and still here I am, trapped, covered from head to toe in fresh deep pools of still warm blood.

I instantly wake from the nightmare, and as I lay there trying to return to sleep, I begin to analyze my dream. Could it be a premonition of things to come? It could be, but I have never been one to have premonitions. I can see how this situation could become reality. The situation exists for a possible horrific conclusion to each mission we run. Could it be a picture from the past, some unknown precognition feeding me tidbits of information? Why? What good would this information bring me? Perhaps it is a warning from the past, a warning intended to keep me from reliving a particular atrocity. Possibly destiny could be pulling me down this path where I am responsible. The blood that I am trapped in was spilled by my own doing. I am trapped by the actions of my own free will as I bathe in the blood of my victims. I will cleanse myself with their innocence and forever bury my sins with their flesh.

Or was it simply a nightmare without rhyme or reason? I'm caught in a loop of my own wild imagination. Still, the cries of the dead are vivid in my mind as they breathe their last breaths. All around me lay hundreds of faceless bodies falling away, leaving empty shells of lifeless flesh. To say the least, I couldn't return to sleep. As long as I'm up, I guess I will grab a quick shower. The water is still warm and feels good with the cool night air. This may relax me enough to get an hour or so of sleep before our mission. It does the trick, and as I return to bed, I'm out like a light.

The morning comes too soon, but our pre-work has paid dividends as Veronica pulls off her brief without a hitch. We were rolling out the gate precisely at our spot time. Things were going smoothly. We make the cross over to MSR Tampa and we are under way. As we reach our traveling speed of sixty-five miles per hour, one of our trucks suddenly drops off the shoulder of the road. It was a huge drop-off of maybe a foot or more. The driver attempts to maneuver back on to the road but overcorrects and loses control. His trailer jackknifes, and his truck flips. We are only three trucks back, and all we could do was watch the situation unfold.

Almost before I can come to a complete stop, Veronica has her combat lifesaver's bag and is running toward the wreckage. I had never seen her move like that, and to say the least, I was impressed. I followed, trailing well behind to give aid or provide security. Veronica quickly evaluates the driver and co-driver and then begins to provide first aid. Another registered nurse that was in our convoy comes up to assist Veronica. They work together, and in short order, they have the two men stabilized. I was truly impressed by the level of cooperation, professionalism, and teamwork these two soldiers exhibited. I felt a little more at ease just knowing that they were with us if anything further was to happen.

We grab their gear from the wreckage and provide security until the medevac arrives. They seemed to take forever. We were only a few miles away from Tallil Air Base. This was a much more established base than Camp Cedar. I would have thought that the medevac would have come from there. Over an hour later, the medevac shows up and takes the two drivers to the hospital for further evaluation. The crew that was supposed to clean up the truck and trailer were there in short order. So with this end all tightened up, we can get back on the road. By now, we were so off schedule that it didn't make sense to even worry about making up time. We would just take our time; rushing could lead to further episodes.

My previous judgments about Veronica were dead-on, but it became obvious that when it came to playing army, she was out of her element. As a nurse, she was top-notch. In this new venue, she had earned my respect. She confided in me that she never had much of an opportunity to drive the big trucks. For that matter, she had little experience even driving a small car. She could drive, but her experience was in a small town with little traffic. Things were beginning to click, and she wanted an opportunity to learn. I was down for that; I would teach anybody anything as long as they have a desire to learn. I would have her drive the next leg of the trip. It was going to be across MSR Sword through Baghdad. Talk about baptism by fire, but she was game.

The lieutenant's idea of the gun trucks came to fruition, and on this their maiden voyage the crew is a bit overzealous. They are chasing the Hodgies at every stop. It kind of looks like an episode of the coyote-roadrunner show. The Hodgies run up to a truck to make a sale and the gun truck gives chase, and while they are tied up chasing one Hodgie, two more make their way back to the trucks. It's far more humorous than effective, and the majority of the drivers are wondering just what kind of monsters the lieutenant created.

At the intersection of Tampa and BIAP, Veronica takes the wheel. From the gunner's seat I have a determination to keep the little redhead girl safe. She has her hands full just operating the twenty-wheel tractor trailer. She looked even smaller sitting in the captain's chair; it looked as if it would swallow her up completely. I guess that added to my desire to keep her safe. I could imagine what my daughter would look like from the driver seat, and there wasn't much of a difference.

As we cross over to MSR Sword, all is quiet. The Hodgies are all still in their little makeshift huts by the roadside, peddling their goods. This is always a good indicator that no IEDs are set up at roadside. If the peddlers are gone, it doesn't always mean IEDs, but if the children are missing from a location that you are used to seeing them in, then you had better watch out. As the first shots ring out, the people disperse. "Contact! Left front, on the overpass. Contact! Left rear from the overpass!" I have to keep Veronica safe, but I can't defend the left side of the truck from the passenger seat. So I crawl out the window and assume a supported position over the top of the cab, focusing all of my attention on the forthcoming overpass. As we near the bridge, I take aim, switch my selector lever to burst, and prepare to rock and roll. That's when I heard it. Shots ring out from the right side of the convoy. Hanging out of the truck with my full back exposed, I knew instantly that I was the target. Our speed made us a difficult target, but today, I was lucky. This was likely a pre-staged ambush. If we would have stopped to engage either the forward or rear gunman, then they would have cut us apart at the flank. This was not luck. This was the way we rolled. We were not in the game to fight; we were in the game to defend ourselves and deliver the goods.

In the midst of all of my near misses adding up, I was beginning to feel more than lucky. Once is lucky, twice maybe, but by the third near miss, I was beginning to feel like I wasn't supposed to die, almost superhuman. This probably wasn't the best role to choose, but it made sense. I had already decided that I wasn't going to make it home. If I were superhuman, I could leave it all on the battlefield and still make it home. Of course, if I didn't, that would be okay too; it's a soldier's life.

With all that happened on this trip, we arrived at Camp Anaconda just before the sun set. It took forever to get unloaded at the TTP, so by the time we return to the staging area, it's long past time to bed down for the night. It was an MRE for dinner, and with the late night last night, I am completely exhausted. No mortars tonight; that's strange. The choppers must have been out patrolling early. You almost miss them. It's kind of like when you sleep with somebody that snores. It annoys the hell out of you, but you just can't get to sleep without the dreadful noise.

In the morning, before chow, Veronica tells me that she needs to pick up a case of beer for our supply sergeant's birthday. She had tried to pick it up on the way up, but with the gun trucks running them off, she didn't get the opportunity. I told her that I was sure that we could make that happen. There had to be at least one opportunity; they couldn't be everywhere at once.

We finally got the opportunity in the Samawah traffic circle. The traffic was backed up, and we were only inching forward. Veronica motioned for the Hodgie to come to the truck and, with beer in hand, jumps up on the step at her door. Just as he handed her the beer, one of the QRF (quick reaction force) boys came in like a linebacker and tackled the Hodgie off my truck. Veronica was surprised to have the case of beer and the twenty dollars still in her hands. What she didn't account for was our slow speed, and she is startled when he catches up to us. Again, he jumps up on the step, but this time, he is greeted with the muzzle of her weapon. "Get down! Get down!" she screamed. He must have noticed by the look on her face that she was just scared enough to shoot him, and he does as he is told. I continue to watch him with his gestures until he is out of sight. "You could have just given him the money and he would have gone away just as fast," I told her. She was still holding the money in her hand, but it never occurred to her. She just pulled off the perfect armed robbery. I could just imagine how he would tell his buddies about how he had just been robbed by a little girl. I continued to laugh on and off the rest of the way home.

When we returned, the laughing stopped as we heard the news that one of our females had been raped. She was raped by one of our own people in a drunken blackout. This was a man who had only been back from leave for a week or so. He went home for the birth of his new son and in one drunken episode ruined the lives of several people. Sober, he was the nicest guy in the world. It's hard for anybody to believe this tragedy. Alcohol, for the first time, was strictly forbidden instead of the "don't let me catch you" rule that had been in effect. I was happy for the crackdown. Several people had gotten out of hand in recent days.

Some were even drinking while on the road in convoys. This had to end badly. Somehow, I don't think it is over for good.

Then we were informed that our brigade commander had called for a battalion formation this evening after chow. All we can think about is that it must have something to do with the recent event. No one is looking forward to this little chat. What else could it be? For the most part, everything had gone well. We haven't even had a company formation since we moved into Iraq.

The battalion formation started as the usual Charlie Foxtrot. Nobody knew what order we were supposed to be in. We would get formed up, then the sergeant major would move us from here to there then there to here. Finally, we seemed to get it together. The sergeant major calls us to attention and then turns the battalion over to the commander. He then tries to motivate us like at some sort of rock concert. He yells out the different companies, then the companies respond, trying to outdo one another. It happens at most of these kinds of formations. It would be nice if someone came out with a new playbook. So the battalion commander shouts out "Where is the 720th?" We raise the roof in response. That's where things go wrong. The next company that he calls out wasn't there, or the next, or the next. He gave up on the cheerleader routine and calls us all to gather around him while he gives us the goods.

First, he talks about the troop from the battalion that was killed on the third of July. We were kind of surprised that he even knew about that after his first fiasco. Then he gives us the normal BS about how good we are doing and how proud he was. I guess if he was any prouder, he may have known who we were. Then for the real news: "I know that you thought that you would be going home after six months, then it was by Thanksgiving, then by Christmas, but the theater commander just came up with a new directive. All units in theater will serve 365 days boots on ground." This was not the news that we were looking for. Some had even speculated that he would tell us that we were going home early. These people were truly disappointed. He then stated that we would all get a chance to go home on leave at some point during our tour. I don't think anybody believed that. He then had us form back up and released us back to our companies. The mood for the rest of the night and even for the next few days was a bit somber. Still, many thought that he was just full of bull and didn't know what he was talking about. That seemed to make the most sense to me.

CHAPTER 8

I return to my bunk, and it is instantly obvious that the camp has fallen victim to our environment. There must be an inch of dust on my cot and the rest of my belongings. It probably looks something like the attic in your grandma's old house, that is if no one had been up there in the past twenty years. It's hard to believe that it was clean only two days ago, at least as clean as you could hope for. I guess there is no time like the present. I have to get this mess cleaned up before I make any attempt to bunk down for the night. If not, I will be eaten to death by the sand fleas. We thought that the mosquitoes were bad when we first arrived and began sleeping with mosquito netting. While we had an early reprieve from the mosquitoes, we were quick to find that the netting seemed to attract any and all airborne dust. Within hours, they were consumed by the powder-like dirt. Along with the dirt came the sand fleas, and they were small enough to go straight through the netting. We soon found out that the sand fleas' bites are far more numerous and more irritating than the mosquitoes'.

The netting was trashed and replaced with bug spray. It worked somewhat, but at least the mosquitoes would leave once they had their fill.

They are telling us that soon we will move to the new tent city. The new tents are supposed to have AC and more modern shower and toilet facilities and even real bunks. With these luxuries, you would think that we would be anxious to move, but all we know is what we know. We have learned to adapt to our meager habitat with the heat, the dirt in the showers, and a nice predictable hard cot. We don't like change. If that means we will have to endure some undue hardship, then so be it. They say that change is the only thing in life that you can truly count on. So why are we reluctant? In any case, we should have a few weeks to get used to the idea.

With Neilson gone and Palo on alternate missions, I seem to have a lot more time on my hands. I have read all of the books that I have, so I guess that I can get caught up on some overdue letters.

Dear Sherry,

Greetings from hell. It's really not that bad. It is quite hot, however. Helen sent me a digital thermometer. It stated on the package it's guaranteed accurate up to 150 degrees. It didn't make it. It lost its mind the other day at 147. I had it in my truck so that I could keep track of the temperature when we go on our missions. The sensor was well outside of the truck attached to the side mirror bracket. I didn't want the reading to be affected by the radiant heat from the truck, so I put it as far out as possible. Most days, the temp stays in the high 120s to the low 130s. I really don't care where you are. Once it breaks 110, it's just plain hot.

We went to see the ziggurat and the city of Ur the other day. This place has such a cool history. The ziggurat was built during the Sumerian times in about 2113 BC. It was the temple of the moon god. I guess there is supposed to be a temple for the sun god in Egypt. These people had incredible foresight for longevity. They estimated that when it was first built, it stood twenty-six meters tall. Now, four thousand years later, with erosion and damages done from numerous wars, it is still just over seventeen meters tall. We walked up the many stairsteps to the top. From there you could see for miles. The temple overlooks the ruins of a palace, a temple built for King Nebuchadnezzar, and the city of Ur, which was the birthplace of Abraham. Abraham was considered to be the father of all prophets according to scriptures.

I'm getting ahead of myself, but it was all so cool. There was even a historian out there who talked us through much of the history. The ziggurat looked like a huge fortress without any doors but a number of tiny windows. The historian told us that the windows were simply to allow the water to escape the building after a rain or even floods. The building itself looks like the makings of a pyramid with the top half cut off. There are also the grand staircases that allow access to the top of the temple. The building was constructed out of many adobe-style bricks that have become petrified over the many years. Some of them still hold ancient writings in cuneiform. They also used a natural tar between the bricks to allow for expansion. The tar was shipped in small boats from c just north of what is now Baghdad. The river once flowed only about two kilometers from the city of Ur. Today, after some rerouting in an attempt to starve the southern people, the river is a little more than fifteen kilometers away. The tar was only used in temples and palaces due to the cost of the goods and transportation.

The last palace was excavated by the Brits in the 1920s. Most of these artifacts are still in Iraqi museums. I'm sure that on earlier digs they robbed many of the treasures that they found and took them back to their homes of origin.

During the excavation, they uncovered the history from two great floods. The first took place in about 4000 BC, and the second flood was from about 2900 BC, which is thought to be from the Noah flood. The historian picked up some seashells from this period and gave them to me. These unbelievable treasures I will hold dear.

According to the writings found, the king actually worked along with the others to create his great palace. The walls of this palace were over four feet thick. The queen's tomb revealed great treasure, including a beautiful golden harp. She had been buried with fifty-nine other bodies. The bodies were likely her servants in life and in death. There were two different stories about the death of the servants. The first was that they were given poison to drink and were buried with the kings and queens. The second was that the servants were simply buried alive. It could have been both as the palace held tombs of more than one king. The palace had a number of large deep tubes buried beneath it. These large ceramic tubes were lined with holes and backfilled with broken pottery and would work as a drainage system so the water would leach out after a large rainstorm.

The temple of Nebuchadnezzar was constructed during the Babylonian times. This was around 2025 BC to 1763 BC. King Nebuchadnezzar's temple holds a great architectural significance. It held what is believed to be the first structural arched doorways in existence. This archway has fallen away over the years, and there is not much of it left. I fear that not too many more generations will have the opportunity to see it in its natural form. I didn't know the story of Belshazzar, King Nebuchadnezzar's grandson, until I spoke to Helen after a dream that I had. You can look up the story in your Bible. It had to do with the fall of Babylonia and the writing on the wall.

In the dream, I was staying in a large motel room. There was a giant chalkboard on one wall. Some children were scribbling on the lower part of the chalkboard while I lay resting on one of the two beds. Then without rhyme or reason, writing appeared in the upper left-hand corner. Each letter was slowly drawn out, and I was mystified by what I was seeing. As soon as the last letter was drawn, the image was wiped away. Then some sort of mist or spirit appeared. It flew around the room a few times then accelerated toward me. I woke up just before it hit, but then I felt as if something had passed through my body. As I lay in my bed, I can feel the mattress settle up against my back as if it was depressed and then released. I had never felt so invaded in all of my life. I wish that I could remember what the writing had said, but I was so intrigued by the writing itself that I never really paid attention to the words. As I told Helen of the story, she remembered the biblical story of King Nebuchadnezzar's grandson Belshazzar and the writing on the wall. It was remarkable that this dream took place right across the street from where the biblical story took place. I wonder if they were as I was, too mystified to see the writing on the wall.

The city of Ur was in complete ruin. They have erected a small building that someone had told me was to mark the actual birthplace of Abraham, but that story was not true. The building was the beginning of what was supposed to be a shrine to one of the gods, but it was never finished. The building is nowhere near the time frame of the other dwellings. They have also recreated a building out of stone that would be a replica of the city itself but on a smaller scale. I understand that the pope asked for permission to come and see the city of Ur and to pray in the birthplace of Abraham, but Saddam declined his request.

If this area ever does get civilized, they will have a great opportunity for tourism. I can imagine that many great men and women have been denied the opportunity to see this world as I have. What a great blessing.

I don't mean to talk your ear off or your eyes off as you are reading this, but I thought that this would peak your interest. I am going to have to go for now. I have to get up early tomorrow for another mission. Take care. Love you, sis.

Love,
Damon

For our next trip up north, the well-rested Young Feller was back at the wheel. MSR Jackson had been cleared for use. This was the first time since the Fourth of July, and we were grateful to once again be off the dusty trail. Young Feller is riding shotgun for the first leg of the mission. This was almost always the case. He wasn't a morning person, and he stayed groggy for the first few hours of every mission. This wasn't all that bad heading up from the south, but when we leave from the north to go back home, I need him to be at the top of his game. Since we were able to avoid Tampa and with no enemy activity, we made it to Anaconda in record time.

We were all off-loaded and back to the staging area by about 1600 hours (that's 4:00 p.m.). This time was remarkable. Others found this a reason to celebrate, and I was correct when I said that alcohol would not be gone for very long. I didn't think it would be this quick. I haven't given in to the temptation, at least not yet.

As darkness falls, many soldiers are already three sheets to the wind. One young soldier, Julio, had way too much to drink and was coming down on himself pretty hard. He had made some mistakes in the past, but over the past few months, I had watched him grow. If it were a contest, I would have to say that he would have won the award for most improved. So when he was coming down on himself, I put him straight. I told him about where

I thought he was before and where I see him now and how he had earned my respect. I guess that touched him. He gave me a brotherly hug and went off to bed without saying another word. Now it was just me, Young Feller, and the old man. The old man was Steve Richardson. Steve was one of the favorites. He was a good worker but not a good leader. I had ruffled his feathers when I became the CC. He had been led to believe that somehow he was mission critical to be the last truck in the convoy. This was the position for vehicle recovery and rear security. But for him, it meant that he didn't have to put up with loading or unloading as this truck was always bobtail (trailerless). He was a seasoned, skilled driver but not a warrior. He belonged in the main body of the convoy, not to mention he lacked the weaponry to be running the rear.

Steve had a bit too much to drink and was in the mood to try to debate me. Every subject, from politics to tactics, I had the facts where he had only speculation. He was complaining about being in Iraq and that we were only here for oil. Armed with more information than most would care for, I shot back with great detail:

> We will never know if the war was about oil or not. We all have our speculations. The truth lies within the people of Iraq. Saddam was truly an evil, vain SOB. The other day, Palo and I were heading to Tallil Air Base to make some phone calls. We stopped at the local Hodgie mart and talked to some of the locals. Every one of them had their own stories about atrocities committed against their families by Saddam and his reign of terror. They told the stories about how Saddam tried to starve them out by rerouting the rivers. Then there were the stories of torture and beheadings and mass graves.
>
> One told a story about a time during the Iraq-Iran war, where Saddam had told his people that they were running

low on funds and if they were to defeat the Iranians, the people would need to bring all of their gold to designated pickup sites. A few weeks later, Saddam was paraded around Baghdad in a solid gold chariot. The entire country was decorated with memorials to himself. Bronze statues, bronze faceplates, or portraits of Saddam were in every little city across the entire country. This man loved himself and loathed all others. He needed to be taken down. If we came for oil, then we came for oil, but the people of southern Iraq will remember that we took down a mad man.

It is a time for a true new world order, not globalization. The last thing the world needs is to put all of the power into even fewer hands. I am speaking of the power of the people—all people. Most people would agree that the strength of America is its diversity wrapped in freedom. America is a virtual conglomeration of ideas, beliefs, and backgrounds held together by the possibility for individual grandeur.

John Lennon could imagine a world where everyone was equal. "No countries, nothing to kill or die for, and no religion too." This would make for very a bleak outlook for human existence. This would mean nothing to believe in, nothing to care about, no differences, and no individuality. I can imagine a world where all people live free and have the ability to seek their own destiny. I can imagine a world where all people would have access to an unbiased education, where history is fact-based, free of political agenda. I can imagine a world where every government represents the will of its people, and I can imagine an enlightening where it doesn't take a natural disaster for people to realize what is going on beyond their front doors. This is why I came to Iraq, this and in hopes of a brighter future for my family. I would guess that most other soldiers would give similar rationality.

> Without war, there can be no peace, only a lawless world where the mighty rule the meek and masses with iron fists, providing a life for their people that was hardly worth living. The people of Iraq understand. I'm sure that we have people back home that will never understand. They are as ignorant as you.

He was arguing just for the sake of arguing, but after this barrage, I sent him away with his tail between his legs. Young Feller wanted to get up and cheer as Steve left. He also wanted to get up and pop him in the mouth, but he had confidence that I would handle the situation. I'm sure that by the time he left that he probably would have preferred a pop in the mouth.

He was talking crazy and almost suicidal that night. I spoke to George in the morning about Richardson and said that I thought that he may need some time off. That's when George explained that I really took the wind out of his sail by moving him to the main body of the convoy, but time off may be just what he needs. I felt a little guilty about putting him through the wringer the night before, not for moving him. That was the right call, and no one would disagree.

As we depart Anaconda, all systems are go. The day feels good. We got out on time, and even the loads were not as bad as usual. Young Feller is at the wheel. About halfway down MSR Sword, Bella drives up alongside of us. I'm surprised to see her like this. Bella is the hardest working person that you would ever meet. She says that she has to be because in a man's world such as the army, you can't be just good. She truly makes up for all of the slackers of any sex. Then she tells me to pull over, that we have two flat tires on our trailer. I tell her that we are going to go to the next rest point. Then she comes back and says that the two flats are on the same axle. That sounds strange to me. I don't recall running over anything. Even if I did, they would have hit the front tires, not the rear. I tell her that we are going to keep going. I can imagine what she must be thinking, but this is not an area that you want to stop in if you don't have to.

I tell Young Feller to use the Jake brake and to try not to brake unless he absolutely has to. If he hits the brakes, then what's left of the tires will lock up and cause undue heat. We could catch on fire or destroy the axle. Sure enough, as we come to a halt at the next scheduled stop, the tires burst into flames. Bella jumps out of her truck in a flash with extinguisher in hand. She quickly puts out the fire. I had already informed the CC that we would need additional time to make the repairs.

I grab my jack as another soldier grabs my spare. Bella has someone grab her spare as she started on the lugs. We worked like a NASCAR pit stop, but things slowed a bit as I had to cut the tire. It was wrapped around the axle. While cutting the tire away, I found something imbedded in the inner tire. It was the projectile from an AK-47. If we would have stopped, we would have been cut apart. As we finished the job, I showed Bella what I had found. She threw her arms around me. She knew as I did exactly what that round meant. We all live to fight another day.

You can bet that this is one souvenir that I'm going to hold on to. Hell, I may even have it bronzed and made into a necklace. It is not possible for me to ever have more respect for Bella than I already have, but there were more words spoken by that one embrace than one could ever hope to speak.

In this one moment, I felt that my entire deployment was justified. I can't think of another individual in the convoy that wouldn't have stopped in the same situation. I thought about it, but something told me to keep going. Surely, if we would have stopped, it would have been the end for someone, if not many. This was definitely an ambush in the making. I have learned to trust my gut and never get in a hurry if things start to go wrong. Everything happens for a reason. Just go with it.

CHAPTER 9

The days are beginning to cool just a bit, but the nights are downright chilly. Labor Day came and went without notice. I can't believe that we have been here for nearly six months now. The days are long but pass quickly, and the nights are short but seem to go on forever. This place has become almost too familiar. The attacks go on so often that they feel, matter of fact, like just another day at the office, not that we are becoming less vigilant. In fact, that's just the opposite. Much of the time, we know when and where they are going to hit us before they even figure it out.

The day finally comes where we must move into the new tent system. We were one of the first companies on the base and one of the last to move. We still would have been content to stay where we were. The new tents are more comfortable. The AC is a nice touch, but it only has two speeds: blow like hell and off. They were not set up on a thermostat either. The bunks are a nice touch, and it is nice to take a hot shower again. They even have a laundry service, I guess, that we can adapt.

George has told us that we must pick a time when we want to go home on leave. I don't want to even go at this point. By the time my date comes up, we will be only a few months from going home for good. I know that if I do go home, it will be hard to come back. I just don't know if I want to put myself or my family through that. I know that they will want to see me even if it will be hard to say good-bye again. I guess that I will talk to my wife about it and then go from there. As it turns out, one of the dates still left is surprisingly over Thanksgiving. It would be nice to be home for that.

The internal conflicts continue to brew. The old man has gone to our command and threatened them. He stated that if they continue to let E-5s run convoys, then he is going to go above their heads to the battalion commander. Taking his concerns under advisement, they said that E-5s could be the NCOIC for our group but not for the entire multiunit convoys. Two days later, they came to me and said that I was going to be the NCOIC for the next multiunit convoy. That means that either they are promoting me or they threw that entire BS out the window. My convoys had always run smoothly. I guess they took the old man's ideas up the chain of command and the command said screw him. I hope this is finally the end.

Young Feller is away on leave, and Julio will be riding with me for our next mission. This should be a fun one. It's a multiunit convoy. Julio and I will be the lead truck. We will be responsible for keeping the pace of the convoy, and Cloudy will be the NCOIC. Cloudy is one of the most intelligent people I know. He knows it too and at times uses this to challenge people to the point of being obnoxious; but most of the time, he's a nice guy.

We had been running missions continuously with the 459th. Our units were equally capable, and we worked great together. The other companies from our battalion didn't seem to be carrying their weight. We had logged more than three times the miles of the other companies. One of the companies that we were assigned with had older equipment that had a top speed of fifty-five miles per hour. Their equipment was always breaking down. Lack of preventative maintenance and just wanting to keep things down so they didn't have to go on the road were the biggest issues. By bringing them into our mission, it was hoped that we could bring them up to our level. It did give us a real day off in between missions. I'm not sure that this trade-off was worth it. Driving at slower speeds and the lethargic demeanor of these people would increase our risk of attack. We had run every mission like we were ready for a fight. Everybody always wore their protective gear, and we ran with our windows down and weapons at the ready. This was not the case for the others, and while they logged far less miles, they have been hit more often.

This morning, the group from one of our sister Companies was slow to get their loads secure, resulting in us missing our spot time. Then, as we get on the road, a civilian convoy has the road blocked. Apparently, they had gotten separated, and their convoy was split in half. The front half, instead of pulling to the side of the road, had stopped and blocked the entire road. Now we were stuck behind them but in front of the second half of their convoy. Now they are turning their trucks around in the middle of the road to go back for their lost leg. What a Charlie Foxtrot. By the time they pull their heads out of the clouds, we are over an hour behind schedule. Another fifteen minutes down the road, one of the other Company's trucks has to stop again to fix his load straps. This is unbelievable! As we are sitting on the side of the road, a tanker convoy passes us. Now we must give them some time to get ahead of us.

By the time we finally get to Scania, our southbound convoy is already there. We radio to them. "How's everything going southbound?" They report that SSG Logan from the 459th lost his truck and trailer to an RPG attack. Then he moved to one of the HMMWVs and then was disabled by an IED attack. Nobody was hurt in either attack, but the equipment was lost in both cases. Talk about a bad day. I knew Logan. I had worked with him a number of times. He was one of the best that the 459th had, and that is saying a lot from this group.

"We'll see you on the flip side. Have a safe rest of your journey southbound."

"You do the same northbound."

Several individuals continue to talk until we are no longer within radio distance.

About five miles outside of Scania, we see several gun trucks in the road firing into a field. Along with them was a fuel tanker with a hole punched clean through. The fuel was still pouring out onto the ground. Our gun truck joins them to provide security as the rest of our convoy drives on. The tanker was hit with an RPG that didn't explode on impact. This was the convoy that had passed us early on in our trip. We should have been in this place at this time. Once again, it appears that we had dodged a bullet quite literally.

By the time we finally reached Camp Anaconda, the sun had set, and it was almost completely dark. What a day! We got so spoiled working with the 459th these guys are a nightmare! *Slow*, *unmotivated*, *uncooperative*, and *unprofessional* would be the first words that come to mind.

When I woke up the next morning, I had that funny feeling in my gut, the one that I have grown to trust. As we depart the gate, I tell Julio, "Get ready. Today is going to be one hell of a day!" He knows what I mean. He told me that he had the same feeling. Fifteen minutes out of the gate, our sister Company needed to stop to resecure a number of loads. "Not again," I say to Julio. We take about a ten-minute break, and Cloudy tells everyone to check their loads. We all oblige his request, and as we complete our checks, we go to assist the others.

Finally under way, we make the conversion from the overpass to MSR Sword. "Where are the kids? There's no kids, anywhere!" I radio back throughout the convoy. "We're about to get hit."

Julio takes his weapon off safe, and my head is on a swivel, looking for the ensuing attack. We clear the area, moving out as fast as we can without stringing the convoy out. We hear that the center of the convoy has cleared the turn, and then there was a loud boom from about a mile back. Cloudy comes on the radio. "Is everyone okay?" Then silence follows. Finally, the center truck comes on. "The truck behind us has been hit!" The truck is a loss, and the crew is injured. The gun truck speeds to their location. The rest of the convoy pulls forward and sets up a security perimeter around the convoy. The gun truck gathers the crew and takes them to a nearby hospital for treatment of their wounds. The lieutenant says that we will move forward to our usual rest point just before the turn to BIAP.

After we were sitting on the side of the road for about ten minutes, I notice a Hodgie pulled off onto the center median. He appears to be working on his car, which is not unusual. These old cars break down all of the time. Soon, another Hodgie stops to pick up the stranded motorist. A few minutes pass, then another earthshaking boom! Cloudy comes on the radio, "What was that?" He was closest to the blast; you would think that he would know if anybody did. Following the blast, everybody around me hits the deck. I am the only one too stupid to drop. Instead, I evaluate the situation and begin positioning our weapons to more strategic locations.

The lieutenant says that we are getting the hell out of here. He says that we will go to BIAP and wait for our crew. We receive word that they will be joining us shortly. Their wounds were minor. One of the men received minor shrapnel wounds in his chest and shoulder. He obviously was not wearing his protective gear. The guy was from, you guessed it, our sister company. Any of us could have been hit, but they usually pick easy targets, and the rest of us were wearing our gear.

As we depart BIAP, I ask Julio, "Are you ready?"

"Ready for what?" he replied.

I said, "We have been hit in the center and end of our convoy. By the end of the day, we will be hit in the front."

He swallowed the lump in his throat and said, "I'm ready."

We were on guard from BIAP to Scania. As we get to Scania, the place is packed. We will not be able to stage in the secure area. We will have to stay on guard for this rest break.

As I am posting security, a black SUV drives up, and Lieutenant Colonel Dow steps out. He is our battalion commander. Lieutenant Colonel Dow was a no-nonsense, right to the point and hard as nails. He was, however, fair. You always knew where you stood with him. He didn't believe in a grey area. He was the one who came up with the phrase "Suck it up. This is war, pussies!" I respected the man not just for his demeanor but he was also a very intelligent man. I didn't like him though. I always thought that he was too much of a prick for his own good.

He asked me how our trip had gone so far, and I gave him an earful. He then asked me to walk the line with him, and I said, "Sure." What the hell else would I say? As we walked through the 720th, we had people posting security and others working securing loads. A couple of people were working on their loads, and he kindly reminded them to keep their gear on. Then, when we got to the sister company, they were all lounging in their trucks with shirts off and no protective gear. It was their man who had been injured already today; you would think that they would take things a bit more seriously. In addition to not pulling security and not wearing protective equipment, they had Hodgies running all over their trucks. The lieutenant colonel came unglued. He asked me who they were, and I was more than happy to tell him. Lieutenant Colonel Dow said, "Get them squared away!" I had been waiting for such an opportunity, so I was happy to oblige him. This was not my unit or my convoy, so I lacked the authority to do anything prior to this point. Many of the troops were hesitant to act even with prompting from the lieutenant colonel. I guess that they had as little respect for authority as what they had for themselves. Lieutenant Colonel Dow was then gone as fast as he had appeared.

We continued south past Samawah. Samawah was the farthest south that I had ever faced enemy contact, but my gut was still telling me that we were not in the clear just yet. Then it comes. "Contact left front!" The gun trucks take up a defensive position. I lay down suppressive fire. The town was too populated to try to engage the enemy from a moving vehicle. They often hid among the general population. As we cleared the area, Julio said, "Well, you were right." I almost forgot what he was talking about. Then I remembered and jokingly replied, "I'm always right!"

Once we returned to Camp Cedar, we were quick to get to the TTP and drop our trailer. This was one mission that we were glad to have behind us. It looks like there is still no rest for the weary. We are told that Colonel Vesco, our brigade commander, will be here again.

This time, he doesn't even make any attempt to motivate the individual companies. I guess he learned from the last time. He calls us around as he sits cross-legged on the roof of a HMMWV. Then he begins by telling us that when we go home next April, we won't be taking our equipment home with us. All equipment will become theater assets. This is good news. If we were to have to find our trailers, we would be searching all of Iraq and probably Kuwait as well. Then he tells us that we are changing tactics. We are going back on the offensive. This means that if someone shoots at us from a building, then the building is coming down. If someone fires mortars from a farmer's field, then the field will be cleared. The idea is to keep the citizens from harboring the combatants. This was more good news. It seems the little man finally had some information that was worth sharing.

Really, this didn't affect the way we ran. As far as Lieutenant Colonel Dow was concerned, we never stopped being on the offensive. He was all about showing force and running hard. We never knew any other way. It was nice to hear that the rest of the theater was going to follow suit. Seeing is believing, so I was still a little skeptical.

After he released us, we broke back down into a company formation. Our company commander was not convinced that we would spend the entire 365 days in Iraq. He had been talking with our command from back home who still said that we should be home by Christmas. We have been inched along since we first got here. My plan was to plan for the worst and hope for the best.

Once we were dismissed from our company formation, we broke down into our smaller peer groups. I am surprised that some of our people actually still believe that we are going home early. If that were true, then we would have been home by now. Our families were fed the same lines back home. Our state leaders somehow think that they can take precedence over the Feds. It makes it hard on the families back home to constantly receive these conflicting reports. I told my family to do as I do, plan for the worst. April will come soon enough, and I will be home on leave in late November. That was just around the corner. I can hold out until then.

Lieutenant Colonel Dow was so disappointed in our sister company that he pulled them from the mission. It was back to us and the 459th. That was the best news that I had heard all day. The bad news was that our day off was gone; even our down day was gone. We would have to conduct all preventative maintenance while en route. This is hard on people and equipment. Young Feller was starting to wear down. I was pushing him as hard as I was pushing myself. Every time I volunteered to take the lead, he got sucked up in the process. It wasn't fair to the young soldier. He should be relaxing with his peers instead of working with the NCOs. I gave him the opportunity to change partners, but he didn't want that either. He liked running with me, just not so often.

Back home, Helen officially takes over as the family support coordinator. She was the assistant before, and that was difficult enough. Our home command unit has consistently put out information that has been far different than what we were receiving in theater. Her job was to keep families informed as new information was passed through the New Mexico Guard Headquarters. It's difficult to be a middle person anyway, but when the information that you receive is in direct conflict with what we are hearing, it turns into a Charlie Foxtrot. It gets to where no one knows the truth, and everything begins to be speculated.

I was wondering if our New Mexico command realized that we were no longer under their command. The Feds had us, and they would do with us what they pleased. The information wasn't always wrong, but what it did more than anything was to foster false hope. Maybe this was their intention, but ultimately, it did nothing except make families leery of any information passed on. This made the job of the family support coordinator most difficult.

I applauded Helen's efforts, and she spent countless hours writing e-mails and making phone calls. It helped her to feel a little more connected, and she made some good friends along the way. In any case, it was a lot of extra work for a woman who had to be mother, father, homemaker, and hold down a full-time job.

CHAPTER 10

George has taken ill, and Baca takes over as temporary platoon sergeant. When Baca is in charge, he wants to let everyone know that he is in charge. He instantly begins to make changes even though his term will be temporary. When someone else is in charge, Baca does all that's in his power to ensure that they fail. Walter takes over as first squad leader while Baca has the platoon, and Baca begins to chastise Walter in front of all of the troops. Walter gets enraged by the lack of respect but understands that that is the way Baca is. In his mind, he should have been the platoon sergeant from the start. It was true that Baca was smarter than George and politics could have had something to do the fact that George was picked instead of Baca, but George had his strong points and was chosen for a reason that would have to be good enough, because you have to have faith in your leadership.

For the next mission, they put Ryan Roybal as the NCOIC. Ryan had spent 90 percent of his total Guard career drunk although he did show his leadership ability when he was sober.

Some liked to call him Ms. Clairol for his almost fanatical need to stay clean. During just about every rest break while on convoys, he would wash his hands and face.

Ryan had never run a convoy in theater, but he enlisted my help and the help of others to make it through. We were all more than happy to lend a hand. Once he got the paperwork done, he could easily take things from there. Then we found out that the XO was going to be the OIC (officer in charge). He had not been on a mission since early on in the deployment. He took a few things away from Ryan, and that had everyone a little disturbed. The officer's job is to hand down the mission. It is the NCO's job to carry out the mission. When officers start to micromanage is when things usually turn into a Charlie Foxtrot.

The XO wanted everyone to get to the staging area earlier than usual to perform rock drills as if this was our first rodeo. Rock drills are where you draw in the sand or use small rocks to simulate what everyone should do in a particular situation. This was normally followed by walk-through drills. It's a belittling way to learn things but something that many young officers like to follow. They must learn it in officer's training school just after they teach that all enlisted personnel are incompetent and should be treated as a lower form of life.

I was tasked again with being the first truck. This was a job that I liked to do. We headed out the gate and easily made our spot time, once we finished our training, of course. We made good time to Scania. We had a nice tight formation, and we looked good. The XO was pleased with our performance to this point. We almost always worked well together. If the XO would have taken more trips up north, then he would have known this for himself.

We pass by BIAP and across Sword. The mission had gone off without a hitch. We were on pace for a record time. Even through Baghdad, the convoy looked and felt good. As I crossed through the gate into Anaconda, I was in good spirits. It had been a while since we had made this trip without enemy activity or some delay. This mission was as near to perfect as I had ever seen. Then I get a call on the radio.

"122 to 143, over."

"This is 143, go."

"143, there is no one behind me," he says as he passes through the gate.

That's impossible! I thought. We were just all together. "Where could they be?" I said to the Young Feller. He then called back to the CC to see what may have happened. After a long silence, somebody came back and said that there had been a bad accident. I thought that perhaps someone had run over a Hodgie on the way in. We were told that the accident was bad and that the XO had picked up one of our soldiers and was taking him to the hospital. We would have to wait for any further information.

Later, we asked what had happened as everything had been going so good. It was a series of events that took place, as it usually is. First, Silva had fallen asleep. It just happened to be his sixtieth birthday. He was the passenger at the time, but when he fell asleep, his helmet fell off his head. Silva's driver was trying to wake him up so that he could put his helmet back on before driving through the gate. The driver's attention was focused on Silva when one of the trucks in front of him stopped for the Hodgie mart. When the driver looked up, it was too late to stop. He yanked the wheel to the left and caught the right side of his truck on the left corner of the trailer in front of him. The trailer then ripped through the side of the truck all of the way to the passenger seat where Silva was sitting. By the looks of the truck, you would have thought that there was no way that he could have survived. When all was said and done, Silva was treated for minor injuries and then released. The truck was a total loss.

When we returned to Camp Cedar, the saga between Walter and Baca continued. We were given an opportunity; one of us from each squad had a chance to win a vacation trip to Dubai.

Dubai was a true oasis with beautiful beaches, hotels, and five-star restaurants. It was like going to Hawaii, but in the Middle East. Walter decided that since Baca was too good to be involved with squad-level decisions that he should be excluded from the drawing. I thought that Walter was playing with fire. I would have abstained from the drawing if I were the squad leader. Walter felt the same way. He wanted one of the troops to have the experience. So the troops' names went into the hat, and Palo's name was drawn. I couldn't have been happier. Palo deserved the trip. He was one troop who was always willing to go the extra mile.

When Baca heard about the drawing, he was pissed. Baca was too self-absorbed to let this stand. I kind of knew that was how he would react. When they held the next drawing, several of us abstained from the drawing both in protest and to give Palo a better chance at winning the second time around. As fate would have it, Palo won the second drawing as well. Things have a way of working out.

I'm pulling back-to-back missions, but this time around, Palo will be teaming up with me. Again, we will be the lead vehicle. This time we will have Palo's SAW (squad automatic weapon). This gun still shoots the same round as the M16, but this gun can lay down up to one thousand rounds per minute. You could literally saw someone in two. The gun truck will actually take point on this mission, but we will still be in charge of pace and such.

As we roll out down MSR Jackson, everyone appears very friendly. It's almost like they had been watching pro-American propaganda. It seems that almost everybody was waving at us or throwing peace signs. It was just a different feel than what I had previously experienced. The children were dressed for school in new shoes and neat uniforms. It was good to see. There were boys and girls from ages of about seven to twelve. It must have been the first day of school, and all were in good spirits. This feeling warmed my heart. I definitely felt a sense of pride as we rolled through. It was almost like being on parade.

MSR Jackson, being a two-lane road, had its own challenges; one being that some of these Iraqi cars and trucks won't go over thirty miles per hour. We must roll faster than that for security reasons. So when a slow-moving vehicle is on the road, the front gun truck will pull up alongside of them and politely wave them to the side of the road. This works about 90 percent of the time. The other 10 percent need a little more prompting. Today, we encounter one of these 10 percent. The gun truck pulls alongside and motioned him over and then had to pass due to oncoming traffic. Once the traffic clears, they pull alongside again. This time he appears to get the message and begins to pull over, but once the gun truck passes, he pulls right back onto the road. Now it was my turn. We pull alongside of him with our tractor trailer and motion him over. He ignores the prompting. Then I jerk my wheel hard right then hard left. Somehow he thinks that he can challenge the big truck, and now I'm tired of messing with him. Again, I yank the wheel hard right, but I would not stop until he was well into the ditch. And for his trouble, he got a couple of nice new tire marks to complement his fancy paint job.

The rest of the trip to Scania was filled with more of the same. People in good spirits, not people who needed some ditch time. It was a welcome and inspiring feeling of true goodwill. I hoped that it would stay with us all day long. Scania was a short stop today. We were delayed by nearly an hour this morning because of bad loads. We had some time to make up.

While we were stopped, I see a solitary man selling sodas under an overpass. I go over to speak to the man. He spoke some English, and when I threw a few gestures into the mix, we were able to communicate quite well. He was an entrepreneur of sorts, selling his sodas at two for a dollar. I offered him a Dr Pepper, and in trade, he gave me a 7UP with Arabic writing. It was a good trade. He introduced me to his grandson. He was a handsome young fellow riding a brand-new bicycle. The man told me that he was able to buy the bicycle with the money he made while selling sodas. We spoke for about twenty minutes, and by the time we left, I felt as if I made a new friend. Just before we drove off, I saw him sell the Dr Pepper to a soldier down the line.

The road was clear all the way through IED Alley and up to the turn to BIAP. We would have to stay on the side of the road for a while at BIAP due to a flat tire on one of the HMMWVs. We are at roadside for about forty-five minutes before we can return to the road. It took about three times as long to change the HMMWV tire as what it takes us to change the big truck tire, and we all wonder why. Now is not the time to question; now is the time to move.

As we cross the overpass from Tampa to Sword, the mood and feeling of goodwill seemed to change instantly. We are about halfway through Baghdad when two explosions rock my truck from the left side. Then I can hear a combination of small arms fire along with automatic weapons.

"Contact right!" comes from the gun truck that stops to draw fire away from the convoy.

"Where?" I reply.

"Two o'clock, three o'clock, now one o'clock!"

We were being attacked from three different locations, and I couldn't see a single gunman. Palo increases to max speed to clear the kill zone while I lay down suppressive fire, rocking the SAW. I never did see a target, but the gunfire was unmistakable.

Once we all clear the kill zone, we stop for a damage assessment in front of one of the army bases. As I walk the line, everybody is okay. The first gun truck had one shot that grazed his hood, but they fired several thousand rounds at a convoy that stretched out for at least three miles, and they only scored one grazing hit. That wasn't the only thing. They must have set the IEDs up backward because the blast went in the opposite direction of the roadside. They blasted out instead of in, probably saving my butt once again. I was grateful for their blunders, but I still wonder just why they miss so consistently. We were back under way in short order and soon through the gate at Camp Anaconda.

Everybody had a story to tell about the attack as we sat down with a cold beer. Once darkness fell, the BS started flying. Some spoke of heroism—this, of course, came from the gun trucks. One guy said that he slept through the whole thing. Another was asleep but was woken up by the gunfire and shrunk down as far as he could into his chair. But the story of the night came from the maintenance truck. They usually ride with one of the professional drivers, but we were shorthanded, so they had to pilot their own truck on this mission. The mechanic who was driving was wearing headphones and listening to his music, and the other was dozing in and out of sleep. The driver hears a few pops over his music, and he thinks that the tires must have picked up some rocks but then takes his headphones off to make sure. The co-driver then rolls his window down to get some fresh air. He finally hears the gunfire as they roll past the gun truck and instantly reacts by rolling his window up in a flash as if he was trying to shut out a swarm of bees. The driver then starts laughing hysterically, and the co-driver doesn't get it. Then the driver asked him if he really thought that the window was going to keep the bullets out. He then realized what he had just done and joined in the laughter.

Only in the Guard. You couldn't make this stuff up. We all laughed together as if it were the funniest thing we had ever heard, and it was. You could picture the whole thing as the driver told the story. The truth was that we literally dodged not just one bullet today but several. I wondered if this would finally change the callous attitude that some of our people still hold. We had a number of people sleeping through one of the most dangerous roads on the route. We had people who were not ready for a fight with windows up, AC on, and headphones blaring. We should have been cut apart today, and only God knows why we weren't.

The trip back to Scania the next morning was uneventful. Uneventful is good, but in Scania, they unveil a new banner. It had an American and a British flag and under the flags the words "Iraqi Freedom—all will give some, and some will give all." I couldn't have said it better myself. That kind of put all of the petty bickering in perspective for me. We were one unit. We all had something to give, and before we are done, someone could very likely give all.

We will be on the road again tomorrow, but this time, we will be heading south to Kuwait for training. They are going to teach us how to deal with IEDs, ambushes, and how to shoot from a moving truck. Hell, we should be teaching these classes, not taking them. This class was actually designed by people who had never been up north for soldiers who are just coming into the theater. Some general made it a mandatory training for everyone. This will be my first trip back to Kuwait since we moved to Iraq in June. This could prove to be interesting.

As we travel through southern Iraq, all we see is an occasional flared oil well pouring heavy black smoke into an empty horizon. Then as we near the Kuwaiti border, two things are apparent. The first is that this area is not moving forward anywhere near as fast as up north. This could be because the area is so sparse and spread out that it would be not only difficult but hardly beneficial to spend a lot of capital on this area. The other thing is that I was right when I said that the gifts will become expected and animosity would occur. Now, as trucks pass, they are met with offensive gestures and rock throwers when gifts are not offered. I am deeply saddened by this turn of events, but I called it several months ago.

This is the first time that I think that I have ever seen the sky in Kuwait. We lived here for six weeks, and it was always covered by a dust cloud or something. I really don't remember, but I know that it feels strange to see it here. We are about an hour away from the base, or at least that's what we were told. Thirty minutes later, we came to the end of the blacktop and onto a dirt road that heads off to the corner of nowhere and where in the heck are we.

I can imagine some American diplomat coming to the Kuwaiti government and saying we need some land to set up a live-fire base so that we can train our troops on tactics. Of course, they are going to say yes, and we will pay dearly for it, I'm sure. Then they probably pay some poor individual to seek out the most desolate part of the entire Kuwaiti desert. This is it. I don't know how, but they found it.

The base is a small tent city, but they have several vendors where you can buy food and souvenirs. They even have a subway; we haven't seen these luxuries since we first ventured into Iraq. Tomorrow, we will wake up way too early, but tonight, we will enjoy some of this lavishness.

I wake up about ten minutes early and spend this time just staring off into the brilliant night sky. There is no moon, but the sky is on fire with more stars than you could count in a lifetime. They are all resting on the deepest pool of midnight blue that I have ever seen. This sky would rival the sky up at the lake where I used to take my midnight boat rides.

I see myself as a dreamer. I want to experience every star, every sparkle on the rippling water, every single flower in a field full of wildflowers no matter how grand or meek. Every wrong I want to right, and every innocent I want to protect. I truly do want to save the world. Each night, I place a tall order as I pray for the sanctuary of the innocent and justice for all. I no longer pray for peace for peace is an act of complacency. The meek of this world need action and hope, not complacency.

During the training session, we learned the art of firing from moving vehicles and close-quarters fire and movement. We spent a lot of the time answering questions about what it is like up north. Overall, the training will prove useful; it wasn't a complete waste of time. Tomorrow, we will go back to our rat race, but tonight, I will take in more of this night sky.

CHAPTER 11

One more mission then it's home for two full weeks. I haven't been home in so long; I wonder what it will be like. I'm sure that I will freeze my butt off. There is talk of snow back home, and we are still in the eighties around here. Of course, the nights are cool, not snow cool but cool to the point of discomfort, particularly at Camp Anaconda, where we continue to sleep without cover, not that cover is not available, it's just we know what we know, and we don't like change. If I'm going to have a mortar in my lap, then I want to see it coming.

I'm not on leave yet and I have to keep my head in the game. With our holidays just around the corner, we don't know what we may be in for. The hope is that all will be quiet, but we all believe that things will go in the other direction. We will have to be very vigilant for the coming weeks. I'm glad that I will be missing some of it.

It's almost 0400 hours in the land of sand and sun as we take off for yet another mission. We have been running back-to-back, and there aren't any immediate signs that things will let up. We have been told of a couple of different scenarios in regard to our leaving. The first is that the KBR (Kellogg Brown and Root), a subsidiary of Halliburton, will take over our mission. They are a civilian contractor who has been running a number of the transportation missions here in Iraq. That would be the best case. If these guys take over, then there is a good chance for us to leave some time in late January. The other option is that another transportation company comes in and we will have to train them. If that happens, then we will be lucky to leave by the end of March. Who knows, by the time anything happens, things could change another dozen times or so. If we get sent back too soon, then there is a good chance that we get stuck on some force protection detail. That's a fancy name for guard duty. If that happens, things will slow down to a crawl. I hope we just stay on the road until we leave here.

The kids are out again today in force. We saw two little kids that couldn't have been over about three or four. They had tattered clothing, no shoes, and dirty little faces. These kids continue to break my heart. These kids were standing next to their young mother as she knelt before a polluted pond at the end of one of the trash dumps. They lived in the dump and made ragged shelters out of what others have thrown away. The mother was scrubbing the children's clothing in the filthy pond water. The children were waving proudly as we passed. Again, this is a story of hope. People should not have to live like this, but it is all too common.

The people of our country are so spoiled. Our poor live lavishly compared to these people. Most of our people who come close to living like these people have chosen a path that took them there. These people never had enough opportunity to make bad choices. Geography made their choices for them. I find it incredible that an area so rich with natural resource could let their people starve in the streets. The money is squandered by the nobles and to hell with everyone else. We have our rich and our poor, but you could never truly understand the difference until you have seen it with your own eyes. A few blocks over, we see some children playing with pipe bombs like our kids would play with squirt guns. I wish that I could wrap my arms around all of them and just keep them safe.

As we pass by block after block of starving children, I tell Young Feller, "I would love to say to the clueless ideologues back home as they sit on their butts, stuffing their faces with cheese puffs and fine wine while protesting the war effort: 'Come live in these people's shoes for just one day. Of course these people don't have shoes to stand in. When is the last time you stood for anything bigger than your own overstuffed gut?' I would love to go home and spend some time cleaning out our own filth. I would start in DC, then I could just work my way west." Then again, I have to admit, even with all of our challenges, we are by far still the greatest nation in the world. Then I thank him for putting up with my rant. Young Feller says, "That's okay. If you do decide to go on that cleaning spree, let me know, and I'll come with you." I think I'm creating a monster in my own image.

Our holidays don't appear to have had any ill effects for enemy activities. There are a good number of people in long lines outside of a few factories, hoping to find work, and the streets are flooded with pedestrians, mostly adult males, but there were a few children. It was reason for concern. Any time these people are in great numbers, mustering for whatever reason, is grounds for added concern. But for the most part, today they are peaceful. What tomorrow brings is anybody's guess.

We arrive at Camp Anaconda after an uneventful day of travel. I bunk down early to make time pass. I figure if I can get a couple hours of extra sleep, then it will feel like I will be home sooner. This never works. I lay in my bunk too keyed up to go to sleep. I can't wait to see everybody. I wonder what it will be like not having to look over my shoulder every minute of every day. Even sleep is light, and you awake with every sound. The fireworks were rocking this evening. The mortars continued until well after the choppers went airborne. Then it sounded like we gave them some fireworks of our own.

I continued to lie awake, peering into the night sky as doubts roll through my mind. I haven't been gone that long, but for some reason, I can't stop worrying. Maybe I have changed and they won't like what I have become. I don't feel different, but I know that I have witnessed a great number of things that could change a person. "Just go to sleep already," I told myself. "Worrying is not going get me home any faster." The prompting didn't help, and I fell victim to an almost sleepless night.

With the sun peeking over the horizon, we are just turning on to MSR Sword. We were the first convoy out the gate this morning, which, as you know, is reason for concern. It appears that the Hodgies must have been out late last night too. They could not get themselves up this morning to arm their IEDs. I'll take a quiet morning every day that they come, which is not very often. This whole holiday thing might just work out for us.

I have that feeling in my gut again, but it is just a bit different than in the past. I am having second thoughts about going home. I am nervous. What if something happens here while I am gone? Perhaps Young Feller will fall victim while I'm away. I don't think I could take that. Perhaps one of our other troops will get shot or blown up. Hell, I may just think myself to death. I'm my own worst enemy. I probably do more damage to myself than what they are capable of doing with an IED. I will go, and I'm going to enjoy it even if it kills me.

My morning begins at 0200 hours, not much different than other days, but today I will be headed south. This will be the longest day of my life and not just because I'm in a hurry to get home. I am in a hurry, but I will be traveling back through time. By the time I arrive home, it will only be hours after I left. I will fly out of Kuwait at 1800 hours; I have a three-hour layover in

Amsterdam, and then I arrive at home by about by 2000 hours. We will be chasing the sun on its journey west around the globe.

The Kuwaiti airport is very conservative. The airport is filled with rich smoke from a number of cigars. I haven't been in an airport that allowed smoking since I was a kid. As I go by the gift shop and flip through the magazine rack to see if I can find something to occupy my time, I notice that they have blacked out the cleavage on every magazine where a woman may be wearing a low-cut blouse. Gambling and pornography were strictly forbidden. That was good with me. If more cultures adopted this attitude, the world may be a better place, or worse depending on your morals.

Amsterdam is the place for you if you are of low morals. The gift store had porn at child level, and nothing was covered. In addition, they of course had gambling and alcohol. Smoking was permitted in designated areas. Just off the airport, they had coffee houses where you could spark up the herb of the day. Some would call this paradise; others would call it wrong.

When I reach the States, it was an eye-opening experience. Just try coming back to the States from a Middle Eastern country post-9/11. Even with my military ID, I was practically strip-searched. I guess they don't want to be accused of profiling. It's amazing how many of our rights we are so willing to give up in the name of safety. It's been a long day, so I guess they can search up whatever cavity they need to, just let me get home. See, there it is—complacency.

When I finally land in Albuquerque, Helen and the kids are all at the airport, anxiously awaiting my arrival. Once I pass the security gates, they are holding up signs with patriotic drawings, American Flags, and the words "Welcome home, Sergeant Toole!" When they first spotted me, they dashed to my side. Ryan (the boy) was all decked out in his little uniform, and Cherestine clung to me like I had come back from the dead. The entire airport erupted in applause. This is not at all what I had expected. It was all a bit overwhelming, but I was so happy to see everybody that the surroundings quickly became dull background noise. Don't get me wrong, all of these people were genuinely happy for my return; for whatever reason, I don't know. As far as I was concerned, I was just away doing my job. I was not the hero that everyone was so happy to see. I think that people are so disappointed with the despicable way that they treated the Vietnam veterans that everyone is way overdoing things. This is disturbing in its own way. If people want to thank a Vietnam veteran, then that's what they should do then do the same with vets from Korea, Granada, Bosnia, Desert Storm, and every other conflict. There are way too many heroes to be wasting your time on me. I'm just a man.

I guess this meant a lot to my family. I feel for them, for the hardship that they must endure during my absences. Every day they worried about me getting wounded or worse. It's no wonder when they see the evening news with all of the death and destruction they report. I had not seen the news in some time. I was appalled to see the reporting of events in Iraq along with the daily body count. This was not the same war that I was fighting. It's amazing that anybody would cheer. As far as the news was concerned, it was all just a waste of money and men.

It was good to be home. The girl must have grown an inch or so, but everyone else looked about the same. They all looked so good, and it gave me such joy to hold them all again. I can't believe that I almost didn't come home. It was a two-hour drive home from the airport, and it just seemed to fly by.

I was glad to see that life had carried on in my absence, but at the same time, it was if I were in a time warp and had some ground to make up. Danny was growing into a fine young man. Diego, my oldest stepson, and his family came over to greet me as well. I will catch up on all the news that I can, but I will be gone again before I know it. They wanted to know everything about Iraq and all that I had gone through. I told them as much as I felt comfortable with, but I really just wanted to know about them and all that was going on here at home.

Once home, we spent some time catching up. I asked proudly, "So did you get all of my letters?"

Ryan is the first to speak. "You can't write. They say that I write better than you, Daddy."

Out of the mouths of babes. That cut like a knife. I could just imagine all of them sitting around laughing as they read my words. I wrote hundreds of pages home, and they all thought that it was one big joke. I didn't say much at the time, but I decided right then that my writing days were over. I wasn't going to pour my heart out just to be the butt of their jokes. I tried to shrug it off, but the way that made me feel, if I could, I would have turned around and gotten back on the plane I would have seriously thought about it, but I knew that I was being hypersensitive about it, but it was an emotional time. Everything seemed so different. Had I been gone for so long?

I stepped outside for a moment to get some fresh air. The night was cool and crisp with snow expected. I thought that I would be freezing here after being in Iraq, but I guess that maybe I have gotten used to extremes and all I needed was a light jacket. A light snow began to fall, and I am in awe of its beauty. After a few moments in the winter wonderland, I return inside. I was able to suppress the incident and get on with enjoying my home and family. It had been a long time coming since Helen and I had a chance to hold each other, and we did make up for lost time. It was nice to sleep in my own bed and eat home-cooked meals. I didn't realize just how much I had missed it all.

My first week at home was almost all in preparation for Thanksgiving. There was one luncheon, however, that I was to attend at the Guard headquarters in Santa Fe. At the luncheon, I met the commanding general; he presented me with his coin symbolizing superior service. He didn't know me from Adam or what I had personally accomplished overseas. The coin therefore meant nothing to me personally. I was honored, however, to present it to my wife, who was much more deserving of the coin than me. She knew the general through Family Support, and the general at least knew what her contribution was. She earned it.

We spent every moment together; the boy and the girl seldom left my side. I loved the attention and the company. Loneliness was a battle of its own in Iraq. I kept to myself a lot since Neilson left. Palo was usually on a different rotation, so I usually only saw him in passing. I can't say that I wasn't close to anyone else as we were all brothers and sisters, but I didn't really hang out with any of them unless we were together on a mission. Even then, it was only while on the road. I spent most of my free time reading or writing.

For the second week home, my mom and dad came from California. They never left home for the holidays, so I saw this as a huge honor. This occasion was different. Her baby was home from the war, and she wasn't going to miss an opportunity to see me. She had been on pins and needles since my deployment. A day didn't go by when she didn't pray for me. She wasn't alone in her feelings or prayers. Everyone was praying for me, Helen and the kids, Helen's family, my family, several of their friends as well as the entire congregation of my church. It's no wonder I felt invincible.

The questions that almost everyone had for me were, are we doing any good over there? Is it worth it? My answer usually went something like this."I have nearly been blown up a number of times. I have been shot at several times, and at night we watch the mortars fly in like the Fourth of July. So is it worth it? You bet your bottom dollar. You should see the children. If you look into their little faces just one time and still don't think it's worth it, then you don't have a heart in your chest." Almost everyone would respond by saying that this wasn't what they were getting from the evening news, and they were glad to get the perspective from someone who was there.

The girl's teacher wanted me to come and speak to her class while I was home. I was honored by the invitation, but I couldn't bring myself to do that. I was okay speaking to people one or two at a time, but I wasn't ready to be in a tiny classroom with dozens of people. I know that Cherestine would have swelled with pride to have her dad talking before her class as I was paraded like a hero. I just wasn't ready to be a hero; I was just doing a job.

I tried to distribute my time with all of my family. I wanted to visit with all of them. I wanted to share my experiences with everyone, but more so, I wanted to know everything about everyone else. Normalcy was missing from my life. I won't deny that life on the battlefield was exciting, but so is a story about everyday things. I would rather talk to Helen about her work or the kids about school or my parents about their travels. I was home if only for a short time, and I wanted to take it all in.

It was difficult to make time for intimacy, but the night, no matter how late, belonged to my beloved and me. We would spend time every night talking softly and catching up where we could. I would hold her in my arms, caress her skin, and taste her kisses. I felt excited, comfortable, and safe. I probably slept more sound than I had in months.

Thanksgiving dinner always begins the night before with the assembly of the tamales. Helen and I have always enjoyed working together in the kitchen. The making of tamales is a job that can be shared. The kids were usually in bed by the time the assembly took place. I have gotten pretty good over time. I am nowhere as fast as Helen, but I know that she appreciates the help. After the completion of the tamales, I grow weary and head off to bed. Helen insists that she must stay up to clean up. She often will begin another project and continue cooking long after I have turned in. Then she will be up before anyone and right back at it. She's a real dynamo, and I gave up trying to keep up with her years ago.

My mom takes over and helps Helen with dinner where I normally would, so I retire to the living room, where I will get to watch football with my dad. I'm a Steelers fan with my second favorite team being anybody against the Cowboys. I don't know who came up with the annual schedule where the Cowboys and Lions are always playing on Thanksgiving, but he should be severely slapped and beaten about the head and shoulders. The Lions haven't won a game in years, and the Cowboys, well, they're the Cowboys. What more can I say?

Dinner is ready by three, and it looks and smells heavenly. I felt extremely proud to slice the turkey this year. This was my dad's job, and now I was carving for him. It seems like a small deal, but it meant a lot to me. We had, in addition to the turkey and tamales, fresh bread rolls, stuffing, red chili, mashed potatoes, sweet potatoes, cranberries, and all of the extras. Everything was perfect.

Thanksgiving is one of my favorite holidays. It's all about food and family. With fourteen of us at various tables, the house was full, and there was more than enough food to go round. Mom, Dad, Helen, Danny, Cherestine, Ryan, Diego and his not so soon to be wife (Amanda), Julian, Maria (Pixie), my sister Sherry, my two nieces Jamie and Kristie, and my nephew Jake were all there. The only ones missing were David (my middle stepson) and his longtime girlfriend, Stacie. We would have loved to have them, but they were living up in Wisconsin and couldn't make it down. We are all close, and I love them all as my own. It was truly a special occasion, and while I enjoyed it immensely, the fact that I would be heading back soon was haunting me. It would be hard to say good-bye again. I dreaded this part from before I even came home.

Everybody gets together for my last night. I kind of wanted to spend this night alone with Helen, but my entire family is such a big part of my life that I would have felt guilty for cutting them out. I will carve at least a small part out where Helen and I can get to spend some time alone. Helen and I made our escape and went for a little walk. Hand in hand we strolled, hardly saying a word. We both knew that our time was coming to an end. Helen stops, and when I don't, she yanks me back. She grabs my other hand; her hands were ice cold. I rub them quickly, trying to warm them. She kisses me, then her tears begin to fall.

"I'm going to miss you," she said.

"I'm going to miss you too. The time has passed so quickly. I wish I didn't have to go. " I pull her in close and try to shield her from the cold, crisp night. The moon is beaming with its near full circle. "I wish this moment could last forever."

"Don't go," she said, but she knew that it was an impossible request. It was growing late, and with our family waiting for our return, we would have to go back.

The next day, they were all at the airport to see me off. It was every bit as hard as I thought it would be. I say good-bye one by one, telling the kids to be good and that I will be home for good before they knew it. It was a tearful good-bye, and with one last group hug, I was off through the security gates. I couldn't bear to look back; I knew that if I did, my own tears would fall. Now was not the time for sorrow; now was the time to go back and finish the job that I started. Then I would be free to come home forever.

CHAPTER 12

The day that I returned to Iraq, the word had finally came down. KBR would be taking over our mission, and our company would rotate back down south. There was a catch to this scenario. If KBR was to take over the mission, then they would need volunteers to stay back and act as the convoy security force for these unarmed civilians. I was quick to raise my hand, and after a little coaxing, Palo had agreed to stay behind as well. He would become my new battle buddy. I couldn't think of anybody that I would rather have by my side.

I really didn't want to move again, but I was happy to have the majority of the company out of harm's way. We were told that we were going to be here until April. We would likely hand the mission off to a replacement company some time before then. The new mission started up even before the biggest share of our company could even pack.

The way we were set up was that we would have a bobtail 915 both in front and rear and two roving HMMWV gun trucks.

This was not very much security for thirty trucks in an all-civilian convoy. If you thought that we were an easy target before, now was a hundred times worse. We had to be aggressive and dedicated to doing all we could to keep them safe. It wouldn't be easy.

Baca would be the NCOIC for our security team. His partner was John Richards. The gun trucks rotated around a bit, so you were never really sure who was going to be on your mission. Baca had mellowed out his leadership tactics once the majority of the company moved out. We were a small detachment of about thirty troops, and Lieutenant Summers was our OIC. That was only fair since he was the one who started the gun trucks in the first place.

Lieutenant was a good man playing officer. He was prior enlisted, and you could tell that he missed being just one of the guys. In fact, he drew more toward the enlisted than other officers for his camaraderie. He was kind of a big kid; he always wanted to play with the boys. That's probably the best way to describe Lieutenant. He was a big kid playing army with skills in advanced tactics. I'm sure when he played back on the block, he must have won most of the time. He didn't play well with his own kind. Other officers turned him off as they did most enlisted soldiers. Lieutenant got it and became an officer probably to change them to his way of thinking. So far he wasn't having much luck.

So there we were, the biggest misfit platoon that the army had ever known with one tin soldier as our leader. The biggest reason people stayed back was because they didn't fit in or just wanted to be away from the command. We were mutts dedicated to duty in the absence of order, and we became very good at it, no more formations, group meetings, work details, and none of the other things that the army was famous for wasting your time with. When we were on a mission, we were 100 percent engaged, and when we weren't, we were on our own to do preventative maintenance; running over to Tallil Air Base to make phone calls or whatever. Our time was our time. I'm sure this sounds like a great detail, and it was, with one exception. The unarmed civilian drivers made an easy target for the Hodgies, and that made them a favorite target. That meant that we were now the favorite target. With only four armed vehicles for a convoy that would stretch out over three miles on the open road, we were few and far between.

We weren't the first civilian convoy escorts. For the most part, all of the escorts before us were MPs. We were truck drivers and had been in convoys for eight months. We knew what worked and what didn't. I'm not saying we were better, but we certainly had a leg up on everybody else. Nobody knew that stretch of road better than us. We had driven that same stretch of road for over thirty thousand miles. We knew the enemy as well as they knew us.

Today is the first time we met the civilian drivers. I thought they were a bunch of whining crybabies. They sure did a lot of bellyaching for drivers who were there of their own free will. The money is what brought them. They could pull down an easy $120,000 a year plus paid vacations and great benefits. It was difficult duty, and they earned their paychecks. They were never made mention of back home, and they damn sure weren't mentioned in the daily body count. They were truly unknowns. I wouldn't go as far as calling them the unsung heroes, but we probably didn't have the personnel to sustain our missions without them.

From our fist mission out, they knew that we were serious about protection and that we knew what we were doing. We quickly became the favorite security force for these civilians. If the Hodgies wanted a shot at these guys, then they were going to have to go through us. Before each mission, we would have a safety brief and lay down the law for these drivers. They were not to engage or enrage the civilian population. A good share of the violence was brought on by vigilante justice and retaliation. The civilians had been known for forcing Hodgies off the road, and when someone got hurt, they would instantly try to hurt one of ours. This was especially true down south. The southern Iraqis almost never made attempts to fire on a convoy unless it was following an accident that resulted in great bodily injury or death. So they had some control over their own safety in this area.

The civilians had little handheld radios and provided us with a set so that we could all communicate. They liked to be on it all of the time, but that was another change we insisted on. They would have to keep the airwaves open for emergencies only. This was a tough one for them to follow, but the civilian supervisor did a pretty good job of policing his people.

After a few weeks, some of our more radical and more timid soldiers fell out, leaving behind a good group to work with. We still had a few problems, but sometimes that's what it takes to be a cut above. Take a great-running, well-oiled machine. When you throw in a monkey wrench, the machine will break down and fall out. But if you take a machine that's missing a few teeth on the cogs and throw in the same wrench, it will likely jump over the wrench and keep right on going. Iraq was definitely a few teeth short of a full cog. Things were always going wrong, but we learned to roll with the punches.

Palo and I would run the rear of the convoy, and we adopted a very aggressive driving style that made our tractor stand up and dance. We would not let another driver pass to enter our convoy. There were times when we almost had to be in three lanes of traffic at the same time. Some Hodgies would avoid us altogether by driving into the oncoming traffic lanes. We were good, but some things you just had no control over. Baca and Richards always had the front running point. We had good communication, and we did work well together.

On our first several trips out, we lost a number of KBR trucks due to IED attacks. When a KBR truck would become disabled, we would send the driver to another truck and then torch the tractor in place. We didn't want to give the Hodgies any usable equipment to later use against us. As you can imagine, this practice was not pleasing to the owners of KBR, and they soon began bringing a recovery truck along with them. Where was the fun in that? We agreed to this recovery only after some prompting from our command.

We ran fast and would often reach Camp Anaconda by about 1400 hours, much earlier than when we ran in all-military convoys. The difference was that we didn't stop very often, and when we did, it was not for long. We knew that every minute spent on the side of the road was a minute that the Hodgies had to set up an attack. So we ran fast, loose, and very aggressive. If they were going to challenge us, there was going to be a price to pay.

Once we were well established, they added another gun truck to our platoon, and they were supposed to be assigned to our team. These guys were misfits among misfits, and we didn't have the same confidence in them as we had in others. We knew that it wouldn't be long before they were tested and they would show their true colors.

One guy from this new team was arrested when he went home on leave for taking an undisclosed pistol home from Iraq. He had smuggled the gun to Iraq when we first came to the county. He had to have known that he would never have a chance to use it. It was a stupid thing to do both coming and going. Another one of these guys was investigated by CID (Criminal Investigation Division) before we left Kuwait as he tried to steal everything he could from the base, right down to the bunk that he slept on. These guys were not to be trusted, and our lives may be held in the balance. On their first trip up with us, things were quiet, and we were glad for that. We didn't have to count on them, but they would still have to earn our trust.

To kill time and fight some of the boredom, Palo and I took up a daily weight lifting routine. It was a grueling pace that worked every muscle group in our bodies. They didn't have much on any of these bases, but they did have a nice weight room everywhere that we would go. This just seemed like the thing to do. We were both getting in good shape. Palo used to say that he was always in shape, that was, if you included round as a shape. Palo was quickly becoming the best friend that I ever had. I could count on him in any situation. He always had my back!

The trip home started out okay, but we were the first out the gate. We were about two-thirds of the way down MSR Sword when all of the rest of the cars on the road were being held back. I radio throughout the convoy said, "We're about to get hit!" My head is on a pivot, searching for the ensuing attack. My adrenaline hits the roof, and I am ready for a fight. But for now, this is not our fight as we have an obligation to keep the rear of the convoy sealed off from a rear attack. I then called the gun truck, and I told them that we needed to have a gun truck engage the car that was obviously responsible. Once they knew that we were going to be hit, they took immediate action and faded back away from the convoy. I don't know if they were saving their own butts, or just confused, in any case they did not engage the known enemy. Then sure enough—*boom*—the truck directly in front of me was hit by an explosion so great that it rocked my truck as well. The truck and driver were down. The car that was responsible drove off in the other direction, and I knew then where these guys stood! If we ever needed them, they would not be there, or at least that was the consensus in the moment

So we were down to three security force units for this long rolling target. We had four, of course, but one was in doubt of their capabilities. Having someone watching your back when you don't know how they will react is almost worse than not having someone there at all. They may just get in the way of us being able to do our job. Later, when we asked them why they didn't engage, they only said that they could not see a weapon. The intent was obvious, and when he turned away after detonation, it should have removed any and all doubt! They really didn't have an answer, so the terrorists live to kill again.

When we returned to Camp Cedar, I told Baca and the lieutenant what had happened and that I would like to have these guys removed from our security force. My request was denied for the reasons that we were too shorthanded to replace them. After all, it was an all-volunteer force. That really sucks! We will have to work harder to cover our own backs since we couldn't count on these guys. They did change the teams up a bit so we didn't have all of the people on the same truck. That gave me some relief.

The next morning, Palo and I were up early to do our workout. We hit the gym for two and a half hours. I felt great. To end the morning on a high note, I jumped up to the chin-up bar. Before I could complete one chin-up, I fell to the ground. My shoulder had dislocated. It was an old injury that crept up to bite me in the butt. It had sent me to the ER three times before. All I could think of was game over! This would put me on the sidelines for sure. My mind was racing. I talked Palo into this mission, and now I won't be there for him. I felt about two inches tall.

Palo was reassuring; he was more concerned for me than himself like any true friend would be. I tried to move my shoulder, but it was hanging down in my armpit. I was going to have to face going to the medical station. Then in one last-ditch effort, I held my arm up with my free hand then rotated it up and around. I felt it snap back into place.

"I can't believe this shit!" I told Palo. "I did it! I put it back!"

"Are you sure?" he asked.

I was sure. My arm hurt like hell for a moment, but then all at once it felt better. I was ecstatic. Palo wouldn't have to go it alone.

I told the lieutenant later what I had done. He told me that I should go to sick call, but it was my choice. I choose to keep playing the game. I told him that I would take it easy for a few days, then I would do some light exercises to rebuild my strength and no more lifting over chest high. You wouldn't have to tell me twice. After a few weeks, I felt good as new. I never took it easy. Palo and I were out on mission the next day, and I never looked back.

CHAPTER 13

Today we have a real day off. Palo and I are planning on going to the Hodgie mart near Tallil Air Base. Then we will probably go make some phone calls back home. I have spoken to Helen every week, but I haven't talked to my family since I was home on leave except for a quick call just to say I made it back okay. That's kind of a sticking point for Mom. She always worries when I am traveling, and I don't call to say I made my destination. It seems kind of funny to me when you consider my destination.

I brought my video camera with me when I came back from leave. I want to give everybody a taste of where we are. I also want to give myself something to look back on in the years to come. At some point, we will have to make it back to the city of Ur. I would love to get that on video.

When we get to the Hodgie mart, we find the people are very friendly. They find the video camera very intriguing, especially the children. There was almost anything that you could imagine available. This was more like a Hodgie mall. There were several tents set up, and each vendor had their specialty items. I set my attention to one shop that specialized in artwork and Egyptian rugs. The paintings were incredible with very precise detail. They would almost jump off the canvas. Still, the rugs were what I was really interested in. They were almost as precise as the paintings. I had never seen any rugs as beautiful as what they were offering, and the price could not be beat.

Since I had the camera with me, Palo and I thought that we could take some time and get the Hodgies' perspective on the events of the war. They were more than happy to answer our questions and seemed to like the idea of being taped while doing so. Maybe they thought that they would find themselves on the news back in the States. In any case, they were very cooperative. Palo asked one of the Iraqi men first about Osama bin Laden. He said that Osama would not show his face in Iraq or he would be instantly killed. They didn't have anything but disdain for the man.

Then Palo asked what it would take for northern and southern Iraq to get along. They said that they had plenty of friends in northern Iraq, but they had subtle differences in ideology. He said that there were over twelve million people in southern Iraq and only Three million people in northern Iraq. The south had been persecuted for the entire reign of Saddam Hussein. The southern people were brutalized and murdered regularly. If they were to have a new government, then in their eyes it needed to be representative of the true population.

Finally, I asked them what they thought about the United States and the invasion. They had a very positive outlook for the United States and the invasion. They had all lost family at the hand of the now former government. They were grateful for the invasion and for the opportunity to start fresh. They didn't want a long occupation, but they wanted us there for as long as it took to set up order and wanted to continue relations with the West.

Palo and I walked away from the visit feeling enlightened. These people became our friends, and we would go back to visit again. I was surprised that Palo was so moved by these people. He never trusted any of them before, and now he had met some, that really shed some light on the positive changes that were taking place. It felt good. We are making a difference. I could see it. Iraq had made huge strides from where they were when we first got there. Now we have heard it as well.

We departed from the Hodgie mall and then went on to Tallil as planned. I first called my mom; it is very early in the morning with the time differential. Mom is always happy to hear from me. I could call her at any time.

We talked for almost an hour. Mom wants to know everything about everything, and since I hadn't spoken to her, there was a lot of everything to tell. We talked about our new mission and how we wouldn't be home until we completed our 365 boots on ground, and Mom caught me up on all of the family. Thankfully they are all doing well.

I hang up with my mom and it's about 6:00 a.m. back home, so I will try to call. Helen comes on the line; she is still a little groggy but sounds excited to hear from me. She tells me about work and the kids. They were all doing well. I told her about our new mission and how I was one of the first to volunteer. She wasn't surprised.

Then the conversation turns a little more personal.

"It was great to see you, but it was so hard to say good-bye," she said. "It was a lot harder on me than I thought it would be." She started getting a little frisky and then told me that she loved me.

I said, "I love you too." The phone went silent for a moment. "Are you still there?"

She then came back and asked, "Do you mean it?"

"Of course I do."

"Then you had better watch your back and make it home to me."

I had a skip in my step as I caught up with Palo. He had been waiting for me for nearly an hour once he was done talking. It didn't seem to bother him. He was great about things like that. Family had always meant a lot to him, so he understood. When he saw the look in my eyes, he knew that I had gotten through to Helen.

He said, "You had better hold on to her."

"I will," I said, wondering why he would say that.

Then I realized that things weren't going so well for him back home. I've known it for a while, but seeing me so happy must have gotten to him a bit.

The rainy season is upon us, and the powdery dirt turned into a deep paste-like substance. By the time that you would walk the distance from the tents to the chow hall, you were three inches taller than when you left. What a mucky mess. Most of our trucks end up stuck in the muck, and we have to move them to more solid ground before the morning mission or we will never meet our spot time. With the rain still pouring down, we go to try to move our trucks. The people who engaged the axle lock before attempting to move were twice as likely to pull out. Then we would get to more solid ground and pull the others out with a chain. It was a challenge to even walk. Many ended up on their butts before they could finish pulling the heavy chain. Normally we would take this opportunity to laugh at one another, but none of us wanted to be out in the crud.

When we returned to our tent, it was obvious that they were not made for the rain. The water poured almost straight through the canvas material that the tents were made from. We draped our ponchos over our bunks and put trash bags over everything else that we could. It was miserable, and this was supposed to last about three months or so. They did have enough sense to put shale around the tents themselves and on the path to the restrooms and showers. Even with that, you had to wear your boots to the showers and back. But it kept the mud down to a more tolerable level.

As we head out in the morning, it is apparent that we aren't the only people that the weather is doing a number on. There were several vehicles off the road and in the ditches, including one school bus. It didn't look like anybody was hurt except for maybe a few people's pride. We were doing just fine as long as we stick to the harder surface roads. I can only imagine what MSR Tampa was like.

When we reached Samawah, our convoy came to a halt. One of the Scorpion gun trucks raced forward to see what the obstruction was. The other gun truck was running up and down the convoy to keep looters away from the unarmed civilians. Normally, our job in this situation was to keep the back door closed off. This could be a real chore. The Hodgies are not patient drivers and would make attempts to take any little passage to inch themselves forward. They would turn a simple situation into a giant Charlie Foxtrot. On top of that, we are most vulnerable when we are standing still, so keeping them at bay becomes that much more important. Today was not a normal day. Baca was sidelined on this mission, and we were the lead truck. So we just kept the convoy inching forward. This blockage turned out to be due to a simple accident, but by the time we are moving again, the chances for IED attacks are extreme. We proceed with caution once the road was cleared and move quickly all the way to Camp Anaconda.

The mission went well once we got through the initial slowdown. That night, we celebrated our good fortune the way that we normally did: a trip to the gym, dinner, and to bed early. It was too cold to stay out for long. The tents that we finally began to sleep in weren't heated or cooled. You had to bunk down early or freeze your butt off. They did keep the wind out and most of the rain. The rain also seemed to keep the mortar attacks down to a minimum. This made the showers welcome on this end.

Anaconda was a well-groomed, established base with real paved roads and several solid buildings, nothing like Camp Cedar. Don't get me wrong, Anaconda was far from paradise. We rarely had to worry about attacks on Camp Cedar. The southern territory was far more secure and less volatile than the north. We had the good fortune to live in both worlds: the mess in Camp Cedar and the nightly attacks at Anaconda. We were kind of like the bastard stepchildren at Anaconda. We had the leftovers. The tents that we stayed in weren't occupied because the troops moved out to more suitable quarters and they just hadn't gotten around to tearing them down.

The next morning, we were running behind schedule due to bad loads. We took the extra time to secure them so that we could run hard and fast home. Then we got behind several other convoys and were held up at the gate. With this development, we decided in advance to forgo our first rest stop outside of BIAP. Once we got moving, we were making good time across MSR Sword and the overpass onto MSR Tampa. We were rocking Dokken on the CD player, then as we pass by our normal rest stop, *Boom!* The percussion from the blast was earthshaking and ear shattering. It seemed to fit well with the music. Then we felt the back of our truck lift off the ground slightly, and the debris peppered the back of my cab. The truck seemed to lunge forward as we race past the blast. The truck directly behind us also had a narrow escape as he was driving into the blast. Palo and I escaped with only a few marks on our cab, while the civilian truck that was driving into the blast lost his windshield. We drove about five miles down the road and then stopped for a brief damage assessment. The civilian truck driver had to kick out what was left of his windshield, but other than being shaken up, he was okay.

It was yet another narrow escape. If we would have stopped at our usual rest stop, somebody would have gone home with a flag over his coffin. We were beginning to feel a little less lucky and more like someone or something was looking out for us.

That was the closest near miss to date. With my ears still ringing, I say to Palo, "It's just not our time." How else could you explain it? We had cheated Lady Death a few times too many to be a coincidence.

We were riding high on adrenaline for miles to come. Adrenaline begins to be something you crave. I understand that it can be more addicting than crack cocaine. Though I've never tried crack, I can say that when you have adrenaline pumping through your veins, your body feels like you're supercharged. Your senses are operating at peak performance. It's like your deepest love, your greatest strength, your keenest sight, and complete awareness all rolled into one, and you feel as if nothing could stop you. You really feel as if you are a superman. I can't imagine getting this feeling off any drug. Hell, you start looking forward to the next attack. Bring it on. I can take anything that you can throw at me.

We would not be challenged again this day. The rest of the journey was quiet and uneventful. That is until we returned to Camp Cedar. One of the other teams was having a party. We didn't need a reason, but I think it was Johnson's birthday. Johnson was the crotchety old bastard who dropped a turd on his boss's desk once upon a time. Other than crude behavior and vulgar language, he was a hell of a guy.

"Toole, you ugly SOB, get in here and grab a beer," Johnson said as Palo and I walked through the door.

"I don't mind if I do," I said in reply. The BS was knee-deep by the time we stepped in. The beer went down easy one after the other until our speech was slurred and the "I love you, man's" were spilling out in every direction as fast as beer spills from a tipped can.

Johnson and I managed to stumble outside to take a leak, and with tears welling up in his eyes, he says, "I see his face every time I close my eyes." Johnson had one of the few confirmed kills in my unit. It was a Hodgie holding an RPG aiming down on his convoy. Johnson shot him before the Hodgie could get a shot off. He saved lives that day, but taking one was haunting him. Johnson was on the edge, and God knows that a breeze could blow him over it. With his domineering, rugged demeanor, he couldn't communicate his pain to our command. As far as anybody knew, he was crass and too strong willed to let that bother him. That's what I thought too until this night. It was not an act; he was crass and strong, but he was also being eaten alive from the inside out.

I told him that I would help him, and that was a promise that I intended to keep. Unlike Johnson, I was not a complainer. I was sincere and compelling. If I went to the command, they would hear the words that Johnson could not voice. I think that was the reason he came to me in the first place. That and the case of beer probably helped a bit. The next morning, I went to the lieutenant. I explained the situation and the fact that he just couldn't be taken as serious as what the situation called for. Johnson was taken off the mission that day, but it would take some time to get him home. He was grateful to me for listening to him when no one else would. I think that he felt that I had saved his life as clearly as he had saved the lives of his team members. He was the hero, not me, and he deserved the respect of being understood.

CHAPTER 14

The bonds formed on the battlefield are as strong as anything that you will ever experience in a lifetime. Even people with whom you have fundamental differences with will put their lives on the line for you. Many of these people who are willing to die in your defense you wouldn't even be friends with back home. Palo and I were different. We had a deep-seated brotherly love for each other. We had gotten to know each other so well that we would finish each other's comments. A simple nod of the head or gesture and we knew what that meant.

Each morning began fresh. The days were cool, and I would say to Palo, "Pretty chilly." He would always respond, "Thank you." It's a New Mexico thing, but no matter how many times he would say it, it always made me laugh. I had a few sayings of my own and even a couple more that didn't start with the letters *f* or *s*. Anytime Palo would ask me a question concerning quantity, I would respond by saying "Oodles." Palo loved this response and always threw it back at me with a little added expression. He would ask me a question like, "How much weight were you lifting?" I would reply, "Oodles." Then he would repeat, "Oooodles?" It was another running gag that never got old.

Each mission we would head out, I would say in rhythmic tones, "*Bock bock bock bock.*" Then I would finish in a high scratchy voice, "It's Chicken Man." Then Palo would always end my cry by adding his sign of the ox. It was simple, just a fist with pointer and pinky fingers extended like a pair of horns. We were off like some sort of masked crusaders fighting for justice in a mixed-up world. I don't know where the Chicken Man thing came from. It was something that Palo had tagged me with somewhere along the way. We had all kinds of nicknames in our company. There was the Owl, the Possum 1 and Possum 2, the Ox, the Little Redhead Girl, Ranger, Ranger Wayne, Tater, the Silver Fox, Young Feller, the Old Man, and somehow I became Chicken Man. These were all within our platoon. There even may be a few that I can't remember right off the cuff. Several people had several nicknames. They all seemed to grow out of a night of drinking, and since we drank a lot, it just goes to figure that we would all have these other identities.

There are new rumors that our replacements will be arriving the country any day now. We will work with them for a month, then we will turn our equipment over to them, and we will be going home. Now ask me why I don't believe the rumors. I still feel like I will spend the rest of my life in this hell. It's not all bad. We have good friends, a lot of laughs, and there is always someone to pick you up when you are down. For many, this was the first and only family that they have ever known. When these people go home, it will be heartbreaking, and I can empathize with them. My family is close and strong, and I will still miss the camaraderie. People will go their separate ways. Some will likely fall away, never to be heard from again. Others will never leave the Guard, and it will be like a homecoming month after month. Still, others will live just beyond the mainstream of our lives, only a phone call away. I can't imagine a life without Palo falling in it somewhere.

During our morning safety brief, one of our Scorpion gun trucks is missing. They are not responding to the radio, so Baca sends the other gun truck to track them down. We will miss our spot time if they are not found quickly. Within moments, the second gun truck calls to Baca.

"Scorpion 4 to 112, over."

Baca responds, "This is 112. Did you find them? Over."

"Yes, they are having some mechanical problems and may need an hour or so to get them resolved."

Baca is infuriated. They were supposed to do their preventative maintenance on their down day. He makes the call and says that we will go on without them. This was almost like going out without gun support as the team we were left with was from the team that had been untested since the last incident. I didn't like the sound of this at all. Baca was right for making the call. We didn't have any backup teams, and we didn't know if the problem could be resolved. So it was better to stay on schedule with one gun truck, than to go out late with possibly still only one gun truck if they could not make timely repairs.

We headed out only a few minutes late in spite of the early morning Charlie Foxtrot. When we arrived in Samawah, an air force convoy was blocking the entire road. They had a mechanical problem with one of their trucks and took up a defensive posture that blocked all three northbound lanes. Baca climbed down from his truck to have a meeting with the air force convoy commander. He was trying to get them to open a lane so that we could pass. The gun truck took off into the desert. They claimed to be seeking a better defensive position, but it was plain to see that they were messing around. Then they got the HMMWV stuck in the mud. We waited for about thirty minutes for them to get unstuck, then Baca decides that he can't afford to keep the convoy still any longer. Again, I think this is the right call. They had more guns on that one truck to defend themselves than what we had left in our entire convoy.

Fighting was not our security. Moving and moving fast was. If we got caught in a firefight while at a halt, we would be cut apart even with all of our gun trucks. So we left them in the mud with orders to catch up once they got themselves unstuck. As we drive away, we are a bit apprehensive, but I let out my battle cry, "*Bock bock bock bock*, it's Chicken Man!" Palo laughs and replies with the sign of the Ox.

When we came to the next town, again we came to a screeching halt. *Will this day never end*, I thought. The city is wall-to-wall people, thousands in demonstrations and nearing riot. Palo jumps out on foot to make an attempt to keep looters away from our unarmed civilians. I jump from the truck and try to keep the people in the rear at bay. All we can do is go out and put on the biggest facade that we can and hope that no one wants to be the first to die. As one car tries to inch forward, I pound a huge dent in the side of his car with one buttstroke with my weapon. Then I aim in on him, then on another, and another, inviting them on as to who wants to receive the first of the hot lead from my rifle.

I can see the convoy inch forward, and I jump into my cab to drive the short distance and then jump back out to take up an offensive posture. Finally, we get to a point where we are moving steady but slow. We are not out of the woods, but it's better than standing still. I was almost glad at this point that we didn't have any more armed people than the four of us. If anybody would have lost their nerve, it would have meant that we would all have been ripped to shreds. An overzealous, cowardly gun truck platoon was exactly what we didn't need.

I picked up Palo; he was about a mile up the road. He was still pushing people away from the civilians and was engulfed by the crowd. He is a hero on this day. Hell, we all did our job and were in a difficult situation, but he charged forward.

Once we cleared the town, Baca comes on the radio, "143, did you pass the all-military southbound convoy as we left the town?"

"Yes, I saw them."

Then Baca says, "I told their convoy commander to send a couple of trucks to the end of our convoy. That way, as we cleared a path, they could forge through the path we cut. The convoy commander said no way. He didn't have enough guns to face the crowd."

I had to laugh. We had just pulled off the impossible. We held a hostile city full of people at bay with three M16s and one SAW. We were outnumbered thousands to one, and no one wanted to be the first to die.

Our gun truck finally caught up with us at Scania. By the time they got to the town, the crowd had been dispersed, and they never knew that anything out of the ordinary had taken place. We had faced similar situations when we were together as a unit. It was tough to get through then, but this was far worse than anything that we had seen before and will go down as another near-death experience.

Palo takes the wheel in Scania and is doing a great job at keeping the back door closed. I think that he is still holding on to some of the excitement and adrenaline from earlier. One particularly aggressive driver comes up behind us on the stretch of road known as IED Alley. This is the six-lane road that stretches from Scania all the way to MSR Sword. There were three lanes north and three lanes south. Palo was having some trouble fending off this one driver, so I called the gun truck to assist. They fade back and take up the right lane. Palo fades to the left lane, leaving a KBR truck blocking center. The Hodgie pulls to the right shoulder, and the gun truck cuts off his approach. Then the Hodgie pulls to the left shoulder, and Palo cuts off his approach. The Hodgie takes the center lane. I am looking at Palo and see that he has his eyes glued to the Hodgie's car completely, ignoring the rest of the road. Then I look over at the driver of the gun truck. The gunners are asleep, and the driver is just as affixed to the Hodgie as Palo. I saw this in the making, and you guessed it. The Hodgie makes a run at the center. Both Palo and the gun truck react by pulling hard to the center. The Hodgie slams his brakes, and Palo and the gun truck collide. The gun truck is nearly knocked completely off the road. His crew is instantly woken up, and both the Hodgie and I are laughing our asses off. Everyone is okay! The HMMWV had minor damage and some nice tire marks. The Hodgie just backed off. I think he got all that he was looking for.

Palo and I continue the conversation into the gym.

"I knew that you were going to collide. I could see it in both of your faces."

"Why didn't you say something?"

"Where is the fun in that!" I said.

He was laughing with me as he had been since right after the incident.

We turned our focus back to our workout. We were taking it seriously. We were watching everything that we ate, ensuring that we consumed at least forty grams of protein with every meal. If it wasn't possible, then we would supplement with a protein shake. Several people who were probably a little envious of our results used to say, "If you run low on protein, I got some extra hanging." Everyone's a comedian.

I had regained my strength after my shoulder dislocation. I was committed to not lifting above my shoulders. It did leave some of our workouts a little deficient, but it was something that we were both willing to sacrifice. I would have supported Palo if he would have wanted to continue working these muscle groups, but he was content.

The night was the coldest yet. The wind seemed to blow right through the tent. The rain was coming down hard and passed straight through the tent. There was no place to run. The sleeping bags that we were issued had a GORE-TEX outer liner that was waterproof, so we just tucked all the way down into our bags. They feel stuffy, and I know that I was just a little claustrophobic. I felt like I was running short of breath by the time the rain let up. I was grateful to poke my head out of the turtle-like shell.

I was happy that we would be facing the open road from Anaconda southbound after such a heavy rain. The road and, more importantly, the shoulders in southern Iraq would have a chance to dry out by the time we reached that area. It was always a mess from Samawah all the way to Camp Cedar.

Today, the road was clear of attacks from Anaconda to Samawah. We always let our guard down a bit once we clear Samawah. Today is not a normal day. The Hodgies spiked a drainage ditch through an underpass as we left town. It caught Baca's oil pan, missed the first KBR truck, and hit the oil pan on the second. They charged forward until the trucks shut down due to a lack of oil pressure. We were lucky to clear the town. It's hard to say if they had anything else waiting for us or not. They probably hoped that we would leave the equipment and they would be able to strip them for parts.

They came to a stop about three miles south of town. We had about two hours of road between us at convoy speed and only about two and a half hours of daylight. We couldn't reach our home base with our radio. They only had a couple miles' worth of range. We didn't have MTS on the HMMWV that was with us. It was on the truck that broke down the morning that we left.

Baca had another decision to make. Do we stay together and risk having everybody out at night or split the convoy up and have the gun truck escort the majority back to safety? It was an easy call. Get as many of the unarmed civilians to safety as possible. I would tow Baca with a chain, and the civilian recovery vehicle would tow their truck back with a tow bar. When the convoy was safely back at Camp Cedar, the gun truck would come back for us to provide additional security.

We were traveling at a blazing twenty-five miles per hour on the two-lane highway. The convoy by now was well out of sight and radio range. We were on our own and crippled, not the way that you would want to be traveling in a combat zone just before dark. We watched the sun dip below the horizon and the moonless night was pitch-black. Our headlamps were covered with mud from all of the daily debris, offering only enough light to illuminate the centerline. With all of the cards stacked against us, I did the only thing that I could do. I pulled out my movie camera and tried to capture the experience for posterity.

We passed by a number of armed Hodgies that were stripping a still-smoldering KBR trailer on the side of the road. I was happy that they didn't seem to want any more from us than we did from them. They were content to get their salvage, and we were content to let them. We were nervous, but we were also hamming things up a bit for the cameras. We had already survived much worse and the worst of the worst on the trip up. It was kind of fun making the film, and if something would have happened to us, they would have a way to know exactly what. When I told Palo this rationale, he said, "You numbskull. You know that if something does happen to us, the only ones who will see the tape would be the Hodgies." He was right. They would strip the thread out of a seat cushion if they thought it was still of some use.

As we near the last little town before Camp Cedar, we hear the gun truck on the radio. They will make it just in time to take on the last possible threat. It was good to see them. They even brought our other gun truck with them. I guess they were able to get it repaired. Now it will be our turn. We will have to make a trip down south back to Kuwait to get Baca's truck repaired. Tomorrow, we will have a tow bar of our own and will be able to run at highway speeds. I was just looking forward to good burger. They had real fast food in Kuwait, and I haven't had a good burger since I was home on leave.

We packed up early in the morning and made our way south. Nothing had changed down south. Nothing ever changes down south. The same little kids were in the same places, waiting for their daily handouts. While one hand was held open waiting for a handout, the other one held a rock almost daring us to not give them something. We had grown used to this and brought slingshots back from the States, the good ones. Once a kid let loose with a rock, he was shot in the butt with a marble. After a while, you only need show them the slingshots and they would drop their ammo. It's a dog-eat-dog world, and the biggest dog usually wins.

We drop Baca's truck off at our maintenance platoon at 1000 hours. Then I head for a double patty of flame-broiled goodness, add double cheese, smoky bacon, crisp lettuce, spicy onion, sour dill pickles, and just a little mustard and catsup, and it's love at first bite. I continue to eat until my belly is stuffed and well-rounded. This one burger had enough protein and calories to last all day, but hell, you only live once.

Baca's truck was completed by early afternoon, and we would have to head back for Camp Cedar. We had another mission to run tomorrow morning. We did receive confirmation that our replacement company was on the ground and going through the Movement Under Fire course. It was the course that we had to go through just before I went home on leave. It was true, and we could head back to Camp Cedar knowing that our time left was growing short.

CHAPTER 15

The morning started as any other—wake up too early, safety brief, then hit the road. We were moving at a good pace until we reached the first town north of Samawah, where we came to a dead stop. There was a dead donkey in the road. This could have been an IED as they did occasionally set them up inside of dead animals. There was no shortage of dead animals in this desert. In fact, most of the road from Camp Cedar to Scania always had the smell of death in the air. It was a putrid odor that would almost burn your nostrils. If you have ever smelled the stench of rotting flesh, then you know what I mean. This was not likely an IED since the owner was still standing over it, demanding restitution.

Scorpion 2 was arguing with the owner while other members cleared the animal from the road. They stayed to direct the traffic until we all passed. Once the final vehicle was under way, Scorpion 2 was maneuvering his HMMWV back to the front of the convoy. He was driving in the left lane and was passing KBR trucks at a good rate then was soon out of sight. Within a few minutes of travel, a call comes over the radio.

"112 to 143."

"143, go," I reply.

Baca's voice comes over the airwaves again. "Do you see the HMMWV?"

"Negative," I reply. Baca then tells us to proceed forward to check things out. We work our way forward until they came into view. The first sight was just of the wreckage and not the HMMWV. I call forward on the radio. "There has been an accident."

"I know," said Baca.

"Man down!" I shouted into the mic.

A gruesome picture begins to unfold. A single front seat from the HMMWV lies empty in the street, its former occupant looked to be pinned beneath the badly mangled taxicab. At first, I thought that she was dead. It was Specialist McCarthy, the only female soldier attached to a very aggressive, almost elite team.

We provided security for the KBR civilians and the rest of the team as Sergeant Davis, a combat lifesaver, began to go to work on McCarthy. Even if he was shaken, he was a better choice to provide aid than Palo or me.

Baca comes over the radio again and says, "I'm turning the convoy around and coming back."

"Roger," I reply.

We look to the HMMWV, which had spun free from the road and came to a halt in a ditch about twenty feet away. We were looking for the final passenger, Specialist Schneider. He was the SAW gunner aboard the truck. He was riding halfway in and out of a makeshift gun turret that was cut into the roof of the HMMWV. We found him shaken and sore but without major injuries.

Traffic was beginning to build in both directions, and Iraqi citizens were gathering at the scene. Baca arrived, leaving his co-driver back to supervise the convoy turnaround. Then he would follow up by holding back the southbound traffic. Baca, being a nurse in his civilian career, took over first aid operations. The crowd was becoming increasingly louder and potentially hostile. They didn't feel like we were providing adequate attention to the Iraqi taxi passengers. The driver was dead and needed no further immediate attention. The passengers were briefly checked and evaluated to be less critical than Specialist McCarthy.

I positioned myself between the crowd and the area around McCarthy's medical team. I strongly urged the crowd to subside, first, with my loud voice, and when that didn't work, I followed up with my weapon. I told them to return to their vehicles and that we would get them moving shortly. An Iraqi teenage boy acted as an interpreter on my behalf. I shouted to Palo, "Clear a path to the south!" He quickly responded by pushing cars to a small secondary road. The route would work fine for the small cars, but the larger trucks and busses would have to wait until we got the road cleared. We then routed the northbound traffic to the right shoulder. With the detours in place, we had the traffic moving and the area cleared. By the time the MPs arrived we had the site well under control. We waited in the area until McCarthy got a medevac out, then we headed back to Camp Cedar. This was the first convoy that didn't complete a mission on the day it was sent out, but after what we went through on our last mission, Baca decided that we would just try again tomorrow.

McCarthy was put on the next plane to Germany to be treated for her injuries. She was stable but was going to have a long recovery. Davis was treated for a back injury, and although he was released, he was in a lot of pain and sidelined. We were again shorthanded, but if it had to happen, then now was the time. Our relief company was just coming on board, and we would begin training them immediately. We may just make it home yet.

This training thing split Palo and me up. I moved to the HMMWV, and Palo kept our truck. At least we will be on the same missions. The people from this new company were not very receptive to the way we ran. They were definitely of the new mentality. We ran hard and fast while they were of the mentality that we should be courteous. They thought that somehow courtesy would work in their favor. They don't understand that these people who are still fighting are not Iraqi. They stopped being Iraqi when they no longer cared if they blew up innocent people, including children. These people were radical outsiders but still hiding among the general population.

From the outside looking in, Palo looked like a loose cannon. I don't really know if it was because I wasn't there to pull his reins or if I just didn't realize how much he truly hated these people. That couldn't be. I know of his disdain, and I had for as long as I could remember.

As we were coming up to Scania, I was running side by side with Palo. We had extra security, so we were working together to keep the rear closed off. A Hodgie was coming down the on-ramp just in front of us. He tries to race ahead and work past the convoy. Palo races ahead and pulls alongside of the Hodgie and motions him over. They are traveling at nearly eighty miles per hour, and our Hodgie is running out of road. He should have just braked, but I think he was intimidated by Palo's aggressive driving. The Hodgie finally jerks his car off the road and just catches his bumper and left fender on the concrete girder. The Hodgie then spins out of control minus a bumper and fender. I radio to Palo, "That guy looked pretty smart with you as his hood ornament." Palo comes back with, "He should have stopped." Then he laughed. I had to agree; he should have stopped. Any aggressive driver could be considered a threat. He just got a little too much enjoyment out of it.

That evening, we were sitting down with our new friends from South Dakota. It seems that they don't think that we belong here. They think that the Iraqi people are barbaric and wouldn't know what to do with freedom if they had it. They were about to get an earful. So I opened up with both barrels.

> Prior to 1776, our nation struggled for independence from a suppressive government. People were searching for security from their leadership and freedom from oppression. Those that dared to take a stand would risk life and limb not only for themselves but for their families. They believed that man was born with a God-given right to be free and without freedom, life would hardly be worth living.
>
> Neighbors found themselves at odds over their loyalties. Many would remain loyal to the king. The people took up sides. Brutal fighting took place within our borders. People stood toe-to-toe as they fought with cannons, muskets, and swords. Blood spilled from the bodies of the dead and wounded over hilltops and grassy plains. Many who tried to remain neutral were caught up in the fighting and joined those who lay in crimson red on the battlefield.
>
> The efforts of the brave men who fought so gallantly for our right to be free would have gone unanswered if not for help from allies. Both the Dutch and French stood by our side to help finance and arm our soldiers.
>
> Once our freedom was won, we would continue to fight one another over ideology and territory. During the next century, we migrated west, forming this nation, fighting the Indians and Mexicans, through civil war and gun slinging outlaws. Even today we argue over political differences, spirituality, and morality.
>
> We are currently the greatest nation the world has ever known. We live in the belief that all people are equally capable and should be given the opportunity for greatness. The way we achieve greatness is to break down barriers and give individuals the freedom to do for themselves.

> These people live much the same as we did two hundred years ago. They have always been under one oppressive government or another. They may fight a bit as they find themselves. We are all less than perfect. We still have murder every day in our streets. So tell me what makes us so much better? What if they succeed? What if they become a powerful ally rich in natural resources? What if every child has a right to make their own choices? How can this be wrong? Love thy neighbor does not end at the borders or across the sea.
>
> All people have a God-given right to freedom and an opportunity for greatness. We who have been so blessed and have the ability to help oppressed people have a moral obligation to do so. We must not be caught up in timetables or fear the spillage of blood. History has taught us that some things are worth fighting for. If we have become so consequently selfish as to turn our backs on others to save ourselves or our wallets, then we will likely pray for forgiveness come judgment day.

They could not argue, or maybe they were afraid that I would never shut up. In either case, I guess that I won. I can't see how anybody that did not feel the same way could serve in an all-volunteer armed forces, especially now. The war has been under way for over a year and is in the making for much longer than that. Only a fool would put his life on the line for a cause that they did not believe in.

Some were in line, and those who weren't faded away into the night. Palo was like-minded. Even if he hated them somehow, he wanted them to know freedom, and he couldn't hate the children. Hell, he even liked every Hodgie that he actually met. He would disagree if I asked him, but I was there. He could lie to himself, but he couldn't lie to me.

We had a number of missions with these people over the next few weeks, but we never suffered an attack. That was amazing.

It's hard to teach something when you lack visual aids. I guess you have to experience certain things and just see how you react when they happen. If they plan to run the way they say, then they will find out sooner rather than later.

As we prepare to head south for the last time, we are confident that we have shown them all we can. The rest will be on them. Before we can get off post, we hear news that they have already suffered casualties. They had been hit and hit hard. The kinder, gentler force was not working. Like I said, some things you just can't teach. I'm sure in their eyes the theater just became a more dangerous place to be.

Camp Arifjan, Kuwait, had grown twofold since we had left. They had an awesome gym and even a swimming pool. This was like Club Med. Hell, Camp Cedar had a phone center that opened two days before we left, and we thought that was good. The people stationed here were unbelievably spoiled. One day, in the chow hall, we were talking about the prisoners at Abu Ghraib. We were laughing at the fact that they were complaining of being so abused. I said, "Hell, if I were in the same situation, I would love to have a pair of female panties on my head." The people at the next table were getting annoyed by our terminology and by the way we made light of the situation. They had never known anything other than the pampered, protected life of Kuwait. They started making comments about our lack of respect. I wanted to give them a taste of what it was like up north. I wanted to rip off their heads and beat them to a bloody pulp. My comrades stopped me from acting by telling me that we were almost home and not to mess that up. It would almost have been worth it, but their rationale was pretty good. I guess calmer heads prevailed.

The next two weeks we spent packing. All of the stuff that we were still taking home even if we gave all of our trucks away was amazing. We had to scrub down all of our gear. We couldn't take any of the Iraqi soil home. I guess their dirt and ours wouldn't get along or something like that. Any hoops that we had to jump through would be worth it. We were going home.

I was amazed that I made it. I never really prepared for going home. I was supposed to die. I began feeling more afraid of going home and going back to a lawful society than facing the enemy up north. What if I couldn't adjust? What if I don't fit in? I have so many questions that only time can answer. We don't like change, and this will be one of the biggest changes of my life, except for coming here in the first place. The army prepared me for war but not for returning home. I can remember enjoying my leave, but that was two weeks. This is the rest of my life. I didn't even like being back in Kuwait with all of the silly army rules and regulations. In Iraq, we made the laws, and we could adjust to our needs. There was no cut-and-dry. Now we had to play by their rules. I was torn; half of me wanted to run back up north, and the other half was looking forward to going home to my family and, of course, Helen.

I guess I can get used to the idea. I do have a lot of reasons for going home. In fact, they are the same reasons for coming here in the first place. That seems somewhat ironic. I came to the land of sand and sun for my family, and now I'm afraid to go home and face them.

I load up my duffel bag and throw it over my shoulder. The bag shifts backward and so goes my shoulder. My bag falls to the ground, and just like before, I snap my shoulder back into place and carry on. It hurt like hell, and I began to think that maybe it was time to go home and begin to heal. The shoulder is a metaphor for my whole life. I need to go home and heal, all of me. When I looked at the big picture, it was all making sense. I was ready to move on.

I called home, and Helen was all abuzz with the news of our coming home. She told me about how they had a huge homecoming planned. Even Randy Travis was going to come and sing for us. It was the biggest deal in her whole young life. I didn't know how to tell her that that was not what we wanted. A hero's welcome should be reserved for heroes. We were just men coming home from a job overseas. I even felt like, since the job wasn't finished, that maybe we shouldn't be coming home, but that was just more of my nerves talking. The homecoming I came to terms with and decided that it was important for our families. They could feel like losing us for a year was worth their while. It would give them closure. If it was important for them, then it had to be important for me. They wanted show that they were proud of their soldier, and they wanted to show us.

Home was so close I could almost taste it. I can't believe that I am finally looking forward to it, whatever it would be.

CHAPTER 16

Things are heating up as we prepare to leave. The Hodgies were having a political demonstration just outside of one of our bases. Things got out of hand, and one of the gate guards open fire on the demonstrators. This caused a backlash from the Hodgies, and by the time it was over, we had suffered the single largest loss of American lives since the beginning of the war. If I could base this on my own experience, I would have to say that somebody lost their nerve. We had been in situations a number of times where we were outnumbered thousands to one, and if we would have fired a single shot, then we would have been mutilated by the population. We kept our cool, and subsequently, we kept our lives.

After the uprising, we were called to a formation by our third battalion commander. I gave up trying to remember names after the first one. We had seen them come and go while we remained in country. This couldn't be good, but we didn't have any equipment. Our gear was packed and ready to ship within two days. Our trucks were handed over to the company that took over our mission, so this couldn't be all bad. It was all bad. He told us that we would be held over for one last mission. With the uprising, they had to bring in more troops to keep the peace up north. Our mission was to take an armored division back up north.

We had to draw the almost unused equipment left by our sister companies who came to the country after us, didn't do very much while they were here, and rotated back before us. Some of the stuff that was left by our sister companies didn't have more than six thousand total miles on it. We hauled supplies for over thirty thousand miles each in the first eight months, and they did less than six in the whole year. Something was definitely wrong with this picture!

The 459th was in the same boat. They were held over for the same mission. We were used to getting screwed. What was one more mission? I had to call home and break the news to my family. They would be devastated or at least disappointed. Everyone in the unit had to make the same phone call. Just one more mission, they said. That meant two, maybe three, weeks. We had been inching our families along since we got here. I don't think they would believe that we would be home in three weeks any more than we did.

With nothing to do except bite the bullet, we began working on the equipment that we had just inherited. The maintenance on this equipment was appalling. No wonder they were always non–mission capable. We repaired what we could and lubed everything we couldn't repair. Then we began to harden the truck cabs with steel plating. All of the stuff that we couldn't get before was now in abundance. The plating might keep some bits of shrapnel from penetrating, but it wouldn't stop a direct hit. The plating would slow us down because of the extra weight, and it made the trucks difficult to defend. We would be like ducks in a shooting gallery. For this reason, many decided against the hardening. Our ability to fight is what kept us alive for 365 already. Why would we want to change? With our rationale, you would think that they would let us run as we have, but this is the army, and we would have to run their way. Every vehicle was fitted with this cumbersome plating.

As we venture northbound and cross the border into Iraq, we find that something new has been added. A sign saying, "Barrels up, slow down, respect civilian drivers." "What the heck is this!" I told Palo. It went against everything that we had done over the last year. No wonder convoys were getting cut apart. I wonder whose idea it was to put this sign up. No doubt it was some colonel trying to make a name for himself. This was the beginning of OIF (Operation Iraqi Freedom) 2. This was a kinder, gentler army than OIF 1, more like a kinder, gentler target than ever before. No wonder they were taking so many casualties. The army had their balls cut off by the theater command.

This is my first convoy that is a mix of both military and TCNs. I think TCN stands for third-country national, but I know that it is the new politically correct term for Hodgie. I hated the idea of running with these unskilled, problematic drivers. Every convoy that I have seen these guys in was a major Charlie Foxtrot. We could not communicate with them, for one thing, and we couldn't trust them, for another.

When we pulled into Scania, we were instructed to check our loads, not that we had to be told. As I attempt to climb up onto my trailer, my shoulder goes out for the second time in three weeks, and I fall to the ground. I do as I have done three other times during the last four months and reset then carry on. I know at some point I will need to have this addressed. But it won't be today. Today we have a mission to run.

The Hodgies, I mean TCNs, were every bit as messed up as I thought they would be. They would get lost from the convoy, make wrong turns, and leave gaping spaces between trucks. I am just about at my wit's end. We have never been like this, not on our worst day. Thank God that we will leave these bastards up north and head home in an all military convoy.

When we return from our last mission, we find out, big surprise, wait for it, this is not to be our last mission. Only two days back and we volunteer to go as the roving security force for a company on their second or third mission into Iraq. What the hell, as long as we had to be here, we may as well stay busy. It's early May, and the temperature is a dry 115 degrees. We are used to the heat, so it doesn't feel like an issue. Palo and I are a bit apprehensive as we are the only seasoned troops on this mission consisting of both military and Hodgie civilian drivers. Now that we have been with the Hodgie drivers, we know that we don't care much for their lack of professionalism. But we have been in a lot worse situations than what we are facing now, after all. We were invincible—or so we thought.

With the new uprising, they closed off MSR Jackson, and we were back on the dusty trail. About one hour in, the CC decided that they needed a break. They were not used to driving blind, and it was taking a toll on them. As we sit idle on the side of the road, another convoy of FNGs were passing us going south. These guys were serious. They were buckled up tight and looked like they were ready for war. This was not a bad posture to carry, except the road is long, and if you have your guard up all of the time, you will be less likely to be on full alert when it really counts. That was something that you learn with time.

Palo had a developed a deep hatred for all Hodgies, and it showed in his overly aggressive driving habits. He loved it when any of them stepped out of line. It gave him an excuse to lash out, and that meant either they came around to his way of thinking or got hurt. He would use our truck freely to run them off the road or worse. I couldn't blame him for his disdain or action, but I never felt the same no matter what they threw at us. In my opinion, they had a right to fight for what they believed in. They had the same right to die for their cause as any of us, and that was okay by me. In fact, I actually had respect for them in that way.

The thought of dying did not bother me, or at least it hadn't. Something has changed, and I don't know why. I feel a fear that before I had not known. It didn't make sense. I have been shot at a number of times, been on fire, almost blown up by IED blasts, and was in many more extreme situations and left without a scratch. So what is fear?

We make it through to Scania. We get the report, but it is the same as always: IED attacks, small arms fire, daisy chains, RPGs, and mortar attacks, nothing we haven't seen dozens of times over the past year. While other convoys are held back, we are allowed to continue for we were our escorts. It bothered me that we were the first convoy to leave this checkpoint in some time. That gave the enemy time to set up their attacks, and we knew it. Our chance for getting hit was almost assured. Palo and I both felt it in our guts, and we were on high alert.

We make it to BIAP with only the normal civilian traffic to control. We have to make a stop for a period. This was the same for all convoys now. We will refuel and take a rest break. While we are sitting there, we run into some of our guys from Second Platoon on a separate mission. As we stop to shoot the bull, there is a sudden uproar, and all of the MPs make a run to the rear gate.

"What's going on?" Palo asked the guys from Second Platoon.

"No clue," they reply. The camp gets the word that no one is allowed to come or go until further notice.

"Wow! This must be big!" I said to Palo. He agreed and we parted way with the guys from Second Platoon and headed back to our truck. We will be leaving once we get the green light.

Then the word comes. Some FNG shot a round from his Mk 19, a fully automatic grenade launcher, into the clearing barrel. The round ricocheted out and went through the windshield of his truck and was imbedded in the driver's shoulder. The round has a built-in safety whereas the round has to spin so many revolutions to arm itself. Lucky for the driver and the rest of the crew it didn't arm in the short distance. What an idiot! He would have a lot of explaining to do. We were glad it wasn't our convoy. Once they had the situation under control, we were cleared to leave. Again, we were the first convoy out in some time.

We depart BIAP then over RPG Pass and cross over to MSR Sword. We are at the last thirty minutes of our journey, a journey that we were facing with great apprehension. The city is active with people, any of which may be a potential threat. I have the SAW at the ready, scanning the distant crowds, overpasses, and the vegetation for snipers and other hostiles. All is going well, and we start feeling that maybe we were wrong, but we knew that we still had a ways to go.

Then for no apparent reason, one of the Hodgie trucks pulls out of the convoy and to the right side of the road. Palo and I can't believe what we are seeing. "What is this guy doing!" I said to Palo. We can't stop here, not now. We radio to the convoy commander that one of the Hodgies had stopped, and the convoy commander radioed back to get him moving again.

"No kidding!" we said together.

Palo said, "We should just leave this stupid guy here to get his head shot off."

"We can't," I said. "Pull over."

The tension is so thick you could cut it with a knife. The hair on the back of my neck is standing straight out as we slow to about ten miles per hour and begin to pull to the right side of the road. As soon as we hit the white line on the side of the road, I look down and see a small pile of rocks and broken asphalt. I start to turn my head away then, *pop,* a flash of light, then game over, I thought as the debris peppers my face and the cab fills with the distinct smell of burnt gunpowder. My body fell into a sudden shock, and I felt a deep sense of shame. I should have seen it sooner, but it was only five feet from my face. I couldn't even get a word out before it blew. Palo and I look at each other in disbelief. We can't believe what just happened or the fact that we are still alive. Only the cap blew; the main explosive didn't discharge. We turn to each other and all we can say is "WOW!" We instantly feel an adrenaline spike then fear as we digest what just happened. Fear quickly turns to anger, and we can't help but think that our Hodgie was somehow involved. For the first time in my life, I feel the hate that has been the drive for so many others all along. I have never in my life felt hate, and I wanted to take that stinking Hodgie apart 5.56 millimeters at a time. I jump from the cab and take up a defensive posture. Palo runs to this SOB and yells at him to get back into his truck, but the Hodgie continues to work on his tie-down strap as if he were trying to stall for more time. Palo then brings his weapon to the ready and bears down on him, his weapon deliberately pointed in his direction, and I only hope this time he follows through. *Shoot that SOB! Shoot him!* kept running through my mind, but this was all of the prompting that the Hodgie needed. He was then quick to return to his truck, and we were off to chase down our convoy that by now was several miles away.

We catch the convoy just before the next overpass interchange. Tensions are still high, and we are still pissed off and very vigilant. We run ahead of the convoy, and the Hodgie falls back in line. We then take a defensive position on the bridge as the convoy passes. We are still keyed up from our very near miss, and we actually hope to find a legitimate target. As the last truck passes, we scurry back to our cab, and we are off again. Then, as we round the last corner that is the road to the back gate at Camp Anaconda, we race ahead of the convoy to the Hodgie mart. Again, we get out of our truck, and we get right in the faces of these Hodgies to ensure that none of these bastards have access to our convoy. The convoy forges ahead and passes into Camp Anaconda without further incident. We both feel a letdown of emotion, and we begin to thank God for our lives.

The next morning, we depart from the Hodgies and head for home. We no longer feel invincible, making this day as difficult as the day before. We make it back to Scania without action.

Again, we can finally let down just a bit. We then pass Samawah, and we finally can settle down. The convoy commander pulls the convoy over for a rest halt in what appears to be a barren part of the desert. But the convoy commander has other than rest on his mind. He calls for a test fire. This is a chance for his troops to blow off steam and some ammo since the trip was uneventful for the most part. Test fires were strictly forbidden in the ROE (rules of engagement), but at commence fire, the trigger-happy gunslingers let it all hang out. A civilian Hodgie pickup truck suddenly appears in the impact area. I call for a cease-fire, and the barrage dwindles to silence. A Black Hawk was patrolling the area and must have seen the pickup fleeing from the convoy and, with the gunfire, assumed he was a hostile. The Black Hawk gets into position, fires his weapons, and the pickup disappears in a ball of fire. Nothing was ever said about the incident again. What's done was done, and nothing we could do could change that.

This was the worst mission that we had been on to date. Even with all of the hate and disdain that I developed for Hodgies, I felt bad for the innocent man who would never see his family again. It wasn't right, and Palo and I agreed that we would never volunteer for another mission with these guys again.

This was my last mission into Iraq. Perhaps this one was just a little too close. In any case, I lost my taste for it. We were supposed to go home soon, and I needed to have my shoulder documented before traveling home. Maybe it was just an excuse; I can't deny that I had been shaken by that last mission. I couldn't take the newly found hate out with me to the battlefield. I truly don't know what I feared most. Was it the enemy, the so-called friendlies, or myself? All I really knew was that I was done, at least for now.

I was surprised to find the mission going on and on. I truly thought that we were just about done when I allowed myself to be sidelined, and when we weren't, it was too late for me. They wouldn't allow me to go back. Now I would carry guilt along with hate and disdain. Palo was on his own and bounced from truck to truck wherever he was needed. He would never again see the level of security that we found in each other.

They put me into physical therapy, on light duty, and on some BS bus detail in Kuwait. I was to ensure that we had busses and Kuwaiti police escorts for all of the new troops arriving in the theater. The Kuwaiti police rarely had the same sense of urgency for the mission that we had. We would get a unit on the ground and want to get them moved out. Often, the Kuwaiti police would want to wait for hours until enough troops came in to fill all of the busses. This wasn't good enough for us.

One day, I had enough troops to fill three of our five busses and went to get our escorts. The police insisted that they must have all five busses filled before they would move. I told them that they must roll out within the next half hour. Forty-five minutes later, they still hadn't shown up. By now, I had had enough of these bastards. I jumped into my HMMWV, and at speeds of fifty miles per hour, I drove into their lot, threw the vehicle into a side slide, and came to a halt just beyond their front door. When they come out to see what the commotion was, I begin to yell, "You get your butts over there right now!" It got their attention, and they did move out. I wish I could say that this was the end of their malingering, but at least it made me feel better for the moment.

It wasn't until later that I realized exactly what I had done. I went flying into the police station in a foreign country, driving reckless and demanding service while being demeaning to them. This would be enough to get you locked up and have the key thrown away in some countries, probably this one included. Can you say international incident? The disdain that I developed for these people was definitely showing through.

CHAPTER 17

Since we moved back to Kuwait, we had full access to a phone center and an Internet café. I made good use of these assets. This was new for us. In fact, they opened up an Internet café on the day we left Camp Cedar, Iraq. The rest of our unit had these things months ago, but it was all new for the stay-behind security force. Some of the computers even had webcams. This meant that my family could actually see me for the first time since Thanksgiving. A lot had changed since then. I had been going to the gym daily and was packing on the pounds. Just over twenty pounds and I was teetering on the two-hundred-pound mark. I looked and felt good.

Helen and I spent a number of hours instant-messaging. We were definitely missing each other. Our IMs were a bit risqué at times, which probably added to the frustration of being away more than it helped. Still, it was always good to communicate.

Once we appear to be getting close to our return date, I begin to have doubts about whether I am going to be able to adjust back into my job and life. Somehow, the job that I was returning to seemed trivial. Life for me had been about life and death, and now fighting with store managers over one or two spaces just didn't feel like it was worth the effort. I didn't know if I could even interact with civilians. The stress of coming home was getting to be overwhelming. This second leg of the war changed me forever; maybe the first did as well.

The thought of being home was the endgame that I had hoped for since my arrival. Now that it was upon me, I felt intimidated just by the prospect of going home. They were asking for volunteers to stay behind for another tour. We had been put through such hell and were told that we were going home since we got here that no one would even consider it. Yet I was more fearful of going home and the unknown than I was of dying.

I was able to put that fear behind me and asked Helen to renew our vows once I returned home. We were making plans to go to Reno, Nevada. We were planning a camping trip with my family and a honeymoon with my lover. I made all of the plans, and most of my family would be there. It was going to be a great homecoming.

As the day approached, my fears began to once again get the best of me. I was looking for any reason to sabotage my return. I was looking at Helen's e-mail one day to see if she had a chance to read my latest e-mails. What I found was one of those junk mail offers from a dating site. I knew in my heart that she was as devoted to me as they come, but I let my mind go wild. Then when I couldn't reach her right away, my mind continued to race. This was the chance for sabotage that I had been waiting for. Within hours, I was ready to cancel all of our plans and volunteer to stay in Iraq. I sent out accusing e-mails, and once Helen saw them, she was so hurt in my apparent lack of trust that I did in fact come close to jeopardizing my return.

After speaking to Helen and realizing how stupid I was, it took some time and profuse apologizing before she agreed to go on with our plans. I had just about screwed up the one thing that I was sure of about my return.

The day finally comes, the day when we are to catch our freedom bird. During the sixteen months of our deployment, we will have set records for miles driven in a combat zone, a record that wouldn't soon be challenged. In the end, everyone from my unit made it home; some were injured, but all survived. We made it through without up-armored vehicles and with Vietnam War–era flak jackets by being fast and ready. I'm sure a little luck and prayers helped along the way.

On the way home, we were applauded by the flight crew as they acted like we were all heroes. This attention that we received before we left was not as welcome now. We weren't heroes, at least I wasn't. I went out to do a job, and I am returning before it is complete. I didn't say anything, nor did anybody else. This was a time to be humble and to reflect. It was a long and, for the most part, quiet plane ride home. Once we got there, there was more fanfare. They had a band to greet us, and our families were all waiting in the wings. Most of us spent the night in El Paso, reuniting with our families. Soon we would have to return to Las Vegas, New Mexico, for a small-town homecoming.

None of us were looking forward to this homecoming. We would all just like to go home and blend into the woodwork. I could see how this was important for our families. They needed closure; they needed to know that we weren't gone for the last sixteen months for nothing. They had been through hell themselves. So this was for them, and that made it okay.

They began by putting us all onto trailers and parading us through the masses. This was a reminder, of course, of times when we were traveling through masses of people at a snail's pace, looking for that potential danger that was always lurking. It wasn't their fault. They were trying to give us the homecoming that previous warriors should have received. At one point, I saw my family in the crowd. I motioned for someone to bring my boy up as he was dressed in his little soldier suit. He was proud as could be to be up there, and that in itself made it all worthwhile.

After the parade, they brought us to the field at New Mexico Highlands University, where they began the festivities by having several people skydive from a Black Hawk helicopter. Once they landed, the speakers began. We had the general, Heather Wilson, and the mayor of Las Vegas. The governor had never bothered to show up for anything we did. The mayor was really funny though he wasn't trying to be. He was awkward in his speaking and used the same catchphrases over and over. Once all of the speakers said their piece, it was time for awards.

No one was particularly surprised by the way the awards were distributed. The highest ranking soldiers received the highest awards though many of them didn't do much. They stayed back at the tents while we led their convoys and took all of the risk. It was all okay. The only thing that bothered me was that I had recommended Palo for a high award, and when the do-nothings received the same award, it diminished what his award really meant.

With all of the festivities over with, we could get on with our lives. For my family, it meant the trip to Reno. I grew up in Sparks, Nevada, which is basically a suburb of Reno. The old joke was always that Reno was so close to hell that you could see sparks. Reno is an over-twenty-one playground, but it was kind boring if you were just a kid. It was close to the mountains and the foothills, so if you were into skiing or dirt-biking, it was great for that.

I chose a fitting suite. It wasn't the honeymoon suite, but it may had well been. It was a huge room with a hot tub right in the room. This room even had a TV in the bathroom. I rented the room for two nights. The first night would be just for me and my lover. The second night, we would have the kids in so they could enjoy the luxurious room as well.

We found one of these "fly by the seat of your pants" wedding chapels that could accommodate us. We didn't want any silly themes, but I guess they did those weddings as well. We chose "Stuck on You" by Lionel Richie for Helen's trip down the aisle. My dad escorted her and gave her away. The vows were perfect for a renewing commitment. I was so happy to have her by my side. We had been apart for so long that I thought this was the perfect homecoming, and it was.

The night back at the room was all about us. We had a lovely reception at my brother Craig's house, and then we headed for the hotel. We left a bottle of champagne chilling in the room so it was ready upon our return. We first had a glass on the couch as we reminisced over our lives together. Then we continued to talk about the day's events while in the hot tub along with some soft petting. Then we reconsummated our love. By the night's end, we used just about every inch of the large room. It was a remarkable evening.

The second night, we let the kids enjoy the room while Helen and I met my sister Sherry and her husband, John. We wanted get away to enjoy a few drinks and maybe even a little dancing. Reno, the town that never sleeps, appeared to be down for the night. We finally found a little club that was hopping. It wasn't my favorite music, and there wasn't a dance floor, but we decided to go in for a couple of drinks. We found a table in the back and ordered a round of brews. The waitress brought us plastic cups, and as we looked around, we found out that we were the only ones with this type of cups. The rest of the patrons had frosty glasses. I made a joke to the others that they must have thought us to be a rowdy bunch. As we looked a little closer at the crowd, it was apparent that this was a place where straight couples weren't exactly welcome. We had one more round then decided that if we weren't welcome, then we didn't need to be there. Besides, we wanted to dance. With the night growing late and our luck running out, we decided to go back to the room for a while.

Back at the room, the kids appeared to have had a better time than we did. There was evidence that they too had used the entire room. Clothes, swimsuits, drinks, and pizza plates were spread out from stem to stern. We picked up a bit then sat in the living area to enjoy one more nightcap. We reflected on the night and had a laugh that the only place we could find in all of Reno was a gay bar. It had been a long day preceded by a late night. We all agreed that we should just turn in early and hit it again tomorrow. Tomorrow we would be heading out to Lake Lahontan for the camping part of our vacation.

We spent just about every holiday out at Lake Lahontan when we were growing up. We had a lot of special memories. We used to meet up with several of my dad's coworkers out at the lake. We spent so much time out there that we basically had our own beach. It took some doing getting back through the rugged roads to the spot, but it was like having the lake to ourselves, or at least half of it. Most kept to the beaches on the improved part of the lake. People would stack up practically one on top of another over there. In my opinion, we had it much better.

We never had a boat of our own, but several of my dad's friends did, and they would take us out fishing or skiing. I learned how to ski behind a seventeen-foot two-tone, green boat with inboard/outboard V8 Mercruiser. Before returning from Iraq, my dad told me that his friend might be interested in selling the old boat. It was still in good shape with a few of its own idiosyncrasies. I wanted a new boat, and this one had so many memories that I had to buy it. The price was within what I was willing to pay for, so Helen and I had a new boat. I don't think that Helen ever had much experience with a boat prior to this, but she seemed to take right to it. I couldn't have been happier than I was at that moment. I was in a place that I loved to go to with people that I loved to be with. For that time, it had felt as if I had never left.

For the next several days, we spent the days on the water and the cool nights with a mixed drink and a light jacket, enjoying the serenity of the night. This reminded me of several nights in Iraq, nights where I would stare up at the stars in the black of night. I would think of home and at the same time wonder how it could be so peaceful in a place so riddled by war.

We spent the last few days with my oldest brother, Craig, and his family. He still had a home in Sparks and will likely never give up his roots. I took Helen and the kids around to show them some of my old haunts, but the area had grown threefold since I lived there, and finding anything that looked familiar was a chore. I found my old house and schools; they were miles apart, and Helen wondered how I ever found them growing up. That was just about all that was left from my childhood. I never really missed it when I moved away. Some of the people maybe and the lake, of course, but that was about all. Being in the military, you learn to pack up and move on without looking back.

CHAPTER 18

Once the fanfare subsided, I was left at Fort Bliss to fend for myself. There were a few others from my unit still there on medical hold. It was nice to see at least a few familiar faces. One of them was Sergeant Davis. He was stuck still trying to get back in shape from his accident. We ended up being roomies. I can't believe that anyone from my unit is still here and someone from my security team at that. Davis was originally from Texas, another Dallas Cowboy fan. He was a good guy in spite of these flaws. He was brought to New Mexico by his now ex-wife, and with no ties, he wasn't planning on returning. Somehow he managed to meet a girl from Arkansas while serving in Iraq. They hit it off right from the start, and he's thinking that that's where he may end up.

I asked Davis how often he sees anybody from our old command. He said that they were by once early on, but he hasn't seen or heard from any of them since. "That really bites!" I told him. "You're telling me," he said. Davis had been having one problem after another with paperwork, awards, and reports needed from our unit, but time after time, they went unaddressed. *Boy, I hope I don't need anything from those ungrateful bastards*, I thought to myself. There were a few others who were hurt worse than us and received the same treatment. It was as if everyone back home was trying to put the war behind them. I was completely disappointed in this treatment; after all, these were the people who we bled for. The least they could do would be to see us through our healing.

Davis said, "Don't give them another thought. They damn sure won't think about you." He was right. If they weren't going to worry about us, then I didn't need to waste energy on them. Davis and I were a lot alike. He had good southern values, and he was also a hard-core conservative when it came to politics. It was a good thing too because when I returned, it was just in time for the presidential elections. As I would watch the war bashing going on, I was madder than a herd of cattle grazing on Astroturf. We would both get completely up in arms and actually yell at the TV during every debate or even for a simple commercial. The lies that were pouring from the lips of the liberal candidate were infuriating. He was downplaying an effort that we were willing to risk life and limb for. Even after all that I had been through, I was completely for the effort. WMDs (weapons of mass destruction) or not, that man needed to be taken down.

While on medical hold, they gave us menial jobs to perform by day, but the nights were our own. I was to ensure that busses made it to the different training sites, and Davis worked in the recreation hall, issuing Ping-Pong balls. These were pretty tough jobs for returning war veterans. We were lumped in with the sick, lame, and lazy. These were the people who stayed behind as the rest of their units deployed. Most of them had a little more than a hangnail, and they were treated as such. What really sucked was that they lumped us in with these guys and therefore we were treated equally bad. What a raw deal, and since our unit abandoned us, we didn't have any recourse.

I started having what you would call abnormal behaviors, and I really didn't know why. I was driving fast and erratic. I continue to check my six every couple of minutes and inspect every bridge for shooters and/or rock throwers. Every aggressive driver seemed to trigger emotions, and I was instantly at a hundred miles per hour, both literally and figuratively. In Iraq, it was speed that kept us safe along with keen senses and adrenaline. So this made sense, except I don't realize when I'm doing it. I'm driving down the highway, and suddenly I am transported back to Iraq. I'm driving down MSR Tampa through IED Alley, looking for the next threat. Before I realize what was going on, I'm miles down the road with no idea how I got there. As I come back to reality, I can feel the beads of sweat running down my face, and my body is trembling. I feel like I'm going crazy. Sane people don't see things that ultimately aren't there.

I don't want to leave the base but then I haven't been home in so long that I don't want to be cooped up either. I spoke to an army shrink, and he assured me that I was just fine. He said that I had developed an addiction to adrenaline and that I should take up a dangerous hobby that could feed my addiction. I was grateful for his insight. All that I had to do was take up a life-threatening hobby and I will be just fine. He said that if I don't, then I will likely end up brushing up against the law at some point.

When I told Helen what I needed to do, she wasn't very happy. I don't see why. I'm just glad that I'm not crazy. I'll do whatever's necessary. I thought that I might have this PTSD that everyone keeps talking about. That would suck. I had flashbacks, intrusive thoughts, night sweats, nightmares, and hyperarousal, but this was all going to be taken away by cliff dwelling. I guess it would, if I were to fall. I often feel like I never really came back, and I wish that I hadn't. The job wasn't finished. How could I come home?

It's a six-hour drive from Fort Bliss to Las Vegas, and I could make it in close to five. I would make the drive home for almost every weekend. It sure beats staying here. Helen and I are planning on buying a house closer to Albuquerque now that I have returned, some place that will be closer to my job and where we can be together. Helen will have to find a new job, but that shouldn't be too hard for her. She is a hard worker and has a lot of experience in the title business. That would come in time, but with the weekend ending, I have to get back to Fort Bliss.

I just got on the interstate, and some jerkoff is on my ass. I slam on my brakes, and he swerves just in time to miss me. Then I see him flip me the bird, and I begin to give chase. This SOB wants to play, and so do I. I pull my favorite killing knife from my pocket and set it on the seat beside me just in case he decides to get brave. This is a feeling that I know, and it feels good. My speedometer pegs out at a hundred, and I am slowly gaining on him. With all of my senses keen, I am aware of everything around me, including the blue lights coming fast in the opposite direction. Then I snap. "What the in the hell am I doing?" I look down at the knife and wonder about my own intentions. I slow down to the limit and then take the next exit. I have to stop and calm down. As I come to a halt on the shoulder of the off-ramp, I jump from my truck and begin pacing franticly. I can feel my heart pounding in my chest. I fear what I may be capable of, but the feeling of adrenaline is still a powerful drug. Maybe that crackpot shrink was right.

I finally calm down and get back onto the road. My hands are still a bit shaky. I crack the top open on an ice-cold soda. My cooler was full of them. I take a big drink, and it burns so good. The Hodgie soda wasn't as good as it is here at home. There was a difference that I couldn't quite pin down. Maybe it was the water, the sweetener, or just the Hodgie labeling, something about it just didn't taste like home. After a few sips, I felt at ease. I jump back into the truck and then back onto the interstate. The road was long, but a wandering mind occupies a lot of time. Before I knew it, I was back on base. I walked in the door, poured myself a shot, then chased it down with the last of my soda. I love being home, but I'm kind of glad that I am still in transition; it's just a lot to take in all at once.

It was football season, and every Monday night, we would find a different sports bar to go to and watch the game. This was about the extent of our night life. Davis was devoted to his girl and I to Helen. One of our favorite sports bars was Hooters in El Paso. I know what you're thinking, but they had our favorite beer on tap, and say what you will but I love their wings. They always had the game on, and the eye candy was hardly noticeable. Life was beginning to feel a little more normal. I had Davis to pal around with during the week, and I was home with Helen every weekend. Then I always had a bottle of Black Velvet to take the edge off. The rest of the world would have to just fall into place eventually.

We finally heard from our command. They were going to have some kind of reintegration weekend up at the Glorieta Baptist Center. I guess too many people were having too many problems and this was their answer. I didn't want to go, but it would be nice to see some of the guys again. This was a church center, so alcohol was forbidden. Yeah, right. This was the first time that some of us had been together, defiantly a call for celebration. There were some people who I didn't care if I ever saw again, but I just stayed away from these people, at least when I could. There were a lot of people who I really wanted to see.

The place was a regular zoo with my entire unit showing up at once. Of course, this description fit my unit well with all of our nicknames. We had the Ox, the Owl, Possum 1, Possum 2, Chicken Man, and there was one guy that we just called Animal. There were probably a few more, but my memory isn't what it used to be. Seeing the guys triggered all sorts of memories, more good than bad. We had some good times together, and these are the memories that you want to keep fresh. Unfortunately, the bad memories tend to hold on just a little stronger. I wonder why that is. I guess that having someone trying to kill you and almost succeeding is just a bit more memorable than a joke that someone told in a drunken stupor.

Possum 1 was a clown. It was always good to see him. He could liven up a room from the moment he walked through the door. He was probably responsible for just about everyone's nickname. There was more to him than his kidding around. He was a genuine soul, passionate, and true. His kidding was usually aimed at himself, but there wasn't anybody immune from getting caught in one of his anecdotes. It was always so damn funny that you never minded; in fact, it was a privilege. If he didn't joke with you, then he probably didn't like you much. He was one of the first people that I ran into.

"So how are you and Helen doing?"

"We renewed our vows and are about to buy a new house. In fact, she's around here, someplace."

"Well, we will have to get together, but I have to run right now."

That usually means that it will be sometime in neverland, but he actually meant later at the conference.

I ran into person after person, and though we had only been apart for about six months, this felt more like a high school reunion. Before we knew it, the time had come to settle down and get with the seminar. They spoke to us about reintegration and how stressful this could be for a family. They said that the soldier's spouse had been keeping the home fires burning and that the returning soldier should not try to jump right in and take things over. They said that we should be proud of our families for keeping things going in our absence and we should just be content to keep things as they are, at least for now. We can work into any changes slowly. Then they talked for almost a full day on spousal abuse and PTSD. They almost made us sound like monsters returning home to conquer our old lives and families.

I could really see the part where we had to be proud of our families, but we needed to get back to our lives. Life doesn't wait for you; you either live or life moves on without you. They make it sound so easy. I had already screwed up their teachings anyway by buying a house. They said no major life changes for at least six months. Well, then this little talk is about six months too late. I don't think that they know what they are talking about, so I spent the rest of the time at the seminar paying only little attention. Soon I would be leaving Fort Bliss, and I would have to return to work. This one-weekend thing did have some good information, but what they should really have done is reintegrate soldiers slowly, maybe by creating some sort of halfway house. A place where it would be mandatory for every returning vet to live, maybe learn a trade, and then go home on weekends to have a chance to get to know your family again, slowly. Particularly for returning Guard soldiers, we all have some sort of obligation to maintain a household, so slowly for us is out of the question.

The entire seminar was nothing but lip service. They told about problems that we would probably all face but didn't offer any practical solutions for these problems. The armed forces have spent years teaching us how to not fear death and how to take another life, but they have never taught themselves how to reteach us to become civilians. Somehow somewhere they have to make this a regular part of their curriculum. They need to spend as much time teaching us to reintegrate as what they spent teaching us how to kill and be killed. The way I see it, it's pay me now or pay me later. The prisons and VA hospitals are full of people who couldn't reintegrate. I'm sure this costs us more in the long run.

The weekend flew by. Other than bits of small talk, I really didn't get any time to spend with my old comrades. Everybody was going in their own ways and catering to the needs of their families. I was glad that I had Helen there. I think if it weren't for her, I would have spent the entire weekend alone. These were my brothers and sisters. We all cared so much for one another, and now we barely had time to exchange pleasantries. This hurt;

life was changing. My family was great, but they really couldn't understand what I had been through, and I don't even understand what I'm going through now. If I couldn't speak to my family and my brothers in arms were too busy, where does that leave me?

I walk alone though I am not. The masses will not see me. They will not hear me. I feel like I am nothing more than a ghost walking among them. I can hear everyone's words. I can see their expression. I size them up to a potential threat level. I can never rest. I am always on guard. How can I stop their haunting voices? I can't make them go away, and they don't even know that I am here.

I feel a fire burning within me. It is a rage that I fear at some point will burn out of control. I'm feeding off the emotions of others, and they are so petty that I may starve. These people are undeserving of their freedoms, and they are so willing to piss them away. Is this what I fought for?

I have thrown up my hands and shouted in silent anger and distress. Why can they not see? The people of this nation have been given a great gift, the gift of freedom. Many have grown spoiled by prosperity. The price of freedom is blood, blood that has been shed for all free men. The price will increase. Now it's the blood of your father, husband, son, daughter, or brother. Stand behind these heroes as they protect the livelihood and future of your children.

Reach down and grab the hand of the less fortunate and pull them up by your side. Let them stand on their own to walk in greatness while they who are unwilling fall to the depths of hell. The overwhelming long-silent majority must speak out and stand up to the vocal minority and take back the rights we are pissing away.

Today there is no innocence; the face of every child is forever scarred by the world we live in. They have been spoiled at birth by the riches surrounding us all. We will no longer do things for our neighbors before ourselves; our needs or, rather, wants are too strong. We will feed them crumbs that fall from our beards and dwell in the feeling as we boast about our generosity.

I wish that I could see some small sign of our humanity that is worth the blood that has been spilled. I know that there are some people from within our nation who are willing to help the less fortunate, but they are few. Most go about their daily lives thinking that somehow they are better than others and deserving of everything that they have even though they have really never done anything to deserve it. Most people will snub their noses at the broken soldier who killed and bled for them.

I guess that I will never change this world although I have done my part. I have looked into the faces of the innocent and promised them hope for a brighter future. Then I helped to pave the way for them to seek out individual greatness. They will have to help themselves from here. That is all any of us can do. Give someone a hand and teach them to walk on their own. It's up to them to do with it what they will.

I returned to Fort Bliss with more questions than answers. They made it sound like we are all screwed up. I don't feel screwed up. I feel like I am seeing things clearly for the first time in my life. . Like I said, I can't change the world. I would like to, but I can't.

It's Monday night, football night. Davis and I will head out to a new sports bar. The game should be a good one, Washington and Dallas. The nights are always fun when Davis and I can choose sides. It's Dollar Draft Night; the game hasn't even started and we have already scored. We both have our vehicles, but on football nights, we always take a cab. That way we can enjoy the night without worry. At kickoff, Dallas runs the ball all the way back for a score. SOB! This may be a long night. Davis rubs it in deep, and all I can do is laugh. I don't much care for Washington, but anybody against the Boys is my second favorite team. I am a hard-core Steelers fan, and I have been since the days of Franco Harris, Bradshaw, and Swann. Three and out for

Washington, then Dallas travels near the length of the field and turns the ball over. I turn to Davis and rub little salt in his wound, but if Washington doesn't start pulling something out of their back sides, I'm going to have to drink the pain away.

"Go, Boys!" Davis yells. It seems as if they're aiming to nail the coffin shut early tonight as they go in for another score. "Oh hell! Give me another draft and one for Davis as well," I told the bartender. I think the bartender and I are the only ones in the place rooting against Dallas. We were in El Paso, so I guess we were bound to be in the minority. Washington finally puts together a drive just before the half, and when it looked like they were going to score, Washington then throws an interception on what should have been their scoring play. The place erupts into a thunderous roar. I congratulate Davis during halftime and turn my attention to drowning my sorrows. "Give me two drafts and a shot." Davis won't drink hard liquor, but tonight, the drinks are on me. That's what happens when you're on the losing end.

By the time we poured ourselves into the cab, Washington had pulled a couple of late scoring drives and Dallas wins a close one 21-18. My ears were ringing all the way home, which was a good thing; that way I didn't have to hear Davis rubbing it in my face all the way home. I would have done the same to him. It was all in good fun, and I had a good time as always. I had to play as if I was a little hurt; it makes it that much more fun for the winner.

My head is pounding this morning. Draft beer and cheap whiskey will do that, and when you drink a lot, it hurts just that much more. At least when you win, you can pretend that it doesn't hurt as bad. Davis gets up like he's on the top of the world, and for that moment, I hate him. This too shall pass. On top of everything else, rain is pouring down. Davis will be in a nice warm recreation hall while I will be outside positioning busses. It's not that bad. I will stay in my truck listening to the radio except for a few moments. After a few aspirin and a bottle of water, the pain is beginning to subside. Soon my hangover will be just another bad memory.

The busses are a major Charlie Foxtrot. Half of the busses were stuck out at one of the ranges, and we would have to make do with what we have. We have to listen to a whiney officer cry about the inconvenience. I wish that I could tell him, "Suck it up! Things happen." But then he would ruin the rest of my day, so I just listen to his complaining. Listening to him, he must have been a Washington fan. At least that would make sense. He would definitely have a reason to cry. Then I think about things and laugh under my breath. He will have to spend the day out in the rain at an open range. There's nothing out at Dona Ana Range, and he will be there all day long. With any luck, they will have a live-fire mission tonight, and he will be out again. There's not much chance for that tonight, but it would have been nice.

We finally got all of these people on their way, so we can go back to the office and begin the planning for tomorrow. Another busy day ahead, but it makes the time go by. I will be heading home by early Friday morning, and my time here is winding down. Just another month or so and I will be finished with my physical therapy. Then I can go home for good. I will really miss Davis, just like the rest, but life must go on.

The one thing I can say about the service is that you have a lot of close friends that move in and out of your life. Sometimes you lose touch, but even when you don't, it's never quite the same. I can say that I have been blessed with a number of close friendships. Most people would be lucky to have one or two friendships like that in their whole life, but the military forces you into situations where brotherhood becomes second nature. My life has been enriched by every one of these relationships. They have forged me into the man that I am, and I wouldn't trade that for the world.

The nights are long. I can't seem to fall asleep, and when I do, I am awakened with terrible nightmares. I find myself lying in pools of my own sweat. I try not to wake Helen for these are my demons. I fear that I don't know what I am capable of as I wake in horror. I don't want to frighten Helen, but a time will come when she fears me too.

I hear story after story of many of my comrades separating from their families. Palo has fallen victim. He probably got married for the wrong reasons in the first place, but it was still sad to see. He had only gotten married to ensure that his daughter would be taken care of while he was away, but I know that his wife still meant something to him. The war had changed him. When we got back, he would only answer my calls on occasion. While I knew that we shared a tie closer than blood, I was also a tie to a time and place that he wanted to forget. This is a struggle that no one should have to face alone, but this becomes the rule rather than the exception. The act of falling back into your life has proven a difficult task. I feel so lucky to have a family that is ready to accept me for who I am or, should I say, for who I am now.

War changes a person; there can be no doubt. They don't tell you that before you go. They spring it on you just before you come back. The army has never done a good job of reintegrating our soldiers. Our world is filled with people who never quite fit back into society. We know what we know, and apparently, we don't know anything anymore. You know that your life has turned into a Charlie Foxtrot when you don't even know where you fit.

I am trying to be content with my new life. Helen sure helps in this regard, but at some point, I will have to find meaning beyond my home life. I can't go around trying to find people to shoot at me for the rest of my life. So I guess that I will go back to work, but I still fear that I won't be able to do the job. In any case, I will have to wait until after I heal from my surgery.

We begin the long process of looking to buy a new house. We are looking just on the outskirts of Albuquerque: Rio Rancho,

Los Lunas and Belen. I have always had a hang-up about living in Sandoval County. There are too many rules and regulations. Plus it's just too damn big. I'm still a small-town guy at heart. Rio Rancho has a big feel to it, and the prices are kind of high as well, so we turned our attention south. We looked at house after house until we finally found a home in South Belen.

Belen is a ranching and farming community that really hasn't grown over the last twenty years. It is south of Albuquerque at about thirty three miles down I-25. It's a main train hub, and you can hear the switching yard from anywhere in town. It kind of grows on you after a while and you hardly notice it. I'm sure that it would put some people off, but we were able to buy a bi-level 1,900-square-foot home for about $100,000. It was twice the house of anything that we looked at and for thousands less.

We would be moving in at Christmas time. Cherestine and Ryan will be moving with us; Danny has decided to finish his high school in Las Vegas and will be staying with Diego.We will spend a few nights in the house before we move in as it is two and a half fewer hours that I have to commute; besides, we are excited about our new dwelling. We have a new home, a new used boat, and now I decided that Helen deserves a new truck. She had done such a good job paying our bills while I was gone that we qualified for a 0-percent-interest loan. I bought her a charcoal color Chevy Avalanche. This made a lot of sense for us as a family; it was part car part truck. I had always liked them from the first one I saw. That first one had all of the body armor, and it was the ugliest, most manly truck that I had ever seen. Helen's new truck looked a lot nicer than that first one, a little less manly but still way cool. Helen loved it as well. Being only four foot something, she always liked a tall vehicle. It gave her an opportunity to tower above for a change.

The first weekend after we closed on the home, we met in Belen and stayed at the new house. We didn't have any furniture yet, so we slept on the floor. For the kids, it was kind of like camping out. In any case, it was nice to be together, and the simplicity and quiet time gave us a chance to just enjoy each other's company.

The next few weekends would be spent packing up the Las Vegas house. With only 1,500 square feet of living space, you would think that it would be easy, but it was 1,500 full square feet. I borrowed a truck and trailer from work to move down. By the time we were all packed up, we had a twenty-eight-foot trailer packed from floor to roof and every inch packed to the gills. Then we still had enough overflow to completely fill the van and Avalanche. Then we traveled in a caravan from Las Vegas to Belen. The boy rode with me in the big truck, Cherestine rode with Helen and the dogs and cats in the avalanche, and Danny drove the van with the fish tank.

Palo came over to help with the move. Palo, Diego, Danny, and I loaded while Helen continued to pack last-minute items. We had additional help unloading as Helen's brother, James, and another buddy of mine, Hector, came to give us a hand. I had moved several times before but never on this scale. I don't know what I would have done if not for the help of friends and family. It was truly an adventure.

We unpacked most of our items, set up beds, furnishings and trinkets, finishing as much as we could on Christmas Eve, and spent our first Christmas together in two years. It was a time for joy and celebration. Helen put on a pot of posole and red chili, which is a long-standing Christmas Eve tradition as we went in search of a local church to pay respect and give thanks.

Everything was beginning to fall into place. Helen found a job at a title company in Los Lunas, the kids were enrolled in their new schools, we had our new home, and soon I would be home for good.

CHAPTER 19

Another sleepless night; this can't continue. Sleep has become a luxury, and I will take it when it comes, but by that time, I am so exhausted that even in sleep it becomes impossible to rest. Every night when I close my eyes, I see the visions of yesterday. I see a desert hell and all that it holds. The sights, sounds, and smells are stained in my mind and cloud my every thought. Every joy is robbed from me at gunpoint. Every relationship has to stand up to the brotherhood of war. Nothing seems important if it is not of life and death. All that I want to do is to live my life. I feel like I deserve that much.

My mind is always racing. It's hard to focus or concentrate on any one thing. It's like I am never completely in the moment. Life was a lot simpler when all you had to worry about was living or dying. We made the laws, and we bent them to fit the moment. There was no cut-and-dry, just a lot of grey area. You had no choice but to live in the moment, and now every moment seems so petty. It's not about life and death; it's about checkbooks, feelings, and mundane monotony. Everything is so complicated. I wish I could go back. Even with all of the good that I have in my life, I don't know who I am or where I fit. I'm just trying to make sense out of a life that has no meaning. Maybe it does and I just can't see it. In any case, confusion is the only constant.

It's Friday morning, and I will be heading home shortly. We will be spending the evening with Helen's family tonight. I really want to see them, but in a way, I don't want to go. I don't know enough about this world to have an intelligent conversation. I guess I can speak of the times that I had while overseas. I haven't said much about it, and I can tell that everyone is dying to know. Maybe after a few beers I will loosen up enough to spill my guts.

Helen was still at work. We don't have to meet with her family for several hours, so I guess I will take a shower and then maybe a nap. This will probably be a long night, so a nap seemed like a good way to pass the time. I lie down and try to sleep but to no avail. What a surprise that is. I toss and turn for a bit longer, and then when I realize that it is just no use, I turn to cartoons. Cartoons are about the only thing that doesn't enrage or annoy me. They are always good for a laugh.

Helen comes home from work and tells me about her day; I'm still a little groggy. Helen says with her head hung low, "I miss Las Vegas. All of these new processes are a pain. I can see where they will be nice in the long run, but it's just so different."

"Look at the bright side. Soon we will be together all of the time. No more commuting."

"That will be nice. I'm going to take a shower. You should take a little nap."

I lay in bed completely spent; it has been a long day. I close my eyes and drift off to sleep. Immediately, I am transported back to MSR Tampa and IED Alley with Palo by my side. We are laughing because one of the Scorpion team members got out to take a leak at the last rest point just before we took off. Then his team took off and left him with a stupid look on his face. We radioed ahead, and the team didn't even realize that they had left him. We gave him a lift back to his truck but can't believe how stupid some people are. There are only four soldiers in a gun truck; you would think that they could count that high. The laughing soon stopped as a daisy-chained IED goes off just ahead of us. We stop, and I see pieces of my comrades all around me. I wake screaming. My body is drenched with sweat, and I'm trembling. Helen comes to me and holds me until the distress subsides.

In many cases, the nightmares are worse than the actual events. We did have people who were injured, but nobody from my unit was killed. I don't know how your mind can put together your worst fears and torture you with them. Hell, life was bad enough without worrying about this stuff happening. Now I have to see it over and over again. The dreams are still better than the flashbacks. At least with a dream, you can come to terms with it. Everybody has them, but with flashbacks, while they are usually not as devastating as the dreams, you are still awake and see things that you know aren't there. It's like a warp in time and place or a hallucination. These flashbacks are really what makes you feel like you are going insane.

I know that all of this is frustrating for Helen. She sees the effects and wishes that she could do more for me. I could tell her how I feel and some of what I have been through, but you could never really understand unless you lived it. She had to live her own hell. She worried every day for a year that I may get hurt or killed. With all that she has been through, I hate to burden her with my problems.

I had to take another shower after sleeping in pools of my own sweat. We show up at James's house a little before seven. James is Helen's oldest sibling and only brother. We are greeted with hugs at the door. Liz is still not here; being late was a family trait, and no one was better at it than Liz. James was truly happy to see me. He is a very genuine man. He tells me that they had all been praying for me while I was gone; I reciprocated by telling him that I know that it helped.

James offers me a beer, and I gladly accept. They ask me what the people were like over there and if they even want us there.

"I should have brought the video that I made over there. It tells a lot of the story. The video started at the Hodgie mart, interviewing some of our Iraqi friends. These were good people. They talked about Osama bin Laden and how they would kill him on the spot if they ever saw him. Then they spoke about our occupation and said how happy they were that we were there. They loved America. They all told stories about how Saddam killed and/or tortured some of their own family members."

James's wife jumps in and says, "Now that's what you don't see on the evening news."

Then she went on about some political rant. Their entire family is made up of hard-core Christian conservatives and we all see eye to eye, but I was overwhelmed from the elections that I just lost interest at this point.

They asked me all about the war, and since this was all that I really knew about at this point, I was more than happy to talk about the subject. I told them all about MSR Tampa, IED Alley, and RPG Pass. These were hot spots, but really, an attack could come from anywhere, and you always had to be on your toes. Once I said all that I was going to say about the war, the conversation turned to more current events, so I kind of melted into the woodwork.

By the end of the night, I was completely drained. It was time to take a long hour drive home. Helen has to say good-bye to everyone, so it always takes at least thirty minutes to get out the door once you decide to leave. I wanted to hear everyone's reaction to what I had to say, but I knew that they wouldn't speak of it as long as I was in the room. They all had a lot to digest. I really gave them a lot to think about. I just hope it doesn't affect the way that they treat me. I'm still the same person that I was.

Helen said, "You make me love you more every day."

"I don't make you," I said, "you just do."

I couldn't help being a brat; it is just my nature. Helen didn't bring up any of the subjects that I spoke about this evening. I think that she heard all that she could handle for one night. I guess it was pretty vain of me to think that the others were talking about me once I left. They were probably more like Helen and heard all they could stomach for now. They probably figured that now that the cat was out of the bag, I would speak more of it when I was ready.

I take our van back and forth from El Paso. Every time that I near Albuquerque, I smell odors like burned ninety-weight oil. I have changed the oil several times already since I have been back. I just can't figure it out. I checked the bearings over and over again; they look just fine. Still, I can't escape the smell. It comes every time I near home when the vehicle has been run hard for at least a couple of hundred miles. I guess that at some point I'm going to have to replace it.

CHAPTER 20

Life goes on, and with the passage of time, the only constant is change. My time had come to leave Fort Bliss and Davis. Somehow it doesn't feel right leaving before him. We had grown close over the years, and this parting would likely mean that we would never see each other again. It doesn't have to be that way, but all too often, life happens and old friends get caught at opposite ends. He will always be a friend, and I will keep in touch, but it will be a long-distance friendship from here on out.

I was back on the road for what should be the last time. I will have to find some form of real life to live. I'm leery about returning to work. I just don't know if I can do it anymore. Has life changed so much over the past two years, or is it just me? How can I be intimidated by normalcy? I have just recently come from a war zone where every day was life and death. I guess that could be the difference. All I really had to worry about was the mission, my life, and my troops; everything else was taken care of. For two years, it has been basic survival, no real BS to contend with. Everyday life is all about trivial BS, beyond family, of course.

At this point, I still don't know if I want to remain in the Guard. They left us. Whatever happened to no man left behind? I do like the Guard and some of the people in it. This is just going to be another decision that I will have to eventually make. I have to take life one day at a time, I suppose, but if you don't plan ahead, the "one day at a time" thing can bite you in the butt.

Life at this point is all about choice, which was one thing definitely lacking over the past couple of years. Perhaps that is the difference. I made choices, but it's just not the same. They told us at the seminar not to make life-changing decisions for a while, and in just a short time, I have purchased a new home and uprooted my family. I'm going back to a new position at work. They had to fill my shoes while I was gone, so things will be different. Hell, perhaps they are taking me back just because they have to. Maybe the position will be short-lived. Maybe I'm just moving too fast.

This has all been weighing heavy on my mind since before I even left Iraq. There have always been more questions than answers. Some questions can only be answered by time. I have been gone for so long that I feel obligated to go straight back to work. It would be nice to take the next couple of weeks off, but the double paycheck will be nice too. They have been patient enough with me, I suppose, that it would only be right if I get back to work sooner than later. I try not to let my internal conflicts show and to be the strong figure that everyone expects me to be. After all, I can either do it or I can't, and I will find out soon enough.

I have only spoken to my boss a handful of times since I left. He could be the nicest guy in the world or the biggest prick that you could ever imagine. He had never been that prick with me, at least not yet. He was always supportive from the day he hired me. I had seen the other side of him, but it was always directed at someone else. I don't know how I was going to react when it became my turn.

I still have the weekend with my family before I have to face whatever will be, and I'm going to enjoy it. We go to the mall in Albuquerque. As we walk through the doors, I begin to feel strange. There are so many people. How can I keep an eye on everyone? Where might the dangers be lurking? We go into one of the small shops, only one way in and one way out. I suddenly feel very claustrophobic. I am on the edge of all I can take; I just want to crawl out of my skin. I have to get out of here. I take my leave and park myself as far away from everyone that I can. As I hold on to the rail near the upper-deck courtyard, Helen comes out to check on me.

"Are you okay? You're pale as a ghost."

"I'll be all right. I'm just not going into any more little shops. I can't take it."

Helen asks, "Well, then do you just want to go?"

"No, do your shopping. I'll just hang out in the foyer."

I was still very uneasy, but at least, this was a level of uneasy that I could handle.

By the time we started home, I could barely contain myself. I would snap at whatever Helen or the kids had to say. I'm driving, but I'm in no way engaged in the task. My mind is racing all over the place, and I just can't stay focused on any one thing. The crowds at the mall must have triggered something inside me. I feel like I'm going crazy. When did it say anything about this at the conference? Maybe I should have paid closer attention.

When I get home, I'm no closer to settling down than I was when we left. I go into the house and immediately take a shot of whiskey. Then I pour myself a stiff double shot and retreat to the backyard. The two things I need most right now are alcohol and solitude. I sit alone in the yard and sip the remainder of my whiskey. I can tell that it is providing at least some relief. The whiskey is gone long before I am ready to return inside. I would like to have another, but I don't wish to get drunk. I just want to take the edge off. I remain outside until a chill grows in the air. I'm beginning to cool down in more ways than one, and I'm ready to return to my family.

"Are you okay," Helen asks.

"I'll be all right. I just needed to settle down a bit."

My senses are always on high alert. I see everything, hear bits of every conversation, and smell every odor and fragrance in the air. I take everything in, but it's impossible to focus on any one thing, so I go into sensory overload. That's when I begin to freak out. They call it hyperarousal. This is the reason for my unrest during the day and my lack of sleep at night. So the beast has a name; now the question is, how do I get rid of it?

It's Monday morning, and I get ready for work. It seems strangely familiar. I anticipated being nervous as hell but, for some reason, I'm not. I may be a little on edge but nothing like I thought. As I get to work, the receptionist gets up, greets me with a hug, and welcomes me back. The rest of the group was equally supportive, minus the hug, of course. I begin to think that this may not be all that bad. My old boss approaches me and says, "Thank God your back, bud. We really need you." *How could they need me*, I thought to myself. I just hope that they're not too disappointed when they realize that I can't do the job anymore.

Jason Miller was the plant director and my supervisor. He tells me that I will now be responsible for all of the convenience stores throughout our market and all stores to the south. This was a great deal of responsibility. I only had three employees assigned to me but hundreds of stores. I was going to be a busy man. I accepted the challenge. I had to give it a shot no matter how skeptical I was. We needed the money, and I couldn't spend the rest of my life running from responsibility.

After settling into my office, I went out to look to see exactly what my market looked like. I headed out to inspect some of my biggest stores of our major local chains. I don't know if I was shocked or relieved as to what I found. We only had one or two shelves throughout the stores. We definitely had nowhere to go but up. Our competition had at least a full door in the cold vaults to our meager shelf. Now I understood how I could have so many stores. We didn't have anything inside of them.

The stores down south were a different story. We had four major grocery chain stores and a number of large drugstores. The south is definitely where I do my volume. I spoke to a few managers to see how we were doing and to introduce myself. I didn't try to make any lengthy conversation with them. I didn't want to talk about the war, and that is still all I really knew. I also didn't want to talk about their trivial pet peeves. In fact, in most stores, I didn't bother to talk with anybody. I would tell the clerk who I was with and go about my business then move on. I knew that I couldn't keep this up, but it was my first day, and I wasn't going to change the world overnight.

It became the way I rolled. I would speak with whom I had to and avoid others when I could get away with it. I was more of a firefighter than a salesman. I would go wherever there was a hot spot and handle local concerns. I stayed away from most regional managers and dealt directly at store level. The store managers seemed to like this approach. I got to know many of the managers who were constant complainers and never really knew those who didn't bother to complain. In my larger stores, I had to build relations; there was no getting around it. These stores were always having some trouble of some sort or another. They were usually petty, but they were a mountain to them, but as far as I was concerned it was still just soda nothing worth getting worked up about.

Soon, I began making a name for myself. I really still don't know how but others were taking notice of my work. I guess that I was able to shift my energy where it was noticed the most; they didn't see what I allowed myself to slip by the wayside every day.

It wasn't long before one of the large companies began to give me a nod, but I was content at the time.

Summer came, and all of a sudden, we were very short on drivers. It was like dominos falling. Once one goes and all of the work falls onto the others, the stress builds until others fall. I began helping out on a truck from time to time, then it was more often than not, and finally it was every day. I was okay with it at first, but when my boss, who put me on the truck in the first place, started complaining that I was beginning to fall behind in some of my other duties, I began getting very irritated with him, and something in my mind snapped. I spent all day every day planning out how I was going to do away with him. My mind flowed in constant circles, and I couldn't shake it. I finally came up with a plan. I planned his death down to the last detail. It would be easy, too easy.

I knew that I had to get away or I would eventually bring my plan to fruition. I then allowed myself to be recruited by the other company who had been seeking me out. When all was said and done, Jason was very hurt that I was leaving after all he had done for me. He couldn't believe that I would go. He never realized that I was probably saving his life. I stayed the remainder of my two weeks in a truck delivering soda pop to grocery and convenient stores. He was grateful for that, but he continued to beg me to stay to the point of being downright pathetic. He sounded like an abusive spouse stating, "I can change. Just give me a chance. Don't go!" I pitied him, but I was not about to change my mind. His display only echoed the fact that I had to leave.

I needed a new start. I told myself that I was going to be more like my old self—confident, competent, and a real go-getter. With that, I decided that I would stay in the Guard as well. I hadn't been to drill since I had been back just over six months. They never really missed me. In fact, they still had me on a stop-loss status. This allowed me to be eligible for a nice reenlistment bonus even though my actual contract ran out in July of 2003. So my life felt like it was heading down the right path.

The paperwork was completed and waiting for my arrival. This is about the only punctual event in the army. Every time I ever needed anything from them, it was the same old story, hurry up and wait, but this event goes like clockwork. The only thing I had left to do was to get sworn in. They didn't have any officers present at my unit during the week, but this was a formality that could not be overlooked. The enlistment was not complete until you were sworn in by an officer.

I called my old lieutenant from Iraq. He was in Albuquerque and more than happy to assist. I met up with him, raised my right hand, and in a flash, it was done. I stayed for a few minutes to shoot the breeze with the lieutenant. He was busier than a one-legged man in a butt-kicking contest, but he took some time with me to catch up. He was in some new pre-deployment company that followed the general around, prepping troops to go overseas. Sounds like a cushy job, but I guess business was good because he was working twelve or better hours a day. I told him about the new job, Helen, and the rest of my family. He was glad to hear that things were going well for me. We wished each other good tidings, and we went our separate ways. Damn, I forgot to ask about Davis. Lieutenant would know what he was up to if anybody did. They were real close. Oh well, maybe I can just drop him a line.

CHAPTER 21

Day 1 at the new job was all videos and paperwork; day 2 was a little better. I was beginning to develop some kind of awkward flow. On day 3, I was activated by the Guard to go to Hurricane Katrina. I can't believe this. We were swept away with only a moment's notice. They are saying that we could be out for as long as six months. The only thing I know for sure is that I was uprooted once again. I have to say good-bye to Helen and the kids again; we have only been together for a few months. At least this time we will be going to help our own people, but we are told of misdoings that include looting and shooting. So how much different is this going to be? We are to report with all of our gear by 0500 hours and be ready to move out.

Morning came way too early. I lived in Belen, two and a half hours away from the small town of Las Vegas, New Mexico, home of the 720th, where I attended Guard. Las Vegas is the meadow city where the mountains meet the plains. Las Vegas is a small town but rich in history with many buildings dating back to the

1800s. They even have the biggest real castle that I have ever seen. It was an old Harvey House built for the railroaders in the late 1800s. It is still a remarkable sight nestled up in the foothills among the whispering pines and small rippling river that flows through the foreground. It's a landscape fit for kings hidden by a town that you could hardly give a second glance when passing by on the freeway.

When I arrived, I was greeted with open arms. I hadn't seen any of these people in months, some even longer. It felt like a homecoming. I hadn't felt this comfortable around a group of people since I left Iraq. I couldn't tolerate a group much bigger than my immediate family for longer than a few moments at a time. It was different here. This was a group where you knew that everybody had everybody else's back. You didn't have to think twice about it; you just knew. They had proven themselves in extreme conditions, so here it was just a given. I was instantly glad that I made the decision to stay in. This was my home away from home and a place where everyone was a part of the family.

Pleasantries were kept short. We had a lot of work to do and a short time to get it all done. We needed to be on the road by noon. We were paired up in two man teams. For me it was the best—Ox and Chicken Man rides again. This time we traded our tractor trailer in for a HEMTT fuel tanker. This was an eight-by-eight beast. I started my Guard career driving the wrecker version of this truck. It had awesome pulling power. It had eight man-high wheels that all pulled together simultaneously. I once pulled a fully loaded ten-ton tractor trailer with its brakes locked up across a dirt parking lot. With the load, it came to nearly one hundred thousand pounds, and I pulled it with ease. These things weren't meant for comfort or speed, just brute force. They would bounce you all over the place at fifty-five miles per hour, which was about top speed. It only carried about 1,200 gallons of fuel, but it would take that fuel anywhere.

I was grateful that Palo and I were kept together. They often split the more experienced people up and put them with the FNGs. For some reason, this was not the case on this trip. I really don't care about the reason; I was just glad that it worked out this way. I would rather have the worst job in the army and work with Palo than have the cushiest job in the army with some panty waste. Palo had earned my respect under fire in the most extreme of circumstances. There is nobody else that I would rather be with on this mission.

Our days were long, but with the slow-moving vehicles, it didn't feel like we were making very much headway for our efforts. We would stop every couple of hours to allow people to take a break, use the restrooms, or whatever. We were supposed to switch out drivers at every stop, but both Palo and I were used to driving much farther at a stretch. We would usually trade off midday. This was still an easy undertaking. The only thing that made it seem long was all of the stops. I would just settle in and get comfortable behind the wheel and we would stop again.

It's the end of day 2, and we still haven't made it beyond Texas. We are all a bit disgusted with our lack of progress. We stage our trucks at some high school in the middle of small-town America. By the time we settle in, it's long past dark. We are given instructions to bed down and prepare to wake up early. Naturally, we do the opposite. Out comes the beer and the bottles, and we are ready to party. The commander disappears into some plush quarters, at least as plush as you can get at an empty high school. In any case, she was indoors and segregated from us commoners. The first sergeant was as well, but once he was sure that the commander was down for the night, he cowardly made his way back out like a naughty little boy to join in the fun.

It was like the good old days. The stories changed a bit since the last time we were all together. Possum 2 was now Pyro Possum. They apparently were on some sort of mission before my return. Things had become a little heated, and they had too much to drink. Somehow Possum 2 doused himself in gasoline and, with the gas can still in his hand, yelled, "Let's burn this mother down!" He was talking about the entire motel and probably would have followed through if it weren't for some intervention. Pyro Possum was always a big drinker, but he was normally fairly mellow.

The war had changed us all. Nobody came back the same as they left. Pyro Possum spent less time in combat than most of us, but he was obviously affected as bad, if not worse, than others. Most never speak of their pain. Hell, most don't think that there is anything wrong with them, and for many, there isn't. They have all been changed in some form or another, but that, in some cases, isn't a bad thing. We all think we know people who have come back and are playing the system for all its worth. They have come up with phantom injuries, mostly PTSD, and they are milking these injuries for as much as they can. Who really knows for sure? Some may appear normal to us but may be privately haunted by their experiences. We all know that fraud, waste, and abuse runs rampant through our government, so why should the VA be any different? This is one of the few areas where I would rather see a hundred cases of fraud than one person who really needs help and not get it. At any given moment, the VA is filled with a higher percentage of trained killers than any one of our prisons. Think about that before you vote against veteran benefits.

The only people that you really know are committing fraud are the people who brag about it and the people who never saw combat. We had a few of both. The people who really get under my skin are the people who put themselves on a pedestal and brand themselves as heroes when they never did a damn thing. In fact, every person that I know who has branded themselves as a hero never did much of anything. I wouldn't bother to spit on these people if they were on fire. I know real heroes; none of them are looking for special praise, and most would claim that they did what anybody would do if they were in the same situation. The truth is that we were all among exceptional people and most would do the same if found in similar circumstances.

Palo wasn't drinking tonight. When Palo didn't drink, I kept my drinking to a minimum. I always wanted to stay on even ground. That seems a little stupid. You would think that at least one of us should stay sober at all times, but that was never the way that it was. If I didn't feel like drinking, then Palo wouldn't drink, and if we both felt like drinking, then we were going to try to outdrink everyone around. It didn't have to make sense; it was just the way it was. We were always in sync and always played off the same sheet of music. It's what made us so close, it's why we could finish each other's sentences, and it's why we knew that we could always count on each other. We were brothers in every sense of the word.

We were up before the first morning sun. I'm sure that several people were still a bit drunk from the previous night's festivities, not me, though I have been there before. I was ready for the day. We planned to make it well into Louisiana before the end of the day. We spent the night only a little more than an hour away from Shreveport. I was surprised when we found out this tidbit of information. We should have been informed and kept apprised of this type of information, but information equals power, and that was something that the commander wasn't willing to share.

From Shreveport, you still couldn't tell the level of damage that the state had undergone. You could tell that there was a pretty good storm but nothing like you saw on the news. As we continued south, it became all too apparent. The interstate was barren. We were the only people on it for miles. That alone left you with an eerie, haunting feeling. As I look to my right, I can see in the distance two lone steel rails. I wasn't sure of what I was seeing at first. The rails were perched on nothing, just rails that appear to be floating about six feet off the ground. Then as I see what is left of a bridge, it becomes apparent that I have been looking at railroad tracks where everything below the steel rails had been washed away. Up to that point, there wasn't even a remnant of the makings of a railroad except the rails themselves. That was the first sign of the sheer power of this storm.

As we continue south, the awesome storm's destruction became more apparent. This storm showed no mercy. I saw some punishing weaponry while serving in Iraq, but it paled in comparison to this. The only thing that may come close would be something in comparison to an atom bomb. Whole buildings were washed away, and the average homes were reduced to masses of broken lumber and stone.

We came to what looked like the end of the world in Plaquemines Parish. The air was filled with a grotesque, putrid odor. It smelled as if everyone in town had their plumbing back up at once, and they did. In addition to the plumbing smell, you had the smell of rotting fish and animal flesh. It was so overpowering that you could almost taste it.

We set up our camp at Plaquemines High School. Class was out for the foreseeable future. We were just above the water table, and a few homes in the area were spared from total destruction, but the ensuing mold problem would likely leave them uninhabitable. This was the saddest thing that I have ever seen. Most of the people got out of the area, but there were a number of families who thought that they could weather the storm. Helping these people with food and water was one of the first things on our list to do. Secondly, we had to rid the pump houses of debris so that they could pump the water out of what was left of the town. Finally, these pump houses would need fuel to operate. That was my job.

We had strict curfews where we all had to be in by dark. We didn't have a problem with that. This area was spooky enough during the day. By now, our supply of alcohol was running low, and it didn't appear that we were going to be able to go to the local convenience store and pick any up. It will be hard to numb these sights out without it. We didn't have the ability to call home. There wasn't a single cell tower left standing. So we were cut off in more ways than one. This was going to be a long tour. We still didn't have any timelines but by the looks of things, we could be here for a while.

In the morning, we were hand selected or "voluntold" for our job assignments. Half of the company was selected for meals on wheels and other humanitarian efforts, and everyone else, less the fuelers, were on pump house cleaning detail. With no pump houses up and running, we were sent out to recon the area. That was good with us. We were going cruising in search of routes where we may be able to get the fuel to the pump houses.

Within a few miles, the roads were replaced by swamps. We had to stay on the hard surface or risk rollover. The soft silt on the road shoulder would never support the weight of our massive truck. Soon, the only visible signs of a road were the tops of the signs themselves. We were driving in over four feet of water and pushing an additional foot or so with the truck. We were committed to finding a high spot. We couldn't turn around, and if we stopped, our engine would become flooded by the water that we were now pushing. All we could do was to hope that the road held out. The water was well into the cab of the truck, and as I look out my window, I can see fish swimming by. This is not a picture that you're used to seeing out the window of your truck. The whole thing is a bit unnerving. After forging through for several miles, we see signs of life. There is a single cow standing on a high point in knee-deep water. She will likely starve to death as she is unable to move from that one spot. God only knows how she found the spot in the first place.

After another couple of miles, the water recessed far enough to where we could see the road again. Palo and I both breathed a sigh of relief. Then off in the distance, we can see a huge ship and realize that we must be nearing the end of the line.

We get a little closer, and I turned to Palo and said, "No way!"

"What?"

"That ship is on the highway."

"Oh my god, you're right!"

We didn't realize the full magnitude of what we were seeing until we got right up on it. This thing was huge and miles away from the gulf. The ship was so big that the anchor was about the size of our truck. We both just stood there for a moment in awe. We took some pictures with our phones and decided that it was time to get back. What an unbelievable day!

When we returned back to camp, everybody had their own stories and treasures to share. One group found a liquor store that had been completely destroyed. Several bottles of booze were just floating in the streets. Most of them were mystery bottles as the labels had been washed away. Hell, we didn't care; we would drink just about anything. We were invited to join our new neighbors. They were the only couple in the area that tried to ride out the storm. They were a nice young couple, real friendly. They invited us to partake in adult beverages with them on their patio. We talked mostly about the storm. It was all that anybody had on their minds.

The couple's home was flooded but may have been all right if it weren't for the four-hundred-pound gorilla in the front yard. It was a large old oak tree that had fallen through their roof, leaving all of their belongings exposed. They weren't sure if their insurance was going to cover anything or not, but they maintained good spirits through it all. We all shared the contents of the mystery bottles, and then they revealed a mystery bottle of their own, homemade moonshine. Only about half of us were game to try some; the others were happy with what they had. It had a hint of coconut, and it was unbelievably smooth. It tasted almost like Parrot Bay rum, but it was a lot stronger. We finished the bottle at their insistence, then all we could do was stumble home.

I woke up still tired and a little cotton-mouthed. I cringed a bit as I waited for the pain of the almost certain hangover to hit, but then, nothing. Wow, that was some good stuff, I thought.

I tried to wake Palo, but he just groaned then rolled over and fell back asleep. I would give him a few minutes like every good snooze alarm and then try again. Ten minutes later, I again rattled his cot. "Wake up, buddy." This time when he groaned, I said, "No you don't. I need to take a shower, so I'm not going to be here to wake you up again." He sat up in his bed, grabbed his head, and then he looked surprised when he didn't have a headache. "I felt the same way. That was the real McCoy," I said. Palo got himself up as I headed for the showers.

Once we had all of the pump houses topped off, we set up alongside the highways and fueled trucks and construction equipment. The contractors were grateful for the help and stated that there would be a little something waiting for us when we returned tonight. Nice, another hookup. These people were all great to work with, and they were truly grateful that we were there to lend a hand. They looked at us the same way as the southern Iraqi people when we first arrived in the country. This is the best part about being in the Guard. It means a lot when you can and do make a difference.

When darkness fell, we went in search of our little something. We found it where they said it would be. It was a full cooler of iced-down beer. Palo and I each grabbed a handle and walked the cooler over to our neighbor's house. There were only a couple of the guys that found their way over that night. "Oh well," I told Palo, "more for us." He agreed as we pop the top on the first frosty brew. We only had a few apiece when we decided to call it a night. The beer was good and refreshing, but the long hot day and the short night last night were taking their toll. We said good night to our neighbors, and they said that they would hold on to our beer for us. We both thanked them again and then turned in for the night.

Sleep still wasn't one of my strong points. I tossed and turned for hours then drifted off to sleep. It wasn't long before I was transported back to Iraq. My dreams are so vivid. I see every sight, every man, woman, and child. You had to keep your eye on every one of them because an attack could come from anywhere. We were driving in a Hodgie and military convoy. I know what's coming, but I can't wake myself up. It really sucks when you know what's coming and there isn't a damn thing you can do except watch. The Hodgie pulls off the road, and I am looking franticly for the ensuing IED, but I still can't see it until that last moment. I finally wake up with the blast. I lay in silence in pools of my own sweat. I lay there for a few moments nearly in tears, and then I get up to take a shower.

My body was still shaking as the hot water spilled over me. I couldn't explain what was going on with myself, and I felt a shamed. This shouldn't be happening. I have gotten on with my life. How could the past still haunt me? After about half an hour, I turned the water off. I was as calm as I was going to get, but I knew from experience that my sleep was over for the night.

Just when we started getting into a routine and really feel comfortable with what we were doing, we get the word that we will be rotating out. Another company from New Mexico will be coming in to take over. We were always the first unit in the state to get deployed. It had been this way since the beginning of time. We would leave our gear behind and would fly back home.

The townspeople gave us a hero's send-off, and the mayor gave us the key to the parish. This was different than when we came home from Iraq. For one, we were not paraded around, and secondly, these people knew exactly what they were thanking us for. We had done our job. All of the pump houses were up and running, and the water was beginning to recede. It would still be some time before the masses could return. I'm sure some of these areas will never recover.

We boarded our C-130 at the nearest air base. We had to wear all of our gear as they sat us in nets rather than seats. It was hotter than hell in there, and with the 100 percent humidity, we were all drenched in sweat. We sat there for nearly an hour, and I couldn't help thinking that it would be nice to be back in my truck right about now.

As we took flight, the air began to cool and cool some more, then while we were still drenched in sweat, the temperature dropped to near freezing. What a miserable experience this turned out to be. If I never fly this way again, it will be too soon. Luckily, the flight only lasted a few hours. I was never so happy to see the ground as we arrived in Albuquerque. We departed from the plane and are loaded up onto busses. Many of our family members lined the streets as we passed. They were all waving and honking their horns. Then they drove in a procession back to Las Vegas, where we would have a brief welcome-home ceremony. We all, just as before, wanted it to be over. In time, it was, and we were released to continue our lives.

CHAPTER 22

When I returned to work, any hope for resuming my training had been squashed. They had moved on, and for me, it was sink or swim. This company while the same type of company that I had worked at before did things very differently. I was like a fish out of water, and I had a few clowns that wanted to test me at every turn. I was never one for writing people up, but if I was going to clean this house, it was all going to start with paperwork.

I went from my three employees up to twenty-two overnight, and it was obvious that I wasn't going to be able to play this role as friendly as I had been able to do in the past, at least not until I get a handle on it. People heard that I came from the military and labeled me to be a hard man to work for right from the beginning, so why disappoint them.

My new boss appeared to be a good guy and was very supportive. It didn't take long to realize that he was a numbers pusher and knew nothing about operations and what it took to get the job done. I worked my butt off putting in countless hours in order to ensure that the job was a success. Soon, our paper pusher was trying to get efficiencies up ad began adding extra cases and extra stops to every truck. Then he was getting on my back to ensure that we didn't lose quality in service. We have time windows to get into almost every store, so something had to give.

Within the first six months, due to the added workload, we lost the majority of our veteran employees. While I was doing everything that I could to keep up morale and provide the best service possible, my boss was pushing for more. I tried to speak with him, explaining that we had a staff made up of mostly new drivers that were doing all that they could. It wasn't their fault; it was his. This didn't sit well with him, and we soon became at odds with each other. Again, my mind was beginning to race.

I was working sixty to seventy hours a week, and in this time, I hardly ever missed a case and I never had a route sit. Virtually everything was delivered every day. This was my job to get the product to the customers. I would lend a hand wherever it was needed, and I even helped my bulk drivers on holidays and busy weekends. No one had done that before me. Many of my employees thought that I was among the best bosses that they had ever had.

One day, my boss called me into his office and put me on a performance plan. This was basically a write-up for managers. He stated that I needed to make better use of my time, but the only example he could cite was a delivery that I had made after hours on my way home from work. I signed his little paper, but he was now the main focus of my retaliation. It was different with him. I didn't simply want to do away with him; I wanted to do something so horrific that he would have to live with it for the rest of his life. Perhaps I could assault his family while he sits by powerless, watching. This wasn't what I wanted to do, but the rage inside of me wanted him to pay.

Again, much like before, I become obsessed and my mind races. What will I do? How will I get away with it? My mind flows in constant circles. It is getting to the point that I am becoming afraid of myself. What am I capable of? I was willing to kill on the battlefield, why not now? The truth is, there isn't a reason; only a penalty for getting caught. Surely I could come up with a scenario where the likelihood of that was minimal. I was mild mannered, quiet, thoughtful, and fun. I would be the last person ever suspected of doing such a heinous crime. Circles, circles, I can't get them out of my head. I decided that I had better get some help.

I went to the office of our senior HR representative so that I could find somewhere to turn. The wheels at the VA move slowly, and God only knows what I may be capable of by the time they get around to helping me. As I sit in her office, admitting for the first time that I needed help, I actually broke down before her. I never cry, so now I feel weak and powerless for the first time in years. I fought to get my tears under control, and when I pulled myself together, I was able to tell her that I needed to know our mental health policies and to find an approved doctor.

I felt like I was going completely insane. I never rested, being hypervigilant made sure of that. I was always on guard and looking for the threats around me. You would be surprised to know all of the places where a terrorist could have the upper hand. Any aggressive driver I came across on the road triggered me and I was off. One day, I was driving on Paseo del Norte, this is a major intercity thoroughfare between Northeast and Northwest Albuquerque. A driver went speeding by me and then cut me off as he passed. The next thing I knew, I was driving at speeds over one hundred miles per hour. This wasn't an isolated incident. This happened every time something triggered me. I couldn't seem to control it nor did I want too. It was a rush, the kind of rush that I got all of the time in Iraq.

Somehow I needed to get a handle on all of the radical and irrational behaviors. The HR rep gave me the information that I needed. So I got in touch with a local shrink. He put me on a number of drugs that were designed to numb me out. I was all for this at the time. I just wanted to get a handle on my out-of-control life. If I had to be completely numb to do so, then that was fine with me.

The drugs weren't biased; they took away sadness, happiness, anger, and desire, including sexual desire. I didn't care about anything. I wasn't suicidal or homicidal. I didn't care if I lived or died, but this was all okay, at least for now. It allowed me to live and do my job without fear.

After about six weeks of seeing the private doctor, the VA finally was able to see me. I had one appointment with the VA shrink, and he wouldn't see me again for three months. After a full disclosure, the VA evaluated me at a 30 percent disability. When my appointment was due, I came in only to find out that my shrink was no longer with the VA. They renewed my prescriptions without seeing me and set me up with another appointment in another three months. When I arrived at this appointment, the doctor was cold and didn't seem to care any more than I did. For a moment, I thought that perhaps he was on the same drugs that I was. He set me up for a follow-up appointment in another three months. When I showed up for this appointment, the doctor was out of town. They didn't bother to tell me or schedule a new appointment. So when I asked when I could be seen, it would be in another three full months. These people didn't seem to have the same sense of urgency as I did. I only had two real appointments in the last nine months, and I was already getting fed up with the system.

A new position opened up at work, and although my boss was reluctant to put me into this position, he didn't have much of a choice. They didn't have anyone else who was qualified that was interested in the position. For this reason, I was given a shot. I was quick to pick up the requirements, and I was excelling as the merchandising manager. My employees loved me; in fact, I never had a single employee quit on me. That in itself was odd for this entry-level position. I had a number of employees that I groomed for promotions and a few that we had to let go, but my crew was well trained and happy. I made record-breaking results in efficiencies, and I ensured that there was always enough help to go around. I was a natural. Even my boss could not deny my successes.

Once I was well established in this new job, the 720th would be activated again for Hurricane Gustav. This hurricane wasn't supposed to be the same magnitude as Katrina, but with all of the bad press the president took over Katrina, no one was taking any chances. So it was back to Louisiana. Palo had left the Guard by now, and Arti was my new driving partner. He was a former marine as well, and we got along well. I still missed Palo. Arti and I have been friends since he showed up at the Guard shortly after our return from Iraq. It just wasn't the same. No one could replace Palo, and I would never want anybody too.

Arti fit in well with the 720th. Arti was quite a bit smaller than I but he could hold his liquor much better than me. I didn't ever really drink very much outside of the Guard. Hell, I didn't drink that much within the Guard, at least not when compared to most. So when we were driving, Arti and I were together but only now and again after hours. I would spend a lot of time on my own, primarily writing when I had a spare moment.

We arrived on location, and we were staged out in a field miles away from any of the action. This is where we would stay for the next two weeks. We never did have any missions, so the whole thing was one big Charlie Foxtrot. I did get some writing done, but that was just about the only good that came out of the operation. We returned home, thankfully without the fanfare.

I returned to work or at least to my office. I could run my operation almost completely from there. I didn't want to see anybody most of the time. Hurricane Gustav and being back at the Guard were a heavy trigger for my PTSD, because upon my return I was on a downhill slide. All of my symptoms were on the rise. I was aggressive and quick-tempered; I had flashbacks, increased nightmares, hyperarousal, and paranoia. I wasn't getting very much sleep, and being on constant alert, I was exhausted. There was never any letdown.

With PTSD, there is nothing louder than so-called silence. When it grows quiet, I hear everything: the choppers flying, the trains crashing, a distant siren, doors slamming, and the neighbors when they do anything. I evaluate every sound for potential threat level and investigate things that I feel deserve attention. I kept my gun loaded at all times and my killing knife hidden at bedside.

I was short with my family. When my boy needed a hug, and he needed a lot of them, I would give him a pat on the head and tell him, "Now get away from me." I couldn't handle anyone being in my space. I began shutting down and closing off. I felt like I had OCD (obsessive-compulsive disorder) to go along with my PTSD. If anybody got close to me, I felt like I was going to crawl out of my skin. I hated the person that I was becoming. I wanted to push everybody and everything away from me.

When Cherestine was nearing her seventeenth birthday, she met her first real boyfriend. She was afraid to tell me at first. She told Helen first, probably to avoid facing me with the news. She had always been Daddy's little girl, and now she was growing up. I met the young man at Cherestine's birthday dinner. He was kind of shaggy looking, not at all what I had expected. He was respectful, and I tried to keep things light to make him feel welcome. I was probably as nervous as he was; after all, it was him who I would have to kill if he ever did my little girl wrong.

Things went downhill from that point on. Cherestine was fighting for her independence and lashing out at the person that she was closest to for most of her life—Helen. I rarely saw Cherestine anymore. She was always locked away in her room. I was upset by the lack of respect that she displayed. She was usually okay as long as I was home, but as soon as I would go away, Cherestine would lash out.

One summer morning, as Helen was leaving for work, she went to check on the kids. Cherestine was to stay home to watch Ryan, but somewhere in the night or early morning, she slipped out of her window and took off. Helen called me as I was already at work, and she told me that Cherestine was missing. I came unglued. I just knew that she had snuck away to see her boyfriend. I came home immediately. Her room was a mess; it was always a mess, so I began cleaning. I started grabbing everything and boxing it up. By the time I was done, she would have a bed, a couple sets of clothes, and that was about it. I even took her door off the hinges.

She came home when I was about two-thirds complete. I didn't even realize how pissed off I was until I saw her.

"Where in the hell have you been?"

"I went to the park."

"You went to see your boyfriend, didn't you?"

"No, I—"

"Liar! If that SOB steps one foot on this property, I will skin him alive!"

Cherestine's tears were falling, but she was nowhere near sobbing. She had grown cold somewhere along the line, and she wasn't going to give me the satisfaction of really hearing her cry. She had never seen me that upset, and I think that she was a little scared. Hell, I was too. I didn't know what I was capable of. Somehow I managed to think before reacting, and I was able to gain some composure.

I finished cleaning out her room, making her help me with the rest. I took away all of her privileges. She was grounded, no TV or telephone. I would let her earn her privileges and things back slowly for good behavior. After about two weeks, she got her first box back and was able to do a few things with permission. Her first day out, she came home late. She apologized profusely, and seeing that she was genuine, I let it go. Her next time out, she messed up again, and I wasn't about to let her make a habit of it. I took her stuff back, and we started all over again at day 1.

She probably decided right then and there that she was leaving, but we wouldn't find out until she didn't come home from school the next day. She was gone, and with her went all of the respect that she had earned over the past seventeen years. The feeling was probably mutual. My heart was broken, and the ache that I felt wouldn't soon go away. She probably felt that she had no choice and was at the end of her rope. She blamed Helen, and Helen blamed herself, but I knew deep down she was hurt by me. I had been angry, closed off, and unapproachable. She couldn't come to me when she was hurting. I wouldn't have heard her; maybe she even tried. I don't know. I was disappointed in any case that she somehow wasn't strong enough to live up to her responsibility. Life was going to get tougher as time goes on, and what will she do then?

We called the police, and we were surprised that when she surfaced, they didn't make her come home, and legally, we couldn't make her either. It was down to Helen, the boy, and me. This was my new family. Helen would continue to try to make amends by going to her shows and seeing her when she could. My rage would continue to grow, but I had to move on.

At work, a sales manager position opened up, and they offered it to that gal that took over for me as the driver supervisor, superseding the progression. When I originally took the position as merchandising manager, my boss told me that this was the natural progression, that I would have to take and succeed at this position in order to move up to a sales manager job. I did everything that was asked of me and more. The current driver supervisor was good, but she had a number of routes sit during her tenure and didn't measure up to where I was on customer service. She was the favorite, so my boss screwed me over yet again.

I probably wouldn't have taken the position if it were to be offered. With me isolating, I really didn't want to have to deal with store managers every day. I was supposed to be doing this already, but I had found ways around it whenever possible. That wasn't the point; the point was that they should have offered the position, and the fact that they didn't, I knew that my days were going to be short-lived if I didn't get out from under by boss's suppressive hand. We had another position that had been open for some time. It was a fleet position, and I would be out of the mainstream. In fact, my boss would be working out of the Phoenix office. This job really was a good fit for now. I interviewed for the job, and with my management skills along with my military experience, they felt that I was a good fit. I took the job, and instantly, it was like a giant weight was lifted off my shoulders. My employees were sad to see me moving on, but they would still see me from time to time.

CHAPTER 23

The new job was easy, so easy that a monkey could do it. I didn't have anyone looking over my shoulder, which was a good thing since with the medication that I was on, I couldn't stay awake while sitting for long periods at a desk. The VA continued to screw me over, so I was frustrated and done. After just over a year of taking antidepressant drugs and not feeling any emotion, I wanted to feel again. I threw away all of my drugs, and soon I was back to feeling like my old screwed up self. That was still better than feeling nothing.

Once I was off the medication, I was able to see things a little more clearly. I began to write again for the first time in what seemed like forever. What I wrote, however, was seemingly full of a little demon they call depression. Following will be a few examples to show how I was really feeling at the time. The first was never titled.

As I lay awake in the early morning, thoughts of days past rush through my mind. I try to relax and return to sleep, but I am burdened by my own cognition. I don't fit within this society. I can get along, but it's not the same as it once was.

This country is so heavily divided between war and peace. Why can't people understand that without war there can be no peace only a lawless world where the mighty rule the meek and masses with iron fists providing a life for their people that's not worth living? I am filled with such rage at those who downplay the effort. I would like to see them live in the trash dumps and at the sewer's edge or in farming communities that were crippled by the rerouting of the rivers to dry up the land and starve the people out. All people deserve an opportunity to seek their own destiny. True peace can never exist without this truth. If you were not there, then you would not see. For or against, they will never understand for they do not see. They are not shown, they are not told, and they will never know. Even many who have seen don't know or understand the majesty of what they have witnessed as they are blinded by fear, homesickness, propaganda, and even death.

I walk alone in a path with many barriers. I am troubled by some of what I have done but more so by what I have left undone. I have returned home from my most passionate quest while I still have the ability to breathe, to walk, to fight. I do not belong among the people of this society, but the rules have forever changed in that other world I once knew. Not so long ago, we made the rules as we saw fit. We were able to adapt as the situation changed. Now we are victims of our own correctness, imprisoned by a world that would frolic at the thought our own demise.

Pray for all. The passion is for all to live free to seek greatness and stand up for those who cannot do so for themselves. Love thy neighbor does not end at the sea or the borders. To live in a world of harmony is not one voice but rather the voices of all. Let them speak and judge them not for their words but rather for their actions or lack thereof.

The next one is titled "I Am Not Blind but Still I Do Not See."

I am not blind, but still I do not see. Visions of yesterday distract me from the here and now. I gaze into the sky, searching for what I know is there: soft flowing clouds resting on a majestic field of blue, ever changing shape to whatever your mind can fathom. The warm glowing sun reaches down to gently kiss your skin, forcing you to look only far enough away to see as much of its brilliance as you can muster. Perhaps the wide spread wings of a powerful eagle soaring through the sky may catch your eye as he lives your dreams of doing the same. I know it's there but not for me. I see an overcast sky with dismal shades of grey covering endless unforeseen possibilities. Structures once thriving with activity are now crumbling masses of charred destruction. The people who escaped the wrath of the powerful weaponry now seek refuge along the streets, creating shelters out of what others have thrown away. Black smoke billows into the sky as if there was some urgency to consume it.

My eyes hold witness to things that will forever cloud and shadow my mind. The rigors of war ignite my passion of good versus evil. Who can deny the joy of a small child when they boast about a promising future or the stories of the grand atrocities committed against one's brother or sister by their own oppressive government. I have little doubt that the act of what we were doing was just even if the true reasons for being there may be somewhat questionable. The lives lost and broken will serve as a reminder that no matter the reason, war is hell. I will be forever plagued about the day my wrath nearly washed away the lives of innocents. I was acting on instinct and training, but instead, humanity prevailed, and the only virtue lost was that which was portrayed in my forever-scarred mind. Some were not as lucky as they found their demise at the hands of foolishness. These are exceptions and not the rule. The difficulty is that the enemy lies within the masses, using them as shields, and therefore collateral damage was unavoidable. That's the nice way of saying the number of the innocent but just as dead is justifiable.

I was eager to play this game called war. I was well aware that I could lose my life, and I was prepared for that, but how do you prepare for being a survivor? They don't tell you that the experience will unlock portions of your brain that are beyond cognition. These areas are aggressive and based on mere instinct and survival like that of early mankind. You are a powerful tool for death and destruction, but then they bring you back to this society where our newfound aggression is not acceptable. They throw you among the masses and tell you that you must merge back into a normal life. They do not know how to cage the animal that they have unleashed. They put you on medication for you are no longer normal. They keep you locked in a prison called the VA and force you to live among the masses. Some believe that they are helping, but the truth is, many are only serving their own egos. They don't know how to help. They maintain control by providing or aiding in your livelihood but only as long as you jump through their hoops. What we really want is to be left alone and free to live outside of society, but if we do, somehow that makes the establishment a failure. They will not stand for that as it does not support their self-serving interests. Oh you are free to come and go as you please, but then they yank your livelihood out from under you when they know that you can no longer function among the nobles.

This one I titled "What Could Be More Insightful than the Words of the MASH Theme Song."

What could be more insightful than the words from the MASH theme song? "The game of life is hard to play. I'm going to lose it anyway. The losing card I'll someday lay." Was this guy a pessimist or an optimist? He makes a point that we all will die. For some, this is the absolute end, while for others, it is the beginning of better things to come. Later, the song states that "suicide is painless. It brings out many changes." But then it states that it is a choice that each individual can make for themselves. Once again, it probably is very ideologically based. Some believe that if one takes their own life, then their soul is doomed, while others believe it is simply the end. These are truly questions that can never be answered.

For me, I can say that I believe that the end is a new beginning, but the beginning of what? Does our life in the here and now pay our ways to a marvelous future? I would like to believe so, but the common man is just that. Man is basking in mediocrity. There are a few who you would call great in talent or intelligence but just as many you would call dumb or clumsy. Truth is, most can excel in some areas but are lacking in others, bringing about neutral fulcrum. The only way to win is to live a full life and look back on your accomplishments favorably or to die in a cause that you can believe in.

There was a time when I looked upon my accomplishments as favorable, but then someone moved the bar. Now the days where I come out even are few and then questionable. My mind flows in constant circles, thinking who should stay and who should go as if I were the grim reaper himself. Why must I judge? Surely, if I were to be judged, I would be one to go. I believe in the betterment of humanity, that every man, woman, and child have the right to pursue a better life or have every opportunity to make life choices. But those who deny basic rights must go. Those who stand on the backs of others to gain power for self-serving reasons must go. Those who keep others down to

> enforce their opinion or self-gratification must go. Those who feed solely on the backs of thy neighbor without personal sacrifice or contribution must go, not to simply go but they should be weeded out of Eden and burned so their seed shall not infect the flock.
>
> There are days when I must fight the urges to act on these thoughts, others when I am so consumed that I am virtually paralyzed by the prison of my own mind, still other days when I can numb the feeling and go through the day in a state of seeming normalcy. Sometimes I truly believe that it is my place in this world to act upon these pictures in my mind. I am told that I was put on this earth for a reason, and that reason is hanging over me like a bad dream.

Life was getting the best of me, and I begin to struggle with memory. It was as if life had ended on the battlefield and a new life had begun. My recollection of the time before the war was like a distant dream, and after the war, my life became all-consuming. The differences between the two people were like night and day. My old self was happy-go-lucky, outgoing, and personable, and the new self was angry, withdrawn, and closed off, maybe even a little cold. I didn't care much for this new me. I used to love myself almost to the point of being conceited. Now I could barely stand to be in my own shoes.

In my eyes, society had gone so wrong. I saw with my own eyes families living like animals, and here at home, the people would sit on their butts, downplaying the effort.

Thoughts of homicide became a part of everyday life. The people who really knew, the politicians who have seen with their own eyes yet play politics with the lives of others must die. These thoughts become all-consuming as I ruminate about playing out scenarios where I take their lives. I couldn't help myself; I had so much hatred and anger that I would do them all in if I could. I watched many of the same people who agreed to send us over to kill and die change up sides for meager political bargaining. The news showing our daily body count along with our politicians downplaying the effort was more than enough to motivate our enemies to keep fighting. They were losing at such a phenomenal rate but knew that if they could keep the fight going long enough, the American news media and the spineless politicians would sway the public's opinion and we would be forced to leave before the job was finished.

My anger and disdain grew by the day. While I made no formal plans, I had several ideas. One was to take out specific congressmen and senators one by one. Another idea would have me take them out all at once, but that was farfetched. Probably the idea I had to take them out at the democratic and/or republican conventions would have been the most bang for the buck, and if I died in the process, then so be it. I didn't put very much value on my own life. I had vowed to defend my country from all enemies foreign and domestic. In my eyes, we had many domestic enemies. This was justified in my eyes due to their aiding the enemy. Soldiers were dying by their words and deeds.

My mind was always spinning in the same circles, the same things over and over again. I become completely obsessed. I can't focus on my work or anything else. The crazy homicidal thoughts were all-consuming. The VA wasn't worried about my ruminations. Their thought was that as long as I kept my thoughts farfetched and out of reach, then nobody was in immediate danger. I felt, however, that I was out of control, and I couldn't foresee getting any better if I wasn't to be taken seriously.

One day, one of our local congressmen was at the local VFW. Again my mind begins to race. I could walk right through the door and kill him in cold blood. I tried to reason with myself about how one life wasn't going to change anything. I would kill him, and then they would kill me, and it would be just another veteran losing his mind. No matter how much I tried, I couldn't get the picture out of my mind. My mind continued to race in tormenting circles. I was coming apart; my life had no meaning if I could not take down my enemy. I convinced myself that he was not a significant target, but I still couldn't get those pictures out of my mind.

I thought that I had better get back to the VA before I destroy everything; but I didn't exactly have a good track record there. What were they going to do, lock me up and throw away the key? So I turn my car toward the VA. Now new circles are forming. I see myself driving my car to the VA, through the glass doors, and into the lobby. I wanted to be taken seriously, and I hadn't been to this point.

It felt like it took all of my strength to stop the car in one of the parking spaces outside. I leave my gun stored in the trunk. I walk to the psych building and up to the second floor. My body was trembling when I walked off the elevator. I tell the secretary at the counter that I need to speak with someone as soon as possible. The triage nurse was available and came out to greet me.

I explained everything to her, the ruminations, the problems that I had been having with the VA, and the anger within me. The nurse listens to everything that I have to say, and as I hear the words that are pouring out of my mouth, I can't even believe how crazy I sound. She hooks me up with whatever shrink was on call, and they begin a small medication regimen. Then the nurse asks me if I feel like I am an immediate threat to myself or others, and when I tell her, "No, not immediate," they let me go. I couldn't believe after all I told her that they would or even could let me go. I silently wondered how many veterans must come in with like stories for them to be so nonchalant about all that I just told them.

The shrink started me on a low dose of Prozac for depression and Lorazepam for anxiety. I was to take the low dose for ten days and then go up to a higher dose. I took the medication faithfully for the first ten days. On the eleventh, I stepped up the dose. Just after noon, I sunk to a low that I had never before felt.

I was filled with such dread and sadness that I could concentrate on nothing else. The feeling passed in about forty minutes or so, and I began to think that I must have forgotten to take the medication. The next morning, I was sure to take it. By ten o'clock, the dreadful feeling was back even stronger than the previous day. Death was calling to me like an old friend. "I can stop the pain," it seemed to say. I felt that I had no choice; I had to go to my car, grab my gun, and shoot myself dead.

I stepped out of my office to get some air when I was approached by one of my coworkers. He said, "Are you okay? You don't look so good." I told him that I would be okay. My coworker moved on and I went back to my office and wrote my good-byes. Then I proceeded to my car. Just as I get to my car, another coworker approaches me to talk about something else. I thought to myself that this plan wasn't going to work.

I got in my car and began driving to the VA. I would take my gun with me up to the ward, and if they couldn't offer immediate relief, I would shoot myself up there. On the way over to the VA, I received a call and I thought, *Why must I get all of these interruptions*? I take the call; it was my commander from the National Guard. While he was talking, I had yet another call waiting. I let that call go to voice mail as I proceeded to talk to the commander. He needed some information, and by the time I was finished giving him all that he had asked for, the ward was closed for the day. I thought about shooting myself in the parking lot right then and there. I got my gun out of my trunk, and with it sitting on my lap, I stopped to listen to my voice mail. It was the triage nurse calling to remind me about our appointment first thing in the morning. Now I was a bundle of nerves. I didn't know what to do. Somewhere along the line, I passed out from sheer exhaustion. I woke up two hours later with the gun still on my lap. I also had another voice mail; it was from Helen. She was going to see her dad. I looked down at the gun and decided that I would talk to the nurse in the morning. I could always shoot myself after that if things didn't go well. I stopped on the way home to pick up dinner, and by the time I got home, I regained my composure and acted as if nothing out of the ordinary had happened.

CHAPTER 24

As planned, I saw the triage nurse first thing in the morning. I still had my gun in the trunk and was ready to follow through if need be. I told her of the previous day's events. I even told her about the gun in my trunk. That was probably not the thing to do. This was a federal facility and therefore didn't operate under the same gun laws as did the state of New Mexico. It was a federal offense to bring a firearm on federal property. I thought that I was going to jail at first when the VA police were summoned, but since I had voluntarily gave it up to the officers, they would just hold on to it for a while.

I found myself in ward 7, the psych ward of the VA hospital in Albuquerque. This is a place where they take everything away from you, including your dignity. It is all in the name of safety, and I don't doubt that all of the precautions are necessary, considering everyone there was in for basically the same thing. When depression bites, it bites hard, and it is near impossible to survive, at least when you're at the point of landing in here. This place gives you a safe haven where you can take a time out from life and gives you time to sort things out for yourself. I can't say that they ever did much for me other than to help get my meds in order and gave me the time that I needed to figure things out for myself.

Most people who still have their wits don't stay for more than a few days in this shoelace-free environment. I was quick to see the people around me who had been in a while and how they were acting, so I knew that if I wanted to get out of there, I would need to put on my happy face and pretend that everything was okay. I thought that I played my roll to a tee. I was due to get out after day 4, but when they said that I would have to spend one more day, it was like a big weight was lifted off my shoulders.

On my last day, I was able to laugh and joke with several of the other patients or, should I say, inmates. It was a day when I was carefree. I knew that I was safe from myself and the rest of the outside world, but I would also be leaving the confines of the hospital soon. This was the first day that I felt like my old self since just before I left to Iraq. It was a long time coming, but somehow I knew that the feeling was going to be short-lived. It didn't matter. I was going to enjoy the day, and tomorrow would bring whatever life had in store.

On the day of my release, what I wanted most was a cheeseburger. I was already sick of hospital food. Then I would call and let everyone know that I was out. I went to a nearby hamburger franchise and ordered a double with cheese. It wasn't the best I ever had, but it was still very good. After I downed the half-pound burger and a few fries (their fries kind of sucked) I decided that I would call Helen first.

I call Helen at her work, and when she answered, I just said with excitement, "I'm out! I'm out!" Her reply was "Good! Now it's my turn to rest for five days." The response wasn't what I had expected, but our relationship had been a little strained. She was busy and stressed out from work and also taking care of her aging father. The fact was that she never even knew why I was in ward 7. She never asked, so I never told her. I wasn't proud that I had almost done myself in, and she obviously didn't need anything else to stress about. I was still hurt by her comment though I knew that I wasn't being fair.

I knew that I was going to have to make some decisions in my life. It was probably the Prozac that pushed me over the edge, but it wasn't what had taken me to the edge to begin with. I felt like I would have to scrutinize every part of my life to make sure that this never happened again. My life depended on it, not that I put a lot of value on my life. At this point, I would love to just rent an empty apartment and live off the floor. I was burdened by all of my possessions as I didn't have the personal strength or the desire to devote any time to anything. My marriage, my race car, my boat, my RV, and my yard, just to name a few, were all in need of upkeep. I felt as if all of these inanimate objects were laughing at me, and I felt very inadequate.

I couldn't even spend time on relationships with my wife, my family, or friends. I kept all of them at bay. I didn't want to give anybody false hope that at some point I may come around and everything would be okay. Everything wasn't okay; in fact, it was just the opposite. Nothing in my life was okay. I was definitely at rock bottom, and I would have to work at rebuilding my entire life. I couldn't let anyone love me. I wasn't worthy. I couldn't have a relationship with the Lord because I wasn't worthy. In fact, I didn't feel worthy of the ground that I walked on. This was not a good place to be, and if I was going to get out of this pit, it was going to be a long climb.

Once I left ward 7, I had so many appointments. I didn't have a clue as to how I was going to manage them and still have time to work. My bosses proved to be very supportive and would give me all of the time that I needed to make myself well again—even after my appointments stretched out over into months and months. I was growing weary, and my depression actually felt like it was getting worse, not better. I had the burden of knowing that I was not keeping up with my job in a satisfactory manner and they were being so good to me.

I begin by working on what was most important to me—my family. Helen and I started a family counseling program that focuses mainly on couples. We take our first appointment, and we are sitting at the far ends of the couch. I had been and continue to push her away. Any advances by her were addressed with stern rejection, which included slapping her hand away from me. It's not that I didn't need a loving touch as much as she did, I just didn't want to give her false hope that things were ever going to get better. As long as I keep her at bay, the less she will hurt if things don't improve and I have to live in solitude.

I have never felt like I could speak to Helen as to what was bothering me. She has a tendency to internalize everybody's problems, and somehow they become her fault. In all of our fifteen years of marriage, I was her sounding board. I was strong enough to share her burdens while shouldering my own. Now that this was no longer the case, I had built a little resentment. I didn't even understand all that was happening to me, so I don't know that I could communicate it anyway. When I needed her most, I didn't feel like I could turn to her. This was when I really began to question our relationship. I internalized everything and was being eaten up from the inside out.

One day seemed to roll into the next, and I couldn't keep things straight in my mind. I wrote the following:

> Another day has passed as yesterday and the day before. Time is inconsequential and passes without notice. Tonight I will sleep and wake to a tomorrow that will have little cognition of the today that once was. Soon time will bush against consequence, and I will pay the price for societal incompetence, and nothing begets nothing in a pay-

> as-you-go world. I once gave my all only to find that it had taken all that I was.

Helen read over my shoulder, and when I got to the "nothing begets nothing" part, she comes unglued. "Pull yourself out of this already!" I wish that it was that easy. There was a time when I didn't fully understand depression, but I tried to be compassionate. I even tried to believe that I understood, but I never really did. I have known several people close to me that had suffered, but I can say now that I never really got it, so how could I expect Helen to?

Helen is normally very friendly. She is outgoing and personable, but she also has a hateful side, much like her father. He was normally a great man. He was the life of the party, but he didn't hold back a word that he was thinking. Helen is much the same. She says what she feels, often not thinking before speaking. She can be snide, and her tongue can cut like a knife. It wasn't typically face-to-face, but when I was in the other room or when she thought I was sleeping, she would say the words just loud enough to ensure that I had every opportunity to hear her. She made a number of comments whereas she accused me of being gay. Her comments probably would have just rolled off me like water off a duck's back if I wasn't so low to begin with. Instead, I let every negative comment drive the wedge between us deeper and deeper.

Helen was probably near her wit's end as well. She was spending a lot of her time focusing on work and her dad, who was now in a home for the elderly. He was still very capable at times but had periods of dementia, especially at night. Nobody wanted him in that home, but all agreed that he needed constant supervision. So Helen would go to him two to three times per week, and when you consider the hour's drive each way, she was exhausted much of the time.

In March of 2010, bad had turned to worse as I found myself in an auto accident. A lady had run a red light; I had a truck on the side of me, blocking my view to the right, so I never saw her. I hit her full-on on the side of her car. I couldn't even begin to touch my brake; it happened so fast. I was dazed and confused; I didn't really even know what had just happened. I was assisted from my car by a passerby and seated on the curb. I didn't even check on the lady; I never even saw her face. She remained in her car until rescue crews arrived. She had to be cut out of her car, and we both went away in ambulances. While at the hospital, my muscles all began to tighten up, and I was in pain like I had never felt before.

Still in pain a week later, I went to get a doctor's release to go back to work, but when the doctor saw me and recognized the fact that I was still in a state of confusion, she sent me by ambulance to a hospital in Albuquerque. I felt like I was about half drunk. I couldn't stand for long periods of time without being so dizzy that I couldn't walk straight. They called it post-concussion syndrome and could offer no time factor for it getting any better. I was out of work and under a constant battle with short-term disability. This wasn't helping out with my other tribulations. My PTSD was at an all-time high. My nightmares were crossing, and I was driving my own car in Iraq. During the day, I couldn't drive myself, so I felt a little imprisoned in my own home. I couldn't even make it to most of my appointments at the VA. The only appointment that I made every week was that of family counseling, where Helen would drive me.

After several months of nothing getting any better, I just couldn't pull myself out of bed. I took my nighttime medication when I woke up in the morning. I just couldn't face the day. I had done this in the past on accident and figured that I could pass it off as the same. Sometime later that morning, I proceeded to take the rest of the bottle of Ambien. I was tired of playing the game. Nothing was getting any better, and I just wanted it to all be over. Then later that day, when Ryan came home from school, he found me unresponsive. Helen had told him to wake me for a physical therapy appointment. When he couldn't wake me, Ryan called my mom, who was a nurse, and she instructed him to call 911.

It took all of the king's horses to carry my listless body down the staircase. They loaded me into the ambulance, and it was back once again to the emergency room in an Albuquerque hospital. I am told that I wasn't out for the entire time, and when I was awake, I was moderately belligerent. I have no recollection of the next thirty-two hours. During the time when I was out, I was able to communicate exactly what I had done right down to the number of Ambien that I had taken.

The hospital had said that it was an accidental overdose, and since I didn't really want another trip back to ward 7, I just let that stand. I know the mind-set that I was in and had been in for a while. It was no accident. All it took was the inhibition of that first one and it was to be all over from there.

I was in the hospital for three or four days, but it seemed like forever. They kept me on a liquid diet for the first few days. I didn't understand the reasoning for that, but all I could do was to request real food and hope at some point they would give in. They finally did, but it was on their terms, not mine.

Until 2007, I was the guy who worked through the pain. I never went to the doctor, never missed a day of work, and never showed weakness. That had all changed. I now felt like my life was an open book, at least as far as the war and recovery. I still had my secrets. I was only going to show the cards that I needed to in order to play the game. Outwardly, I would portray an open book with everything under control, while inside I was silently going crazy, or at least that was the way I felt. I was confused, scared, angry, and paranoid.

I would close my eyes and hear the choppers in the air as if they were searching me out. I would plan my escape, and if they ever found me, I would make a plan to fight things out. My plans to fight always ended in my death, but I wasn't going to go alone nor was I ever going to spend time behind bars. Being at war, I would imagine, is much like prison. They tell you where to go, when to go there, where to eat, when to sleep, and even when to shit. You fear for the lives of your comrades more than your own. That part may not be too much like prison, but I never intend on finding out. I have said some pretty incriminating things about some powerful people. Anything is possible.

When the trains crash, it's like hearing a distant explosion, and I silently wonder if anybody was hurt. Belen is a main railroad hub, and switching goes on all day and night. I don't hear them too often during the day, but it was always at night when I would hear the mortars fly.

My heart sinks every time the dogs bark. This is a warning that something is occurring that is out of the norm. I'll take any form of warning I can get. I get up and check the windows and doors. The funny thing is that I'm not looking for terrorists but, instead, the way too long arm of the law. They are men in uniform that have all of the facts and have the power to twist them as they see fit. We are not free. We have given up that right by incorporating laws for "the good of the people." We have allowed our government to become too strong as we piss our own rights away. Call me paranoid; maybe I am. Try living in fear and then see how easy it becomes.

At this point, I still don't know where my PTSD comes from. PTSD occurs when a person sees or experiences something so horrifying that the mind can't process it. Most people see the occurrence, process it, feel the emotion, then let it go. People, most often warriors, don't have the time to or ability to stop and process the moment; they must stay engaged in the fight, so the emotions get suppressed only to haunt them later in life—or so I am told. In any case, I have been involved in dozens of such occurrences. How do I pin it down to just one. Maybe it is accumulative; it could be one occurrence on top of another and another and still another.

Our family counselor had been telling me about an inpatient treatment program that she thought would do me a world of good. She wasn't the first to tell me about the program, but she was the most persistent. She was a counselor for the program, and she had seen the results. I had never given the program serious thought because I was trying my best to hold down a job. I couldn't just take three to six months off, but now I was out of work anyway because of the accident. So I quit fighting it and agreed to give the program a try. The program only had so many slots, so now it was a waiting game.

While waiting for an opening in the program, the drugs that I had been taking didn't appear to be working, at least for sleep. I would lie awake for hours, and it appeared that I was becoming immune to the Ambien. The doctor tried a few alternative drugs that have similar effects. The first was an antihistamine, but those always had a wakening effect on me. This time was no different. The next drug they tried was Trazodone.

My first night on Trazodone was crazy. I was drowsy, but I couldn't fall asleep. When I finally drifted off, my dreams began instantly. They were so vivid. I drifted in and out of sleep, and I couldn't figure out where the dream ended and life began. In my dreams, I was still lying in bed, awake and paranoid as if I were traveling back and forth through some obscure alternate universes. I never really knew what of the night was real or imaginative. If it was real, then somebody was staring through my upstairs patio door, attempting to break in. He paused a moment when I grabbed my killing knife and met him at the other side of the glass door. He then ran away into the night. I also overheard my neighbors discussing how to hide a body that he had killed over a drug deal. All of these things could have happened considering the area in which I live. I will never know for sure. All I know for sure is that I felt like it was a sleepless night.

That was the first and last time I ever took Trazodone. Once I was back to my regular drug regimen, I woke up in the middle of the night completely paralyzed. I couldn't move any part of my body. I tried to call out, but my voice could only form a low groan. *So this is it*, I thought. Now, on top of everything else, I'm going to be paralyzed. All I could do was to lie there and wait. It only lasted a few moments, but it felt like an eternity. Then all at once it went away. I lay there in silence, trembling and half-haggardly happy that I could move at all.

CHAPTER 25

The STARR program was an inpatient program that was supposed to help people with substance abuse as well as PTSD. Don't ask me what STARR stands for; I gave up on memorizing government acronyms a long time ago. The program wants to get people sober so that the PTSD training can really sink in. You are tested throughout the program for drug and alcohol use, and any positive results could get you booted from the program. That wasn't a concern for me, but everyone hates to see a brother fall.

The first week of the program I spent by myself. It was the Fourth of July weekend, so the counselors were off, and most other patients were out on pass. Pass privileges were only granted to people who had completed the first two weeks of the program then it was up to the discretion of your counselor. I brought my computer with me, and for the first two weeks, all I did was stay alone in my room, playing solitaire. I only came out for meals and an occasional class.

I hadn't been very social in quite some time. I preferred staying alone and quiet with no one to disappoint but myself. I was always polite, and I really didn't snub anybody. I was just a man of few words. Other patients were good about giving you your space but still offered support and friendship. We were all there for essentially the same thing. We all had similar circumstance; we were all brothers in uniform or at least were at some time. The patients were mostly vets from Vietnam, Iraq, or Afghanistan at ages from nineteen to about sixty-five. Many of the older guys had suffered for most of their lives. They self-medicated with illegal drugs and alcohol to make it to this point in life. Many of them had destroyed any chances of having normal family lives due to anger and addiction.

I know that there is a lot of fraud, waste, and abuse in any government program, but this proved to me that if only one out of a hundred truly need the help, then it's worth it. People who go through these programs typically are in desperate need.

The program started off slow. I think that it was probably due to the holiday and the fact that my councilor was still trying to move to the Albuquerque area. We had a few short sessions to do my initial assessment and to let me know what to expect from the program. The PTSD part of the program was essentially four phases. The first was Invio (meaning in life); this training was to get you out into the world, doing things that most people would take for granted, like riding a bus or going to Wal-Mart. The next part of the program was classes developed around what PTSD was as well as coping skills. Another step was the interpersonal group. This was where all of the patients were brought into the same room and were challenged to share very personal things with the group. It could be about your past experiences or your challenges with life or the program in general. The last part was the most difficult for everyone in the program. This part was called immersion therapy. In this phase, the counselors see you one-on-one and try to take you through your most horrific memory and make you relive it step by step and over and over again. It is said that if you can relive the memory over and over, you will eventually habituate to the memory so that it can no longer haunt you.

I wanted to get everything out of this program that I possibly could, so I began writing down all of the things that I could remember about my deployment to Iraq. I decided to write it in book form, but I changed my character to a fictional person that I created for the story. I guess that I did that so I wouldn't really have to own it. I could step away from detail just enough so that I wasn't there. I wrote during every spare moment. I captured things that I hadn't remembered in years. If it was immersion that they wanted, I was jumping in with both feet.

It wasn't long before I came up with my most horrific memory. I remembered things that I don't even know if I understood them as they were happening. Hindsight is truly twenty-twenty. I learned a lot going down memory lane. I learned that I could kill face-to-face if need be. I learned that no matter how strong or brave I was I could still be scared and weak. Worst of all, I learned how to hate; I had never truly hated another being until this day, and I have hated myself ever since.

I began my immersion therapy. My most horrific memory had to do with the time when I faced the IED only five feet from my face, the one that the main explosive never discharged. I spoke through the memory detail by detail until I was trembling in my seat. Until that moment I never really knew how bad it had affected me.

This was what got me. I figure that it was because once we reached our 365 days boots on ground, our freedom bird was within sight; I felt for the first time in months that I was going to make it—I was going to live. I had come to terms with death, and it was okay until I let my guard down, and then I was sent back into Iraq. It never quite felt the same after being so close to coming home, and I never fully understood why until I began to write.

I was learning a lot in my classes, and I had made some new close friends: Ernie, Tony, and Tom just to name a few. Tony and Tom were Vietnam vets, and Ernie was an Iraqi vet like me. We never really spoke of our deployments. We had counselors for that. We all had the common thread, and we all spoke the same language. We all knew without speaking a word that we were all living in a similar hell. I guess that with the military background, it made it easy to form a brotherly bond.

Finally, after about a month, we were breaking into the intense therapy that I had feared yet welcomed. While sitting as relaxed as I could be, my counselor told me again what was about to happen. He said, "We are going to record this and every session so that you can play it back throughout the week. We are going to take your most horrific memory and go through it slowly. I want you to try to picture it in your mind as if you are actually there. Throughout the session, I will ask you for more specific details to try to take you deeper and deeper into the memory. Let's begin at Scania and end where you come to the gate of Camp Anaconda. Whenever you're ready."

I begin to tell the story and try to tell it from a third-person perspective. My counselor stops me and tells me to speak as if it is happening right at the moment. He said, "Tell me what you see, tell me what you smell, and tell me how you feel." I start over, sink down in my seat just a bit, and picture the event in my mind. As I go through the event, I can picture the area, I can see myself and Palo driving in southern Iraq. I can picture all of the debris along the highway and watch everything from the catbird seat. As I approach the area where the IED was, my counselor asks me what my SUDS level was. Once again, I gave up on acronyms, but SUDS is a way of measuring anxiety on a scale of zero to one hundred. At this time I was around a seventy. I finish the story, and he asks me again for my SUDS level. I said that it is about the same, about seventy. I think that I am done for the day when my counselor says, "Okay, again, but this time let's slow it down." I was really taken aback by this statement.

I begin again. This time as I recall more detail like the sound of the engine, what music we had playing on our makeshift CD player, and what smells were in the area. I was beginning the journey of being transported back to a time and place that I hoped I would never see again. This time, as I approached the IED site, my body began to tremble uncontrollably. My SUDS level was through the roof; I used to joke and say that SUDS were the number of beers required to calm you down after the memory and my level was currently at about a ninety. I kept with the story as I saw the IED for the first time. I saw my head turn as I tried to yell out to Palo of the forthcoming blast. This was the first time I ever realized that I actually saw the IED just before the explosion. It was so vivid now. My heart was racing as I continued through the scenario and didn't let down until I passed through the gate at Anaconda. Then I heard the frightful words "Okay, again." This time, as I heard the words, I was pissed. I thought for sure that once I was truly able to get back into the memory, it would be over.

We went through the mission a total of five times, and each time, the memory was more intense than the last. I continued to remember small details and add them to the mission with each pass. My SUDS were easily at a hundred by at the end of the fourth pass and didn't come down until he said that we were finished for the day. I am left with a nervous twitch that is a constant reminder of my first day of recall. I think I can say that the first day of recall may have been worse than the actual event. When the IED actually happened, I didn't have the time to fully evaluate the incident. I had to react to the next potential threat and the next after that. I never had the opportunity to completely digest what had happened, hence the beginning of my PTSD.

It took hours to calm me down from that first session. I was chewing Copenhagen and smoking cigarettes as fast as my buddies could deal them out, but after several, I got sick to my stomach and had to quit before I threw up. I didn't normally smoke, but at the time, I felt like it was the only thing keeping me remotely sane. I didn't speak many words to my new friends, just two letters: *PE*. The constant thrashing of my foot explained everything. PE, or primary exposure, was the name of that beastly therapy. It was also referred at times as immersion therapy.

I continued PE for the next nine weeks. I developed a few techniques over time to lessen my own pain. I would stall each recollection by adding more and more trivial details. This would extend the story without necessarily adding to the stress of the remembrance. We only had so much time for a session, so I knew that if I could stall, I wouldn't have to hear the words "Okay, again" quite as often. It wasn't that I didn't want to get everything out of the therapy that I could, it was simply self-preservation, live to fight another day. The practice only worked for a few weeks anyway as the concept changed from the full mission to just the hot spots.

Hot spots were easier for me anyway. The full story would drag me down deeper into the memory than just working on the explosion. We would go over the hot spots many more times, and by not going so deep into the memory, it didn't take very long to habituate. My SUDS were dropping from the now eighties back to the seventies by the end of the sessions. I was making good progress according to my therapist. I had to admit, the longer I was in the program, my nightmares were lessening in frequency as well as severity. They had my medication dialed in with constant visits to the resident shrink. The combination had me feeling more like my old self. I was still messed up, and my trembling foot is still a constant reminder.

Helen was such a support throughout this process. I had been so cold to her for over a year now, and she still came to visit me twice a week to start with, which was no small task considering that she was going to visit her dad two days a week. She had no time to herself whatsoever. When she wasn't visiting her dad or me, she was running a household and working a full-time job.

We were allowed to leave the hospital and go home every weekend. This was a nice change from therapy and it gave me time to visit with my family. On occasion we were given a pass to stay away from the hospital for longer periods of time and I was allowed to go home every weekend after that first two weeks even a couple of long weekends for special occasions, such as the wedding of my oldest stepson, Diego. He married the mother of his daughter and longtime girlfriend. It was an event that cut through all of the stuff I was feeling and made my heart swell with pride.

After the first week or so, I began seeing the error of my ways concerning my wife. She deserved so much more than I was giving. We would have a lot to work on once I complete this program. I would have to become a person deserving of her love and support, and she would have to forgive me for being the ass that I was for so long now. It was going to be a long road ahead, but I still had to get through right now.

I continued to write almost day and night. I was completing three to four chapters a week, and every week, Helen and I would sit in a quiet room in the house and read through my creation. She would help me edit along the way as grammar, spelling, and punctuation were never my strong points. Most of the story she knew, but now and again, I would surprise her with details. At times she laughed, and at times she cried, and with every evoked emotion, I knew that my words were powerful and my story was one that needed telling. Even though my book was still fiction at this point, most often, what hit home was true.

There was some relief from the demands of therapy. New Mexico Trout is a private organization that devoted much of their time providing therapeutic fishing trips to the VA and other entities. They would come in just about every week and provide fly-fishing training to hospitalized vets and then take them on a fly-fishing outing about once a month during the peak fishing season. One day, I had a particularly difficult PE session, and that evening, I was feeling like I probably needed to go back to ward 7 for a spell. I knew, however, that we had a fishing trip the next morning, so I decided that I would hold off. The trip took us into the Pecos Wilderness to a private pond. The setting had lush, deep meadows, steep pines, rolling hills, and a rippling river just a few feet away. It was so serene and intoxicating that it took me away from my problems and provided more of a relief than any therapist ever could. I returned from the trip invigorated and ready to continue the difficult work. Don't let anybody ever tell you that nature, with a little help from New Mexico Trout to take you there, can't perform miracles.

With the help of the STARR program, I was finally in a place to take back at least some of my life. I was even the president of the patient organization for a spell. It was a confidence builder that gave me the opportunity to show some leadership and organizational skill, skills that I would need if I was going to get back to work.

I was rapidly approaching the end of my short-term disability, and I didn't know if I was going to be able to finish the program before I would have to return to work. I called my boss, who I had only spoken to a handful of times over the past six months, and he allowed me to return to work for one day so that I would officially return to work off disability and then go on vacation for three weeks to complete the program.

I was very apprehensive about returning after being away for so long. I worked for one day and was in a state of near panic when I returned to the hospital. I don't know how people ever make it when they leave the program and can't return after a fall. This was the way that the program was set up. Most people graduate from the program then are sent back into the world to sink or swim. The program is so good, but the end of the program is so final that it doesn't allow for regression. When you're done, you're done. I was lucky and a very unusual case as they wanted me to complete the program, so I was able to work a couple days then return to the program a few days and was essentially weaned back into society. If not, I would have been a certain failure.

On my graduation day, I thought that, as writing had been such a big part of my program, I had to say good-bye with a poem or at least something written. It went like this:

> Did you ever have one of those dreams where you started to fall and the fall just kept going until something finally woke you up? That was my life over the last several years. I was in a long free fall, and there was nothing I could do to find the end. I tried to wake myself up by putting myself into an endless sleep a number of times, but the end would not come.
>
> I continued to fall until my brothers reached out their arms. You caught me and told me that I had landed, but falling was all that I knew. So you told me that I could stand. I don't know how. So you showed me, with some help at first. Slow and easy was the mark. You said that it would be okay and that if I fell again, you would be there to catch me. And then you did and you did again and you continued to catch me until I felt steady on my feet.
>
> "Now you must walk," you said. But I didn't know how. "We will teach you." And so I stepped out with small steps at first, but I stepped just the same. "We are here, and we will catch you if you begin to feel weak." And so you caught me and you caught me again and again until I could walk on my own.
>
> "Now you must fly," you said, but I was afraid. "Life is a scary thing, but you must live, and to live, you must fly," they said. But I don't know if I can. "We will teach you,"

> you said. So I flew, and I fell. You caught me and sent me out to fly again. So I flew, and when I returned, you caught me, so I flew again and you caught me and again and still again.
>
> Now my time has come to fly on my own. I am stronger now because of you, my brothers. You, my brothers, taught me how to stand. You, my brothers, you taught me how to walk, and now you, my brothers, have taught me that it doesn't matter how high that I fly. Because of you, I will never have far to fall. Thank you for all you have given!

It was a fitting good-bye to comrades who see you through such a rigorous part of your life.

CHAPTER 26

I was back to work, not that I had much to do. All of my work had been farmed out while I was away. Now that I was back, I didn't really have a job, only a title and a lot of downtime. I was developing a lot of good work habits, like listening to music and surfing the net. I felt guilty for collecting a paycheck for the amount of work that I had been doing.

I felt a hell of a lot better after my stay in STARR, and I was riding high. My meds were in order, and I felt like a new man. I was ready to tackle life's challenges and work on other parts of my life. I had some ground to make up when it came to my family. They had been so supportive during my recovery.

Just before leaving STARR, I spoke with my family counselor. I told her about an indiscretion concerning a young female from Guard and asked her if I should divulge this information to Helen. She told me that that was a decision that I would have to make on my own. She said that if I was going to tell Helen, then I should tell her during a family session.

I decided that if we were going to have a real chance for happiness, then we should begin without secrets. At our first session after we returned to family counseling, the question about the possibility of other women came up. I said, "Not women, but there was one woman." The hurt instantly showed in Helen's face. I continued, "I never slept with her, but she helped me through some difficult times. She may have saved my life." Helen was deeply hurt and angry with me. I tried to tell her that the other woman was nothing more than a fantasy that I held on to when I was grasping at straws. What Helen heard in my explanation was that I had an emotional affair and the reasons probably hurt more than the indiscretion itself. She heard that when things were at their worst, I turned to a stranger instead of her. She was right. There was no excuse that would justify what I had done. In the end, all I could offer was that I wasn't really in my right mind, and I apologized for hurting her.

The affair overshadowed every appointment for several weeks, and just when Helen was coming to terms with the whole thing, she was looking through my e-mail and found an e-mail containing a letter that I wrote to this other woman. It was a letter like what you would expect to see in a Harlequin romance novel. The letter had a plan as to where and when we could meet to consummate my fantasy. I never gave her the letter, and I had thought that I had destroyed it. If there ever was one letter that I hoped Helen would never see, it was that one. Helen was crushed once again. She had every right to be. I couldn't offer any excuses. I was wrong. The only right thing that I did was not giving her the letter.

Helen was torturing herself by reading and rereading the letter. Finally, our counselor and I convinced her to destroy the letter and to quit tormenting herself. It made no difference that she destroyed the letter; she had every word memorized. I was beginning to think that I had screwed things up beyond repair. The issue was at the forefront of every counseling appointment and just about every conversation that we had. I told Helen that I would spend the rest of my life making it up to her, but the issue had become all-consuming, and I could only apologize. I was completely in the wrong, but unless she could find it in her heart to forgive me, we wouldn't have much of a life together.

We completed our family counseling, but Helen was still left feeling that issues were unresolved. She was feeling down, depressed, and less than adequate. She felt like the family counselor, being from the VA, was more concerned with the veteran and less with the rest of the family. She needed a counselor of her own away from the VA. She found one close to work and went to a few appointments but felt guilty about the cost of her appointments, so she cut them in frequency. Her counselor agreed with Helen that what I had was an emotional affair and that it was just as bad as if I had a full-blown affair. Again I couldn't argue. I had no defense, and I never tried to manufacture one. I do think things would have been worse if I had a full-blown affair. I don't think that she could ever forgive me or me myself if I would have taken it all of the way. I don't even know if that would have been possible. Our relationship was one-sided and a fantasy of a foolish old man. It was never real, and she never reciprocated except for a little flirtatious prompting. The only thing I ever really knew was that she seemed to like the attention.

I was wrong on so many levels that when I step back now with a clear mind, I can't even believe that I could put my family through it, or hers, for that matter. She was over twenty years my junior, was married herself, and had small children. In all likelihood, she was playing me for the fool that I was. In any case, by this time, it was long behind me.

I was feeling good. Work wasn't challenging me, so I decided that I would go back to school and maybe become a psychologist then go back to work for the VA. They helped me so much that I felt it was time to give back. I took two classes: algebra and Spanish. I was on top of the world. I felt not like my old self but a lot closer to it than I had felt in a long time. My after-STARR counselor was using me as a peer mentor, and I even ran the group a few times. That felt good. I was already giving back.

I was still isolating at work. I wasn't good with conflict, and I still couldn't risk being angered. I got this far by keeping myself uninformed about the world and politics. Getting angry could bring everything back. All that I had worked so hard for would be lost.

I began school and realized that this was going to be no easy task. I was doing hours of homework and studying every night. I was having a lot of difficulty remembering anything. I didn't know if this was caused by my TBI (traumatic brain injury) or symptoms from my PTSD or side effects from the medication. All I knew was that something was drastically different than the last time I was in school.

I started writing again, but this time my writing was more upbeat. It showed that there was hope and life after PTSD and depression. I called this one "Depression Bites."

> Have you ever been in a place so dark that it actually consumes every bit of light that comes your way? Every little bit of good is washed out by despair. How can you move when you're already in up to your neck? People who don't understand the magnitude of depression will tell you to suck it up and drive on. A sponge can only hold so much before the contents spill out. The stronger you are, the more you can hold back, and when this dam breaks, it usually spills out in blood red. Is it any wonder why you can't make it out on your own?
>
> Depression is real. It steals life not just from the people who ultimately take their own lives but for everyone that it touches. I was once in a place where death was calling to me like an old friend, an old friend that you didn't want to disappoint or the friend that you just could never say no to.

I was saved by what I like to call divine intervention; you can call it what you will.

On the day that I was going to do myself in, my attempts were foiled by a series of unusual interruptions. It was an unexpected visitor then a phone call then a near stranger that just needed a moment of my time, not just once but over and over again. I could have ignored the interruptions, but I had it all planed out so perfectly. So I made a new plan, and again my plan came unraveled like a spring in a child's cheap toy.

Disheartened by my best-laid plans, somehow I found a glimmer of hope in one of the calls that allowed me to hold on for one more night. If my screams were not heard, I could always finish the job. So I held on. The next day, my cries were heard, but I was not full ready to accept the help that was being offered. So a bandage was put on my bleeding heart, and I was sent back into the world, where I would wait for the dam to break once more.

They sent me back into the world with all the king's horses and all the king's men to watch over me and to give me aid and support. That wasn't enough. The dam did break months later, and I can't tell you why I am here to tell my story. The pain was so overwhelming and I so weak. I just couldn't fight any longer. I wanted it to be over. I wanted the pain to stop, and I wanted to stop hurting the people who I still managed to care about.

So how do you do it? How can people so desperate find a way out? You have to want to. You have to want to enough to do the work that it takes to drag yourself out of hell. You need help, and you have to be willing to accept the help in whatever form it comes in. For me it was medication and one hundred days of intense therapy, but for you, it may be something else. I'm not a doctor nor do I play one on TV. Look to the professionals; get a second opinion and maybe

> a third. Accept what they tell you no matter how difficult it is to hear. Then work on the solution.
>
> You are too important to simply go away. Somebody needs you; if not now, someone will eventually need to lean on you, and you will need to be strong enough to hold them. If you ever find yourself as low as I was, then you've got nowhere to go but up. Seek help and ye shall find. I found mine at the Albuquerque VA.
>
> God hasn't forgotten you, and you are worthy of his love.

When my family started reading this, they thought, *Here we go again.* As they finished reading, they were pleasantly surprised. I was still struggling with school. Everything that I learned during the week only stayed with me until we got past the test for that chapter, and my midterms showed it. I studied my butt off and just barely passed after doing well on chapter tests and class work.

I was still feeling okay though I was beginning to question my ability to live up to my own expectations. In December of 2010, the Guard finally sent me to a medical board. As I was sitting before this board of high-ranking officers and noncommissioned officers, they asked me to explain where I first got my PTSD. This was the first time that I was faced with this event since I left the STARR program. My body began to tremble as I told the story, and before I finished, my SUDS level was as easily as high as it was during PE. I wasn't expecting that. I thought that I was over that. Why in the hell did I go through three and a half months of hell if it was all going to come right back?

The board immediately knew that I was an extreme case and put me on basically a no-duty profile. This was the beginning of the end of my military career. This was bittersweet news. The military had been such a big part of my life for so long, but most of my comrades were already out of the Guard. I was struggling with my training, and I knew that I would not be allowed to be deployed. I was a liability more so than any kind of help, and who wants to stay where they are not needed?

My next obstacle was my final exams. I studied day and night. I even took my books into my office to study during the day. I couldn't remember anything. I know in my heart of hearts that my Spanish teacher manufactured my grade. She gave me a B in her class. I had a C in her class before the final, and the final looked to me as if it were written in a foreign language. It was, of course, but not one recognizable to me. Algebra was a pass-fail class, so I have no idea how I did on that final, but I had enough points in the class from weekly grades that I only needed a D on the final to pass. I guess I got my D. I passed the class, but I knew once again that I did not do well. I took the spring off and decided that if I went back, I would only take one class at a time.

My world began to decline. The military board ignited my PTSD once again, and school stress put me over the top. My bubble had definitely popped. My after-STARR group watched as I began to self-destruct. The only thing that was holding me up was the fact that I was doing much better with my family. Helen still had an occasional breakdown over my affair, but for the most part, we were becoming closer than we had been in some time. This was when I wrote the following:

> I am a failure. Before today, I felt confident, like the old me, but I was reminded that I am not. I don't know if I ever will be. Today was a blow to my ego, and I feel as if I have regressed to the days when I first entered the STARR. Will life for me be a continuous game of solitaire? I just want to rip things apart. I have failed my work, I have failed my family, and I have failed myself.

Now in early spring, it was apparent that nothing was happening with my Guard medical board, but month after month of standing around watching as people worked around me was making me feel even more worthless. It was near the anniversary of my car accident and when my world came unraveled. I was again fighting depression. I was thinking that I could get out of the Guard in May, when my contract expired, but that would be like throwing away seventeen years of my life with nothing to show for it. Really, it was more like twenty years, but because I was in and out of the Guard a couple times, I had a few years where I didn't earn enough points toward retirement to count for a good year.

We were about to be doing well in other ways. I was to receive a settlement from my accident. We would end up with just over a hundred thousand dollars after paying off the lawyers. We had accumulated a lot of debt, however, with me being out of work for the majority of the year and owed over fifty thousand in debt. Helen and I were both working, and we were about to have some money in the bank for the first time in many years. I bought a new Harley Davidson Heritage Softail Classic. I had been looking for a while, trying to decide on a color and options. One day, we went by the Harley dealership, and there it was. It was called Marlow, which was a dark, metallic reddish-brown with bright copper flames. It was a limited edition numbered 71 of 200. It was gorgeous. We hadn't had a chance to clear our debt as of yet, and I didn't know if we would qualify for a loan, but I had to give it a shot. This wasn't just a bike, it was a dream. It had only been on the showroom floor for an hour before we got there, and someone else tried to buy it but didn't qualify. When they came back and said that we qualified, my jaw nearly hit the floor. It wasn't mine just yet. I had to come up with 10 percent down, and I didn't have it. They gave me ten days to come up with the money. I said that I would but my money from the settlement was still two weeks out. We didn't have another payday until after that, but I had to have that bike.

I called my sister who was always in pretty much the same financial situation that we had been for some time. I wanted to get her thoughts as to how I should go about asking my parents for a loan. I hated asking them for money; they had helped me out so much when I was younger that I couldn't bear to ask them for help. My sister said that she was in a position to help me out just so long as I could repay her within two weeks. I was flabbergasted. It was going to happen. They sent me a check for the rest of the down, and within a week, I was an owner. I was so excited when they brought it to me all polished up like a new penny that I drove off with the kickstand down. The salesman was yelling, trying to tell me, all the way out of the driveway. I did feel a little stupid once I figured out what he was trying to tell me, but I really didn't care. My money came through just days after I got my bike, and I was able to pay my sister back with interest.

The first thing we did was pay off our debt. That felt almost as good as riding off on my new Harley. What a relief!! The next thing we did was to buy a CD and stash forty grand. We put the rest into savings. I did want to put more money down on my bike, so we did that and just kind of sat on the rest for a while.

CHAPTER 27

With a little money stored away, we started making plans as to what we would like to do this year. Taking the grandchildren to Disneyland seemed like a good place to start. We would go on the Fourth of July, when everyone had a long weekend and the kids were out of school. Next, I booked a cruise to the Bahamas during Christmas vacation for Helen, Ryan, and I. We talked about going on a cruise once before, and Helen didn't seem to like the idea. She never said why, or maybe all I was hearing was the word *no*. This time we were in different circumstances. When I told Helen what I was planning, she was ecstatic.

We had a lot going on. Helen and I would go on several short motorcycle rides. Helen loved the bike as much as I did. When we would just go for a short trip, by the time we were nearing home again, I could hear her singing on the whispering wind. It was great to see her so happy. We had been through a lot. The motorcycle gave us time for us. We've had kids our entire lives together and never really had any time for just us. This was better than any therapy.

We weren't thrill riders; we were cruisers. We were in complete harmony with our surroundings. The views seem so vivid, the mountains and fields by day and the stars at night. It's amazing to see the sun rise by day and set at night. It's like your favorite camping place with the breeze rushing past your face and ever-changing scenery. Every aroma brought you in connection with where you were. We have a stretch of road that has a number of different restaurants, and as you pass you can smell the sweet treats—smoky barbecue and succulent seafood. It's like going to the state fair with the heavenly aroma of the food court. The country roads are even better, especially after a light rain. The earth has been freshly washed, and you can smell the rain, the cut grass, and an array of floral heaven. Even the feel of the air itself ties everything together. There are pockets of warm and cool air as you ride down the highway. You will be riding along, and the air will suddenly feel cool, and just as it becomes a little uncomfortable, you hit a warm patch that covers you like a soft blanket. I couldn't imagine not riding anymore.

Work wasn't getting any easier. I get so tired. I spend much of my life exhausted. This feeling got a little better when they were adjusting my medication at STARR, but it feels worse now than ever. Maybe I'm just bored, but it seems to hit at any time of any day. It doesn't matter what I may be doing or not doing. I just wish I could get it under control. The only time of day when I can't fall asleep at the drop of a hat is bedtime. Then I just lay there imprisoned by my overactive mind. Even with medication, it takes hours to get to sleep at night. I guess that the haunting has always been worse at night, so I go to bed fearful of the memories.

Life is just so crazy. I wonder what it would be like to live life again free of the past and PTSD. Sometimes I get a little jealous of soldiers who come back from war and live a normal life. When you get right down to it, one soldier's bag of s— smells pretty much like another's. I guess I get too caught up on what is going on on the other side of the fence. Does anyone even care what's on my lawn? So why would I care how somebody else lives? I guess it boils down to life—it isn't fair, and no one says it's supposed to be. I just keep fishing for answers that don't exist.

For Guard this first weekend in March, we have a MUTA-5. That translates to Friday evening through Sunday afternoon. Things are brewing whereas my unit is about to be split up; half of us will be going to Santa Fe, and others will be moving to a new battalion but staying in Rio Rancho. I plan to stay with the company that I started with so many years ago even though I will have to drive a little farther. The NCOs in Rio Rancho have always been a little pretentious and feel that they have always been better than everyone else. In my opinion, it has been just the opposite.

The new battalion commander is coming in to meet with the leadership of my company to get a feeling for who will stay and who will go. This meeting drags on well into the night on Friday. We are all held captive until they pull their heads out of their butts, and they decide to release us at about eleven but want us back by seven in the morning. I was on my bike that night; it was colder than hell by the time we got out of there. It's about eighteen degrees, and I had an hour's drive. By the time I eat and take my meds, I know that they won't wear off until about eight thirty. I get up at five the next morning to get myself ready. I'm on the road by six and decide that I'm too sleepy to risk taking my bike.

Before I reach Albuquerque, I am already making involuntary lane changes and running the ribbed edges of the road's shoulders, which were shaking me awake before I go completely off the road. I've heard this was called driving in braille. I keep telling myself that I'm okay, but I'm still under the influence of my medication and not thinking clearly. By the time I reach the far end of Albuquerque, I'm doing all I can to stay on the road. I nod off for some time, and when I awake, I am driving in the middle of two lanes and traveling over one hundred miles per hour. The realization of what could have happened snapped me awake until I got off the interstate. It was still about fifteen minutes until I arrive at the Guard; I have some distance to drive. I fall asleep again at a traffic light until I am awoken by the sounds of other drivers' horns. Finally, I make it the rest of the way, but it wasn't pretty.

Just before lunch, my commander calls me into his office and said that it was reported that I was driving erratically on the way to Guard this morning. I think that he was expecting me to make up some story, but what he heard instead was "Hell yes, I was doing everything in my power to keep my car on the road." Then I told him about my medication, which he should have been well aware of. My medical records have been an open book for months now, and my command was well aware of my situation, not that they were doing anything about it. I was no closer to being out of the Guard now than when I was before I went to the medical board. My commander didn't let me drive myself to lunch and wanted a report of how I was doing before he let me drive home that evening.

I risked life and limb to get to Guard, but all I was allowed to do was watch the clock slowly tick by for two and a half days. Being in the Guard with the reminders of days past really messes with my head. I always struggle for days before and after guard drill. I really wish that they would get it together and do something. I don't know how much more I can take.

My drowsiness continued to plague me. I had a doctor appointment in mid-April. My doctor told me that since I had private insurance, I should go outside of the VA for sleep disorder studies. He said that the VA was backed up for months and it wasn't likely that I would have even a consultation until near the end of the year, if then. So he wrote me a prescription for a sleep study, and I would go outside of the VA. Even the private sector was booked up, and the soonest appointment I could get was for late May.

In mid-May, Helen's dad passed away at the age of ninety-two. He was a great man! Helen and I had our first motorcycle rally in mid-May just shortly after Alfredo passed. We thought about not going but then decided that Alfredo would want us to go; this would also give Helen a chance to clear her mind. We were going to meet up with some of our friends from Amarillo in a small New Mexico mountain town called Ruidoso. We were going to the rally, but our friends had plans to take our travels away from the group and do our own thing. It was all new to us; we were just excited about being out. Ruidoso was only about two and a half hours out of Belen; our friends were looking at about a six-hour drive.

We got there a couple of hours before them and secured our pre-rented cabin. It was a nice place just off the highway but well into the woods. The cabins around us were quiet. This was known to be one of the first rallies of the season, but it was a lot smaller than the one that takes place there over Labor Day. There were still more bikes than we had ever seen in one place at any one time, but the town was not overcrowded.

By the time our friends showed up, we were settled into our room and my bike was spit-polished to a glimmering shine. My bike was always neat as a pin. I cleaned it before and after every ride. This wasn't uncommon; most riders are proud of their bikes and like to keep them in showroom condition. I knew that my bike turned heads; everywhere I had ever gone, people gawked at my bike. It wasn't necessarily the prettiest bike there, but it towered over other stock bikes and stood its ground against custom paints.

When our friends showed up, they cleaned up and settled into the cabin. We then took a ride up to Mescalero, the home of the Inn of the Mountain Gods casino. I had been by there once before, but the place hides its elegance off the main road among the shivering pines. It even had its own private lake. I had heard this place was something, but growing up in Reno, I thought of it as just another excuse to throw money away. It was far nicer than I had ever expected, and I'm glad that we took the time to go in. After a short tour, we headed back to Ruidoso to eat dinner and plan the next day's events.

We decided that we would make a big loop the next day. We would go first to Cloudcroft, then to White Sands, then on to Alamogordo, and then back to Ruidoso. Helen and I bundled up for the road. We always wore our leathers and helmets. We were new to all of this but wanted to be prepared for anything. Our friends both had really nice Honda trikes, they didn't wear helmets or feel the same need for all of the equipment that we had. I will admit that we were probably not quite as comfortable as our comrades, but as the temperature began to drop as we got up into the mountains, I knew that we were far better off than they were. We were still a little uncomfortable while they froze their butts off.

Cloudcroft was a small Old West town. It only had one street dedicated to tourists and shopping. Other than the items in the shops, it really looks like a place straight out of the history books. We took about an hour and looked in all of the different shops. We got a few small souvenirs, then we were to leave the cool air of the mountain town and head down to the hot desert of White Sands. As we were coming down the mountain, White Sands glimmered in the distance. The white sand looked like snow from a distance. I had never been into the national park so we decided that we would take a closer look.

We took off one of our inner layers and unzipped our jacket vents. It was hotter than hell when sitting still, but once we got moving and the air flowed through our jackets, it wasn't too bad. As we rode through this blinding sand paradise, we saw people on snow sleds gliding down the hills. The roads, though well maintained, had pockets of deep sand that we had to manipulate.

I'm sure this was much easier for our three-wheeled counterparts. We took a few pictures and completed the excursion at the gift shop where we started. The rest of the trip was basically taking in the scenery along the road other than stopping for ice cream in Alamogordo.

Once back in Ruidoso, we took in the hub for the rally. It was basically just shopping at an indoor swap meet that catered to bikers. We picked up a couple of mementoes. We had dinner and picked up a six-pack and headed back to the cabin. As we sat on the porch, drinking a few beers, the deer began to come right up to us. As long as we didn't bother them, they didn't seem to care that we were there. There were probably about a dozen and a half of them, and they came within about twenty-five feet or so from where we were sitting. It was really cool, definitely the perfect end to a great trip. Tomorrow we will have breakfast and then go our separate ways.

We said good-bye to our friends, then Helen and I drove around Ruidoso a bit before heading home. The trip was more fun than we had ever imagined. We hadn't had a weekend away from our kids since our honeymoon almost eighteen years ago.

When we returned home, the next thing that we had to do was to pay our final respects to a great man. We didn't so much as mourn his death but instead celebrated his life. Alfredo lived a long full life, and he was the kind of man who wouldn't want anybody to make a big deal out of his passing. In fact, his final wishes were to have a meager service and a smaller burial. His wishes were to be cremated and to lie at rest in the family plot next to his beloved.

The family planned a viewing of his body along with a short prayer service. He was a devoted Catholic but opted not to have a rosary in his behalf. At the final service, Alfredo's son-in-law David and his nephew Carlos sang a tribute to the man whose heart was full of song. People came from all across the country to pay tribute to Alfredo. The last four remaining siblings of a family of seventeen children were all in attendance. At the reception following the service, Alfredo's nephews led the family in a chorus of "Las Mañanitas." This was a song that was sung at every family gathering and was a fitting way to end the celebration of his life.

I had my first sleep study appointment, and it wasn't much more than a consultation. The nurse had me fill out a survey while I waited for the doctor. When the doctor came in, she reviewed my survey and asked about my history. I told her that I was tested a couple of years ago for sleep apnea and the results were negative. She had me set up an appointment for a nighttime sleep study. Of course, it was another month away. A week later, I received a call from the sleep center, and they changed my appointment from a night sleep study to a daytime wakefulness study. I couldn't imagine what that meant, but time would tell. I guess that I will find out in late June.

In mid-June, the fires in eastern Arizona were raging out of control, and with the largest fires in Arizona history threatening the New Mexico border, the National Guard was mobilized and sent to the western border. This was going to be nothing more than a glorified camping trip. We were ready to react if the fire jumped the state line. We would then evacuate nearby towns, but until then, it was a waiting game. On the first morning, the winds were pushing the inferno straight toward us, and we woke up to a heavy blanket of smoke covering the entire valley. By early evening, we could see the flames dancing across the horizon. We thought for sure that we would be evacuating the small town of Reserve, New Mexico, by morning, but by night, the wind had shifted, forcing the fire back into Arizona.

Within a few days, the majority of the company was sent home. I again was to stay back along with a small group of soldiers. We were to stay back just in case. We were responsible for a couple of guard posts, but that was our only duty for the next week. The duties were supposed to be handled by the MPs, but they complained that we weren't doing anything while they were performing guard duty. So we took our turn until the battalion commander came by and said that there was no need for the detail. We were good with that and shut down for the remainder of our stay.

Soon it was our turn to go home. I was hoping that with the extra duty that they would count this duty for our annual training (AT). That was scheduled for next month. I was going on vacation one week prior, and I wasn't looking forward to coming back to that. This duty was bad enough. We didn't ever really do anything, but I was the noncommissioned officer in charge, a duty that I was not supposed to be performing. I figured that AT would hold more of the same.

I was back to work for only one week before I was scheduled to go on vacation. With AT directly to follow, I wouldn't return until the last week in July. During this week back, I still had a number of appointments to include a full day for the sleep study. My job was virtually on autopilot anyway, so it wasn't like they missed me much when I was gone. Most never saw me when I was there.

My daytime wakefulness test was an all-day affair. They had me stay awake for two hours, then they put me in a semi-reclined position, dim the lights, and tell me to stay awake. They have you hooked up to all kinds of wires that measure virtually every movement of your arms, legs, and face. They then measure how long it takes you to fall asleep. Of course, they don't tell you that. All they say is to lie there and do all you can without moving to stay awake. Then they would repeat the process every two hours. It never took more than a few minutes and I was out like a light. Before I left, the technician told me that I failed the test, but she didn't tell me what that meant. I had to schedule an appointment to see the doctor for the results, you guessed it, in another month.

We had a grueling schedule for our vacation. It included Helen; Ryan; my oldest stepson, Diego; his wife, Amanda; and two of their kids, Julian, who was twelve, and Maria, who was ten. We would be traveling for the first two days. My sister lived in Torrance, California. From her house, we would go to Disneyland the third day, go to the beach on the fourth, and take in a Dodger game that evening. On the fifth day would be a short travel day to my mom and dad's house in Madera, where we would meet up with my brother's family and visit for the rest of the day. On the sixth day, we would be going up to Yosemite National Park. The seventh day would be our first and only down day with my mom and dad. Then it would take two days to get back home.

The plan went off without a hitch. We began July 2 and traveled to Kingman, Arizona. Kingman was about a seven-hour drive. I was driving my motor home and pulling my motorcycle in my trailer, and Diego followed behind in my car. We stayed at a nice hotel, swam in the pool, and relaxed for a bit before heading to my sister's. My sister's house was about six hours west of Kingman. We weren't really pushing very hard on our travel days, but I figured that with the kids, it was a good distance without making them resent the trip.

We arrived at my sister's place in the early afternoon. My sister and I caught up on old times while the kids took a swim in the pool. Then it was barbecue for dinner and drinks at poolside. We made our plans for Disneyland the next day, which would be the fourth. I wasn't looking forward to a packed playland on the Fourth of July, but it was what fit in our plans, and I had to do it for the kids. PTSD and crowds don't work well together. I would have to load up on antianxiety meds and hope for the best.

From our first steps through the gates, Maria was mesmerized. This was her first time in the Magic Kingdom. Instantly, she began her transformation to look like Minnie Mouse. She was so cute. Maria is small for her age and just adorable. She is definitely Grandma and Grandpa's girl. Julian is a great kid too! He had been to Disneyland before. He and Ryan stayed together and took in all of the rides that Maria wasn't quite ready for. We all went from one ride to the next, from Frontier Land to Space Mountain and everything in between. I was doing okay; I lost myself in the faces of my grandkids. That was until the light parade and fireworks. We all got separated, and we spent hours looking for one another. I don't do fireworks, and with the crowds, I was just at my wit's end. At the end of the day, somehow I survived. We got home rather late, but you can bet I took a few stiff drinks before I took my meds and turned in for the night. The next morning, we would go to the beach.

Nobody wanted to get up the next morning. I think that Disneyland can suck the life out of you. We all needed time to recover. My sister Sherry got up first. I had been awake for some time, but I didn't want to be the first up, so I stayed in bed until I heard her stirring. We had a cup of coffee and planned out our day. After about ten, everyone else was up and running around.

First, we would go to the beach for swimming, and then later we would go to the wharf for souvenir shopping and a late lunch/early dinner. It was a warm midsummer day. The sand was scorching hot under our feet. There was a slight breeze coming off the Pacific, making the ambient temperature feel cool. Ryan, Julian, and I went straight into the surf. The water was cold, and I had to ease into it. Ryan and Julian jumped right in. I have always hated cold water, but when you're a kid, you let your desire for fun override common sense.

I finally worked my way into the cool water. I was showing Ryan and Julian how to bodysurf, not that I was much good at it but it was always a good time. It wasn't long before we were all riding waves. The kids were having a blast.

Helen entered the surf and was instantly swept away. Every time she tried to get up, the next wave would send her falling back into the water. It wasn't long and she was laughing so hard that she didn't have the strength to fight the powerful waves. I went over to help her up. She was only in a foot of water, but as the waves crashed in, they more than covered her. Even with my help, she still struggled to her feet; the laughing didn't stop until she was completely out of the water.

When we got back to the vehicles, Helen tried to rid her swimming suit of at least some of the sand. When she stretched the elastic, a small crab fell out of her suit along with the sand. For the rest of the day, it became a running gag that Helen had crabs.

We headed to the other beach, and once we found parking, we headed to the shops. There seemed to be more cars than people at this beach. The shops for the most part were void of shoppers. I was glad about that. I don't care much for going into shops, but when there are crowds of people, I get very uneasy. It becomes too much, and I have to get out. I'm sure at this point most men wish they had a good excuse to get out of shopping; PTSD has its advantages.

We went to eat at the wharf. Fresh crab is a favorite for my family. I was really disappointed; the crab, instead of being fresh and sweet, was bland and maybe even a little bitter. I don't remember having it any worse, and being right on the beach, it really sucked. Not everyone was as disappointed as me, but I was just expecting better.

It was boys' night out at the game that night. The ladies all decided to go back to the house to do whatever it is ladies do when they're together. We were eating Dodger Dogs and watching the home team get spanked. I have been to professional sporting events before, and with the exception of football, I have enjoyed Triple-A teams better than the big boys.

It was another late night, but we didn't have to get on the road too early tomorrow. It's only a three-hour drive to Mom and Dad's; we'll get there when we get there. No rush. At least that's what I thought. That morning, the lovely city of Torrance gave me a parking ticket for having an oversized vehicle in a residential area.

We arrived in Madera at Mom and Dad's by early afternoon. My brother Craig and his family were down from Reno. They would be going with us to Yosemite tomorrow. Tonight was a night for drinks and relaxation. I had a bit much to drink, but I'm a happy drunk, so it was all in good fun. My granddaughter was the real beneficiary of my drunken state. She lost a tooth that night, and I paid her ten dollars for it. I knew what I was doing; it was a silver tooth, and you just don't come by them every day.

The next morning, we were off to Yosemite. Helen and I were going up on the Harley; we would go up in a small three-vehicle caravan. Dad was planning our route. He wanted us to see some new sights and give Helen and me an adventure on the bike. It was definitely the long way. The road was a mountain road with a lot of tight switchbacks. It was a fun ride, but we were afraid that the kids may grow weary. We probably should have topped off our fuel tank before we ran out of small towns, but we thought that we would be fine just filling up as we left Madera. Wrong.

Yosemite was gorgeous. They had an above-average snowpack, so all of the waterfalls were still in full glory. Craig's wife, Lori, had the trip all planned out for us. She can be a little controlling at times. There were things that Helen really wanted to see, but they weren't on Lori's agenda. We all had a great time and saw some of the most beautiful sights that nature has to offer.

We got back to Mom and Dad's just before dark. Craig and his family were adamant about heading for home that night. We were all tired from the trip and tried to get them to stay the night and hit the road in the morning, but that just wasn't in the cards. So they packed up and hit the road for another five hours. It was good to see my brother again. It's always far too long between visits.

We all relaxed the next day. It was, of course, the only down day during the trip. I got to visit for a while with my mom and dad, and they had a chance to get to know their great-grandchildren. I'm kind of sorry that the trip was so rushed that we didn't get a chance to do more of this, but you have to do what you can with the time that you have. Tomorrow we will be back on the road, and we will finish the trip in the same way that we began. We would be on the road to Kingman then home on Sunday.

Monday morning I head out to Santa Fe for my annual National Guard training. I'm dreading this trip. Even after our great vacation, I am now hoping that my exhausted body ends up in a mangled mass of steel and debris on the side of the highway. I can't shake this feeling of trepidation. It began the second that I donned my uniform.

I see the pictures in my mind. I relive the past. I cower at loud noises, and I rely on numerous medications just to make it through the day. I am healed. Or so it would seem. The VA looks at me as a great success story. It is true, I have come a long way, and I have worked hard at my own recovery, if recovery is what you want to call it. I have developed a few coping skills, and I do enjoy more days than I used to. I still struggle with life and death though I doubt that anybody would notice. Overall, I would have to say that most days I am strong enough to live with myself, but painful reminders blindside me at many turns.

I have a strong desire to help others live a better life and to help them understand that while they may be crazy, they can still live a fairly normal life. The definition of PTSD is a normal reaction to an abnormal event. It feels a lot like crazy to me. I really can't explain things. My life is good; I enjoy my family, my newly revived relationship with my wife, and many other things. It's not that I am not happy but I just don't feel like I have the strength to go on. I am always tired. I try to get involved, but much of the time, I just want to be left alone. They call this isolationism. I miss the people who are close to me, but I really don't feel like talking.

I have made several hasty plans to do myself in. I have recently driven when I was drowsy, hoping that I would crash. I have thought about taking pills again. I really don't believe that I want to die; I just want to go to sleep and perhaps never wake up again. When you get right down to it, I guess there is not much difference.

According to the doctors, I'm not supposed to do anything except for administrative duties. I'm not the kind of guy who can sit around and watch as others work, so I don't mind lending a hand once in a while. The problem is that it never ends there. Once I start doing little things, they expect me to do more and more. This was the case for annual training. I started off by pointing people in the right direction, kind of like a spotter, I guess. Within days, they had me leading convoys. What a disaster. Things got all messed up. By the time I returned, I didn't have a clue if I still had all of my people. Trucks were going every which way. Some groups were told to leave once they were loaded; some were told to stay in groups. It was a nightmare. Then, when I got back to the Santa Fe training facility, they're having sim wars. The sound of automatic gunfire and the occasional explosion going off threw me over the edge. I told my command that I needed to go to the VA hospital. They took me the next morning, and by noon, I was back in ward 7.

The shrink in ward 7 kept trying to adjust my medicine, but I fought him at every turn. I was having a setback, but the last thing that I wanted was someone to adjust my meds and mess me up again completely. At some point, they realized that they weren't doing anything for me on ward 7 and sent me back into the world. My battalion commander wouldn't let me return to annual training, so I went back to work.

On July 30, I had my results from my sleep study. My sleep doctor said that I had extreme somnolence and that I should not be driving at all. I told her that I didn't seem to have a problem staying awake while riding my motorcycle. She said, "Good, at least that way you will only kill yourself." I thought that was a rather snide comment, but she was trying to get her point across.

I should not be driving—period. One week later, she sent a letter to my employer, and just like that, I was out of a job.

CHAPTER 28

What now? I'm out of work. The doc said that I can't drive or operate machinery; that cuts everything I had ever done in my life. I set up an appointment at the Santa Fe Vet Center. I need to get some counsel on this. They are a really good agency to help you understand what your benefits are and what you need to do. They put me in touch with the American Legion, who spoke on my behalf to the VA. They told me that I needed to file for unemployability. They said that this would raise my benefit to the same as 100 present. I did what I was recommended and just hope it comes through before I go through the rest of my savings.

I tried to keep a positive outlook. I wrote this as I came to the realization that I may be able to beat this struggle.

PTSD, I CARRY YOU WITH ME

You take me away to a time and place that I would just like to forget but you won't let me. As I grew stronger, I thought that you would grow weak, but you do not. You grow along with me as a troublesome reminder that I am not nor will I ever be healed. The power that you possess is strong enough to take me away without notice and put me under your spell. You grab all of my attention, leaving me defenseless in the moment. You are stronger than I.

I see the desert in everything that I do. Leave me alone to live my life; your time has passed, but not really. You follow me in visions, showing me pictures, one moment at a time. There are voiceless faces of starving children, women doing backbreaking work, and shoeless men carrying the weapon of the day. I no longer fear you, but you disrupt my day with regularity. You are stronger than I.

As I walk through the day carrying this pack full of memories, depression, intrusive thoughts, and flashbacks, I try to focus on today. One moment at a time please. Lord, help me hold on. So I go forward, and each agonizing step reminds me that I am all alone and no one can carry my burden but me. With my mind heavy and my heart broken, you are stronger than I.

I have the passion and desire to go forward, but I cannot deny the past. I must go forward, and I will carry the heavy load with me at every turn. From time to time, I will pass a brother who is carrying his own load. We can join our strength and set our bundles down for a moment. We will gather our strength then head off in opposite directions; each load will be lighter for a spell. Hope builds, but you are still stronger than I.

In a moment of despair, when I just don't think I can go on, I step forward once, then once again. I now find myself two steps ahead from where I thought that I could go no farther. I stop and ponder a thought. Who has been carrying this heavy burden through thick and through thin? Who must go through the day burdened by the past and by depression? Who has taken the last steps when he knew

> that he could go no further? Who faces each day when he would rather run and hide? I may carry you with me, but nothing is stronger than I.

The struggle goes, on but if I can believe in my own words, then I'm strong enough to carry this burden. Some days are easier than others. I always have a fleeing thought that maybe suicide is a viable option. It's not, depending on who you ask. Depression is like that; it's a monster that takes many prisoners. I don't know if the depression feeds my PTSD or if my PTSD feeds my depression. It doesn't matter, but its bad enough to fight one of these monsters, but both are a real challenge.

Now in August, Helen and I are finally going to celebrate our anniversary. We will be heading to Las Vegas, New Mexico, and treat ourselves to a night for just the two of us. We head out on the motorcycle and ride up to Vegas. We will stay at the Plaza Hotel, and as the name implies, it sits in the historic plaza. The building was erected in the late 1800s and still holds much of its elegance from this period. We rented the honeymoon suite and planned to take every advantage of it. The room was a large two-room suite with a four-post canopy bed as the centerpiece. The ceiling was at least ten feet high and was made of pressed tin with a nice design. The walls were all painted white. The room just had a fresh clean feel to it, and it was very inviting.

Shortly after we checked in, we thought that we would take a ride up through Gallinas Canyon. It was a beautiful ride through the tall whispering pines, painted rock, and lush green valleys. The winding road that leads up through the canyon gives you the opportunity to see all of the glory from every possible angle. As we begin the journey, a light rain begins to fall. The drops feel like tiny pinpricks on our cool faces, but other than that, we are well protected from the elements.

We travel Gallinas to another little area called El Porvenir. El Porvenir has a walking path that takes you well into the forest.

The path follows a pretty little brook. As we reach El Porvenir, the rain stops, so we get to walk the path with the smell of the freshly washed earth. We take a seat on a log adjacent to the stream. We gaze into each other's eyes and just enjoy each other's company and our surroundings. This area is so serene with tall pines, thick underbrush, the brook running over anything in its path, the birds singing, and the elk bugling, welcoming us to their habitat.

We take in all of the beauty that we can muster before heading out in time to make our dinner reservations. There is another back road heading out of here. The road is part dirt and part pavement, so we are a little apprehensive after the rain, but my experience with this road was that it had plenty of gravel on it for traction. It's a beautiful ride, so I think that it is worth the risk; anyway, if it gets too bad, we can always turn around.

As we make our way down the mountain, all is well. It looks as if our plan paid off. Once we clear the mountain, we can look forward to lush green rolling hills and beautiful horses and sturdy livestock on the many ranches in the area. We get to within the last hundred yards of the paved road, and the dirt road we're on turns into a mucky mess. We can't turn back now; we are far too committed for that now.

We start down the steep muddy path, and already we are picking up too much speed. I lightly apply the brakes, and this causes the bike to start fishtailing. I put my feet down to try to steady the bike. The added resistance keeps us from picking up more speed but does nothing for the control. *This is it*, I thought, *we are going down*. Somehow, by the grace of God, we made it. A hard-surface road never looked so good.

We get back to Las Vegas and our hotel just in time to get cleaned up for dinner. The restaurant is one of those fancy places, the kind that have every weed in the garden thrown into the salad. I'm usually not one for this kind of place. I'm more at home where people toss the peanut shells onto the floor and they have every beer known to man on tap. We ordered a bottle of wine with our dinner; we each had a glass then took the rest of the bottle up to our room. The next part of this book would not be suitable for all readers, so I will forgo the details.

We leave after breakfast the next morning, and we head out off of the beaten path. We head toward Mora; Mora is a tiny town a little higher than Las Vegas but still at the base of several mountain ranges. It's a stunning valley. There are a number of old ruins haggardly standing, lumber shells of what used to be small homes. From here, we will head up the mountain to a ski town called Angel Fire. The road to Angel Fire has been known to have huge herds of wild elk blocking the road as they glide past you without giving you a thought. You can often hear them bugling from Eagle Nest Lake, a near neighbor to Angel Fire.

Eagle Nest is a local fishing haven where people fish for trout and kokanee salmon. I have gone snagging with friends in early winter. Snagging is where you throw a weighted treble hook as far out into the lake as possible then jerk the hook through the water in hopes of snaring spawning salmon. It sounds cruel, but these fish are sterile and will die after the spawn. So the snagging actually keeps the lake clean and disease-free.

From Eagle Nest, we will continue up to Taos. Taos is a real tourist town known for great skiing and Native American art. We have gone through some of the shops before and fished some of the local streams, but today we are just taking in the scenery as we ride on through. Next we will be going to Santa Fe, the City Different, as they like to call it. This is our state capital and has also been referred to as the San Francisco of the Southwest. I try to avoid this city as much as possible. It is probably our biggest tourist towns. It's not that it's a bad city, it's just not for me. From Santa Fe, we will pick up the interstate and head for home. We will be back to Las Vegas in two weeks for a motorcycle rally. We had an incredible time this trip, one we will always remember.

I try to have something planned for every day. It doesn't matter how big or small, but as long as I accomplish something, I will maintain my self-worth. It could be doing the dishes or writing my book; everything helps a little.

Danny and Ryan are constantly at odds with each other. Their constant bickering is driving me crazy. Ryan for the most part is a good boy. At fourteen years old, I always know where he is and what he is doing. He is at an age, however, that can be unnerving. He has so much energy that he is always bouncing around. He likes to tease people and hates to get teased in return.

Danny is a good boy as well though he isn't a boy anymore. He is different than Ryan. He is very reserved and often depressed. His mood swings affect everyone in the house. He lashes out at the people closest to him. I know that he is only releasing pent-up energy. I was there myself only a few years ago. I lashed out at my family. The cost was losing my daughter, and Child Protective Services called on me for my son. I can't afford to lose another child, so I became very passive. It's not that I don't want to lash out; I just can't afford the consequence.

When Danny lashes out, Ryan looks at the treatment of his mother and himself as unfair, and he takes it very personally. When Ryan acts out, Danny feels that he should be condemned for his actions. I look at it as time served. Often the unrest within the household is more than I can stand. I have talked to Ryan a dozen times or more about his behavior toward Danny. Ryan tries to explain how he feels when Danny's behavior and angry outbursts disrupt the family. I try to explain it, but depression is something that you just don't get until you get it.

I can't really tell Danny that it is okay for Ryan to disrespect him because it's not, but it's also not fair that Ryan should have to endure Danny's wrath when he isn't feeling well. It's a double-edged sword that only time and maturity can solve. I hope that someday they can be friends as well as brothers, but that will take some healing on both sides. I just hope that at some point they both realize that they hold equal responsibility in the void. I love them both very much, and I hope that I live to see the day when they can learn to live in harmony.

The bike rally in Las Vegas was incredible. They said that there were over ten thousand bikes there. I can believe it. At times they were parked handlebar to handlebar on both sides of the street in the downtown plaza area.

We went on what they call a poker run. This is a game where often hundreds of motorcyclists participate. They all travel to the same five locations and draw one playing card at each of the five stops just like a dealt hand of poker. I think the high and low hand win the prize. At one point, we stopped at this guy's house; he had a barn in back that had been converted to a custom-car display room. He had all kinds of old custom cars and bikes that he had restored himself. It was really cool. The man had a refrigerator filled with beer and soda pop and welcomed the thousand or so riders to help themselves. No one took advantage of the situation. All of the bikers were grateful for the hospitality. Before we left, Helen spoke to the homeowner to see if she could bring the boy and his friend back before leaving town. The man said that would be fine, and Helen was sure to take him up on that. When Helen took the boys over the next day, she said to the man, "I hope that they didn't leave you too much of a mess the other day." The man told her that when everybody left, there wasn't so much as one can out of place. That was amazing; I have seen worshipers go to a religious function that weren't that respectful.

Again, we had a great time, and it left me open to going to some other larger rallies someday. I never thought that I would enjoy them. I hate crowds, loud noises, and shopping. All of these things are present at the rallies, and for some reason, I don't mind.

CHAPTER 29

With the summer behind us, we have one more extravagance before us: our cruise to the Bahamas. We still take short rides on the Harley. I have been using it as my daily driver. I still go to the VA at least twice a week. I would like to say that at some point I have hopes of being done with all of that, but I don't know that I ever will. I still have many rough days. I still isolate away from friends and people in general. I'm halfheartedly looking forward to the cruise; I just don't know how I will react to all of the people in close proximity. We had everything paid for prior to losing my job, so we decided that we would go forward. We are bound to hear from the VA soon; hopefully they will have some good news for us.

As we prepare to leave Albuquerque, the temperature is in the midforties during the day and colder than hell at night. We will be embarking from Baltimore, Maryland, then on to Cape Canaveral, Florida; from Florida, it's off to Nassau and Freeport,

Bahamas. We will be leaving on Helen's birthday and returning Christmas day.

We were off on a journey unlike anything we had ever done before. We have a full day of travel to get to Baltimore. We leave Albuquerque at eight in the morning and arrive in Baltimore at ten at night. Gotta love discount tickets. I have reservations at the Baltimore airport Marriott. It was a nice place but pricey. We had room service once we arrived as the restaurant was closed by the time we got there. That turned out to be okay because in the morning, we had a meager breakfast in the restaurant, and it cost almost as much as our dinner the night before.

I had arranged for transportation to and from the airport to the ship in advance, and it worked out fabulously. The driver was waiting for us at the airport and transported us directly to the pier. We waited in a lobby for about forty-five minutes when they told us to embark the huge cruise liner. When we reached the top of the gangplank, they hurried us to the dining room for lunch. They said that our rooms weren't quite ready, so this seemed to make sense. As we sat down, the maître d' showed us to our table and placed each one of our napkins in our laps. We had a choice of three or four appetizers, entrees, and desserts. The dining room was miraculously elegant. The entire ceiling was like one giant glimmering chandelier.

After lunch, we had to chase Ryan around the ship as he was in a flurry to take in all that he could in the first few minutes of the journey. It was up this staircase, then down this one, then out this door, and in this one. We could barely keep up, and he would get upset if we fell behind. He was nervously excited. We all were, but his impatient manner was not only exhausting, it was irritating. Helen and I understood his excitement, but while we did have time to kill waiting for our room, this was not our idea of relaxation.

Soon our rooms were ready. Then we had to search ours out. Once we found the room, we let ourselves in and found our luggage already there. The first thing we did was unpack, and before we could go any further, a message came over the loudspeaker saying that we would all have to attend a safety brief in our perspective rally points.

After the briefing, we were off again to inspect the ship. We seemed to be going in circles, and even when we did find something, we soon got turned around and forgot where anything was. I was getting a little flustered when we came across a man wearing a pin that said Ask Me. I'm a man, and traditionally, I won't ask for directions, but by now, I was so frustrated I went up to him and simply asked, "How do I find everything?" The man laughed but then said I needed to be a little more specific. I told him that this was our first time on a ship and we didn't even know what to ask for. He seemed to understand and pointed out a few hot spots and showed us how to manipulate our little ship map. He was helpful, but it was still days before I felt comfortable with our temporary habitat.

Ryan was set up to go with a teen group before we set sail, and I was afraid that he may not even give it a try. I could tell that he was a bit apprehensive about going to the orientation, but after a little prodding, he did finally go. Ryan met some new friends right from the get-go, and we would only see him at mealtime with any regularity. They had things on the teen's agenda until all hours of the night. This gave Helen and me all kinds of time to explore what we wanted to do.

We went to see the comedians, the variety shows, and one of our favorite haunts was the piano bar. Our first night alone was plagued by Helen's memory of my affair and her endless questions about things that she didn't want to hear the answers to. It still comes up from time to time; I wish that I could make it all go away, but some things only time can heal. I can't blame her for the way she feels.

The memories seemed to fade, and we were both able to enjoy the rest of the trip. At one point, we went to a show that had pyrotechnics as part of the show. That sent me over the edge. I sat with the feeling as I had been taught in several of my PTSD classes, but this did nothing for me. I was in full-on crisis mode. At one point, I found myself alone on the balcony and contemplated throwing myself overboard. I really try to think about the people who care about me and what my actions would do to them. Many times, I have such a low self-worth that I can talk myself into believing that in the long run, they would be better off without me. This was not the case this time; I wanted this to be the experience of a lifetime for both Helen and the boy. I came back inside and rode out the feeling while lying down on the bed. By the time Helen came out of the restroom, I pretty much had myself collected.

We get to our first port in Florida, and we had our first excursion. It was an airboat ride through the Everglades. We were going to see alligators in their natural habitat. It was a lot of fun, and when we got back on land, we had an opportunity to hold a real alligator. He was tamed, of course. When he came out, he waved to the crowd. The small gator reminded Helen of her little dog back home, and she couldn't wait to cuddle the little creature. The gator at this point really reminded me of her little dog as the alligator urinated a bit on Helen. How many people can say that they were peed on by a real alligator?

We still had some time to kill before having to return to the ship, so we hopped on a shuttle down to the beach. Ryan and I again attempted to bodysurf; the surf wasn't anywhere near what it was in California. The waves were a good size, but they broke out in much deeper water than we wanted to be in. We caught a few good ones, but that was about all. We still had a lot of fun.

The next day was a day at sea. Helen and I were getting to know the ship pretty well by now. We would go out every night for midnight pizza and ice cream on the lido deck. We found every show that we wanted to see, and we spread our time out all over the place with the exception of the casino. We weren't big on gambling.

We went to a private beach in Nassau called the Blue Lagoon. The water was a beautiful crystal blue. You could see the bottom of the lagoon from even the deepest points. I went in the water for a while, but it was still a little cool for my taste, so I spent much of the day just lounging. I will get my time in the water tomorrow in Freeport when we go snorkeling.

The next day, we board a catamaran and take about an hour's ride to a dive site. Again, the water clarity was unbelievable. When we reach the dive site, everyone seems to be a bit apprehensive, so Helen, a complete newcomer to this kind of swimming, was the first out. I followed her to try to keep her from drifting too far, but she was pretty comfortable swimming the reef. There were so many fish, all kinds and colors. It was like nothing I had ever experienced. After a while, we came back to the craft for a spell. We got dried off, and I decided that I had enough, but Helen wanted to go out for a second trip. She was the first in and the last out. She had a blast!

We had one more day at sea, then we would arrive back in Baltimore. The cruise went by so incredibly fast that I couldn't imagine ever going on one that was shorter than the week that we spent. The entire experience was magical. The food, the shows, the atmosphere felt as close to heaven as you will ever feel on earth.

Our trip home was long and stressful as one of our planes was late arriving into Houston. When we arrived at the gate, we looked at our tickets to see what gate we departed from. It was clear across the airport, and we only had ten minutes until boarding time. We hitched a ride with one of these people-mover people who drove us to the transport. I tossed the man a tip, and we got there just in time to catch the rail. We rode the train to the proper concourse and then ran to the gate. We arrived and didn't see anybody. The boy went to ask what the deal was. Before he could return, I saw the panel that said that the gate had been changed to the other side of the concourse. We had just come from there when we got off the train. Our hopes were almost crushed at that moment, but we had to try. We were off and running once again. Ryan was well ahead of us, but I was moving as fast as I could without leaving Helen behind. We arrived at the gate just as they were closing the door; we made it. This was a stressful end to a near-perfect vacation.

Before we could even make it home, I received a phone message from my sister stating that my grandma had passed away. She was just shy of ninety-four years old. My grandma was a stern and independent woman. She had her ideas about how things should be, and no one was about to change her mind. She was still driving up until just weeks before her death and was living on her own in an independent home settlement. She enjoyed the camaraderie with many of the other tenants.

Helen loved my grandma. They had developed a special relationship over the years. They had a lot in common. They were both creative, both were great cooks, and both of them loved gossip. They liked to compare notes about my mom. My grandma was defiantly her own person. We all loved her though she made it difficult to do at times. Rest in peace, Grandma.

Helen received news that her job would be ending on December 31. Now we would both be out of work. We have a house full of people and no one working. Cherestine, her daughter, and her boyfriend moved in around October. Cherestine's boyfriend was working when they moved in but then lost his job near mid-November, so the house was bursting at the seams. We loved having our granddaughter with us. We hadn't seen her in almost a year, and now at age three, she's getting to be the cutest little angel.

Now that I am home with the year pretty much behind us, I am faced with some challenges for the new year. My brother needs some help in California with his business. His wife has been going through some difficult times medically. He needs some help to keep things afloat while taking care of her. He wants me to go down to help him, and while I'm in a good place to help him out physically, I'm not sure that I can handle things mentally. I want to help even though it would mean leaving my family behind.

I looked at this as perhaps a sign from God that it was time to move to California. We could live near my parents and help out where we could. At one point, my dad even thought about putting a down payment on a house for us. The kids could stay here and pay us enough rent to keep the payment going. It just seemed right. I brought Helen and Ryan to California for Grandma's funeral and to check out the schools and employment opportunities. Ryan loved everything about the idea of moving, but Helen had doubts. After all, her grandchildren were all in New Mexico. That was my main drawback as well, that and my doctors. Helen found a great lead on a job her first day out. This was definitely in the cards, or was it?

Cherestine and her family, who were going to rent our house, decided to go back to South Carolina. The job that she was applying for fell through the cracks, and Helen would stay unemployed for the foreseeable future. At least she qualified for unemployment. There were seven of us in this house trying to live on one unemployment check and my meager disability. All of my signs from God were crumbling as fast as they came. Now if we wanted to move, we would have to sell our home in Belen. That wouldn't be an easy task with the market the way it is.

So I stayed in California to help my brother. I thought that perhaps if I was performing fast-paced labor that my drowsiness would subside. My brother repairs and installs car wash equipment all over California, and at times, it spills over to Nevada. My primary purpose for going down was the fact that he had several new car washes to erect. For the install, we were working long days. I don't mind working hard; in fact, I prefer to work constantly until the job is finished. The work didn't do anything for my drowsiness. I was even more exhausted than before.

My depression was getting worse again as well. I don't know if it was the sleepiness or missing my family, but I would do okay for the most part, but then I would get hit with periods of absolute dread. I had to do all I could to fight the old feelings of doing myself in. Sometimes I didn't do very well. In any case, I lived to see another day.

I would go out to California two more times before the end of March. Each time, I felt that old feeling. In fact, after my second trip, my councilor thought that I was ready for another trip to ward 7. I know that she was right but really didn't feel like going at this time. Hell, I just got home, and I felt that I needed to reconnect with my family.

I have decided that it is worth the fight to live my life instead of ending it. My family needs me. Knowing this, I have toyed with the idea of cutting my eyes out. I even had my knife blade resting on my eyeball. My thought process behind this was that I need to be here for my family but maybe, just maybe, if I didn't have to see things that are constant reminders, then I could live with the consequence. The way I was looking at it, it was my eyes or my life. I tried one day, but it was just too painful to follow through.

By the next week, I had an appointment with my shrink. I told him what I had done and said that I thought that I needed to go to ward 7. My doctor disagreed with me this time. He didn't think that ward 7 was the right environment for me at this time. I was kind of surprised by his thinking. I guess that he knows best. Earlier that day in group, I was very uneasy. My counselor thought that I needed to go back to the ward as well. She seemed as surprised as I was that my doctor didn't feel the same way.

My shrink said that I need to get into the suicide prevention group in addition to my other groups and counseling. I think that he is right, and I will pursue this path. My counselor has me going through another session of PE (primary exposure) therapy. We are currently working on the situation where I almost shot the woman and child early in my deployment. People can tell me over and over again that it's okay because I never actually pulled the trigger and that I made the right decision. So why fret about it? The fact is that I can tell myself a thousand times that something is irrational, but that doesn't change the fact that I see their faces vividly in my mind's eye on a daily basis. It's not just them. It seems that a number of things still haunt me, but since we can only work on one thing at a time, currently they are on top of the list.

CHAPTER 30

Life with PTSD is a struggle. I'm still waiting to hear from the VA about my unemployability. I'm still waiting for the Guard to put me before the medical board; it's all about baby steps. I just recently had to extend my contract with the Guard so that they can eventually throw me out. We will be going on year number 3 this June.

I know that there are others who continue to tussle with the VA and military. My advice to you would be to stay in the fight. It's frustrating, to say the least. I always have said that people who really have PTSD could never stand to put up with the BS of going through the VA process. If I can do it, you can too.

I have gone on with my life, but even now, eight years later with extensive therapy, I can't shake the past. There are a hell of a lot of vets from Vietnam and other wars or combative conflicts that have struggled longer than me. War has destroyed so many lives, lives of the soldiers and the families of the living and the dead. Help is available now that before never existed. I would urge anyone who knows one of these struggling heroes to put them in touch with their local veterans' hospitals while there is still time to enjoy life. There is a lot of BS they will have to face, but haven't they lived with a lot of BS for most of their lives? I know dozens of people who have made it. They are receiving duly earned benefits. It's not a handout or welfare. Ask yourself, has being in a combat zone negatively affected my life? If the answer is yes, then you need to fight for the benefits that you deserve.

I was of the mind-set when I began the process that I could handle anything life had in store for me. It was others who first recognized my PTSD. I just thought I was handling things fairly well, but the people closest to me knew that I was not the person that I once was. I knew it as well, but who could go through that hell and come out the same person? If the person that you have become is an alcoholic, drug addict, or a shut-in, then the VA can help, but only if you are willing to do the work to help yourself.

I wrote "Brother My Brother" for my brother-in-law who is a Vietnam veteran.

BROTHER MY BROTHER

Brother my brother, you walk by my side as we go forward into hell. I know that you have my back, so I do not fear. But still, we caution as we do not know if we will kill today nor do we know if we will live to see another day. We understand the mission for it is simple—travel the chosen path and survive. If you fail, you die a hero, but your blood will forever stain the minds of your comrades, comrades who must endure the horrific burden of life for all of the living and the dead.

Brother my brother, I am here for you. I will walk by your side. Together we will survive the hell of today. We can wash our stained minds with whiskey and wine then celebrate our victory, the victory of life. As the whiskey fades, we are left wondering once again who the real victors

> are. The dead no longer carry the burden of life. They no longer see the horrors of the past or the politics of today. They will not be shunned by the lack of understanding of friends and foe.
>
> Brother my brother, forgotten by others as you sleep in the park or under a bridge. You are haggard and your mind broken, but the masses will not see you. They will live their lives in fear that somehow you will do them harm. Has God also forgotten you, or will you someday find the salvation you deserve?
>
> Brother my brother, continue to seek for the hand that is before you. Your brother will lift you when you are down. Your brother will understand your pain as only he has walked in your path. Share your strengths with him and lift each other. Know and understand your pain is the price of freedom in a less than perfect world.

After all that I have been through, I am not an antiwar advocate. I don't think that we should go to war at the drop of a hat or for political reasons, but some things are worth fighting for. I hope that if we ever get the call to go overseas again, that the people who send us would have a good enough reason that they would send their own sons and daughters over to join the fight. They won't, of course, but they should.

I have recently read that there is a navy doctor who says that he can cure PTSD in some cases. He has sent some soldiers who had PTSD back to the battlefield. To this I say BS! PTSD can go into remission, but after years of programs and intense therapy, I am no better off than I was to start with. I have good days and bad. I struggle with life and death, and while I have been in these programs with many others, I could say the same for them. We learn to live with PTSD. There is no cure and no easy answers.

I was of the mind-set at one time when I would have said that I was cured just to get myself back on the battlefield. Of course, I never planned to return. I wouldn't be surprised if the good doctor is facing the same situation. Some soldiers would do anything to get back to the battlefield. War makes sense to those who know no other way. When you leave to come back to this real world, it feels unnatural. You never completely fit in, and all we know is what we know, so we have a tendency to go back. In my opinion, they are only prolonging the inevitable. Everyone must come home at some point, many with PTSD and many with a flag over their coffin. This is the tragedy of war. Never forget.

I will leave you with this untitled writing that seems to wrap things up in a pretty little package.

> For years now I have been consumed by the war. It has all but taken over my life. How can I have a conversation with any civilian when war is all that I know? I am forever caught in patterns. I feel comfortable talking with other veterans because they understand. It is impossible for others to be truly empathetic, so here is where the circle gets confusing.
>
> I went off to war, where I learn to survive in a hostile environment. This changed me at my very core. I then come home, and I am expected to be the same person that I once was by my family and friends. Try to make small talk out of do-or-die; it doesn't happen. The events of normal people's lives become trivial and petty. So I regress. Only talking to other veterans becomes a reminder of yesterday, days that I often would just soon forget. So I regress. Now I am isolated, shunning those who could never understand and avoiding those who would.
>
> I have been asked the question, "If you only feel comfortable around other vets, then why not take advantage of that?"

My best friend, my comrade in arms, my battle buddy, a man that I love like a son, will barely speak to me because I am a reminder. Men who I lived with for several months of my recovery I see in passing. We will make small talk and agree that we should get together. We never do because to one another we are reminders. Stages in life come and go, and as I pass from one to another, it seems that I have to give everything up to move forward. Why get close to anyone who will at some point just become a reminder of where I once was?

It would seem that recovery feeds isolationism. I make a good point, and all that I have spoken is truth, but it is only part of the truth. I am capable of moving forward and bringing a piece of past with me at every turn. I avoid because it is easy. There isn't anyone to approve or disapprove and no one to disappoint other than myself. So why try? I am in recovery to get a new sense of self. I have learned that my life has meaning not always to myself but always to someone. I have learned that by educating people from the past, I can bring them with me on my journey to the future. The rewards of rekindling my relationship with my family have been phenomenal. I know that I am not alone nor have I ever really been. I was just so overwhelmed that I could not envision a future, so I didn't want to bring them along.

Not everyone that comes into my life will be welcome as I move forward, but that is okay too. I have gained enrichment from everyone that I have allowed to touch my life. I will take what I can with me on my journey, and I won't fret about what I can't. Life is one day at a time; dreams are only what I make of them, and now is what I can hold in my hand.

Godspeed!

GLOSSARY

BIAP: Baghdad International Airport (formerly Saddam International Airport)

Bobtail: Big-rig tractor without a trailer

Carilla: Spanish for ribbing or joking

CC: Convoy commander (usually an NCO in charge of convoys)

Charlie Foxtrot: Cluster f—

Charlie Foxtrot: When everything goes wrong (usually happens when officers get involved)

CID: Criminal Investigation Division

Daisy chains: A number of IEDs in a row all wired to go off at the same time.

Depression: Extreme Despair that carries on for long periods of time (usually requires medication and can be life threatening)

FNG: f—ing new guy, someone fresh into the country

Hodgie: Actually means nobleman, but it was used as a derogatory name for Middle Easterners

HMMWV: Wide-stance, four-wheel-drive vehicle, replaced the Jeep in the 1980s

IED: Improvised explosive device, can turn your best day into a Charlie Foxtrot

IM: Imaginational therapy, same as immersion therapy and prolonged exposure

Immersion therapy: Takes you deep into a memory so that you can habituate to it

Habituate: Acclimate, until subject no longer bothers you

KBR: Kellogg Brown & Root, a subsidiary of Halliburton, civilian contractors

KIA: Killed in action

LT: Lieutenant, low-ranking officer, can be your biggest ally or worst nightmare, not much in between

M16: Basic riflemen's combat arms, fires 5.56 mm rounds, single-shot or three-round burst

M915: Freightliner tractor used by the military

Mk 19: A fully automatic grenade launcher capable of doing much damage but not very useful when enemy is hiding among civilians

MP: Military police

MSR: Main service road (supply routes)

MTS: The military's sorry excuse for GPS

MRE: Meals ready to eat (excrete), barf in a bag

OIC: Officer who thinks that he is somehow in charge of a mission

OIF: Operation Iraqi Freedom

Oodles: Plenty

Pogie bate: Junk food

Prolonged exposure: To go deep into a memory over and over again

PX: Post exchange (shopping mart)

PTSD: Post traumatic stress disorder, unhabituated traumatic memories that terrorize your everyday life

QRF: Quick reaction force (same as gun truck or Scorpion team)

ROE: Rules of engagement, designed to make a kinder, gentler armed forces

RPG: Rocket-propelled grenade

SAW: Squad automatic weapon, fires 5.56 mm rounds at up to 1000 rounds per minute, could actually saw a man in half

Scorpion 1: Lieutenant responsible for setting up gun trucks

Scorpion 2: Part of the QRF, probably the most balanced of all Scorpion teams

Scorpion 3: Another way of saying *worthless*

SOP: Standard operating procedure

Spot time: The time a convoy should be rolling out of the gate, important to stay on so that the enemy knows what time you're coming every day

STARR: An inpatient VA hospital program for substance abuse and PTSD

SUDS: Subjective units of disturbance, rating your anxiety level from 0 to 100 (or my definition, the number of beers it takes to get through a memory)

TCN: Third-country national (Politically correct term for Hodgie)

TTP: Trailer transfer point (where to go to get your messed up load)

XO: Executive officer (second in command)